Voyage to Atlantis

For 2,000 years Atlantis had tantalized the mind of man: Was it a myth or a memory? Did it exist and, if so, where? How and why did it disappear? Here, at last, is the full first-hand account by the man who led the scientific expedition that found Atlantis and revealed the way it became "lost" – in the greatest single natural disaster witnessed by man –a cataclysm so great it has left its indelible impact on the myths and legends of several cultures. Not since Schliemann discovered Troy has an archaeological event so gripped the world's imagination.

Voyage to
Atlantis

James W. Mavor, Jr.

Collins
FONTANA

First published in Great Britain by Souvenir Press 1969
First issued in Fontana 1973
Second Impression August 1973
Third Impression February 1974
Fourth Impression June 1976

Made and printed in Great Britain by
William Collins Sons & Co Ltd Glasgow

Acknowledgments

This book was inspired by the dream of Atlantis. It is the story of the contributions of many people.

In addition to those mentioned in the narrative, I offer my gratitude to my wife, Mary, who was responsible for a large part of the research on which this book is based, and without whose patience and understanding the book could not have been written.

Edward B. Garside provided editorial assistance which not only was invaluable in producing the book but has been my literary education as well.

I am grateful to Edward F. K. Zarudzki and Dr. Hartley Hoskins, colleagues at the Woods Hole Oceanographic Institution, for permission to publish certain of their scientific results and for assistance in the preparation of Appendix C.

The United States Navy has given permission to publish the seismic and magnetic records from *Chain* cruise 61 reproduced in Plate 3.

Robert Kane has kindly permitted the use of his topographic and section drawings of the Akroteri region.

Dr. Paul M. Fye, director of the Woods Hole Oceanographic Institution, has given personal and institutional moral support to my project since its inception in 1965.

Frances Williams of the Woods Hole Oceanographic Institution created most of the many drawings and maps from sketches of mine.

I am indebted to Dr. Christos G. Stergis, who made many

Greek translations for me, and to Barrie Dale, micropaleontologist of the Woods Hole Oceanographic Institution, who analyzed specimens of Theran soil, taught my wife and me to speak Greek, and maintained a lively interest in Thera, though unable to travel there with us.

I am grateful to Dr. Harold Edgerton, whose participation in the project, counsel and encouragement I have valued greatly. His aerial photo of Thera is reproduced here by permission.

I wish to thank William Wetmore who provided assistance in preparing the early drafts of the manuscript.

I wish to express appreciation for editorial assistance to my publisher in the persons of Arthur C. Fields and Steven Frimmer.

I am grateful to Sigurgeir Jónasson for permission to publish the photograph of volcanic lightning.

Permission to publish quotations is acknowledged as follows: A. C. Black Ltd. for the quotation from *The Sea-Kings of Crete* by James Baikie, 1910; W. W. Norton Co. Inc. for the quotation from *The Archaeology of Crete* by J. D. S. Pendlebury, 1965; Penguin Books Ltd. for the quotations from *Prehistoric Crete* by R. W. Hutchinson, 1962, *The Voyage of the Argo* translated by E. V. Rieu, 1939, and *The Odyssey* translated by E. V. Rieu, 1946; The New American Library of World Literature, Inc., for the quotation from *Three Great Plays of Euripides* translated by Rex Warner, 1958; Cambridge University Press for the quotation from *Discontinuity in Greek Civilization* by R. Carpenter, 1966; G. P. Putnam's Sons for the quotations from *Larousse World Mythology* edited by Pierre Grimal, 1965.

I am grateful to the Archaeological Society of Athens and to Dr. Spyridon Marinatos for permission to publish the results of the 1967 Thera excavations.

I am grateful to Charles Innis and Mimi Head of the WHOI graphic arts group, Mr. Innis for counsel and assistance and Miss Head for the drawing of the snake goddess.

Claudine Marquet translated the work of Fouqué which was so important to the project.

All hand lettering of the illustrations was performed by my wife, Mary.

My thanks go to Mrs. Judy Ashmore who typed the manuscript.

I am indebted to Professor Galanopoulos who supplied the monkey head photo and permitted reproduction of figures from his published papers.

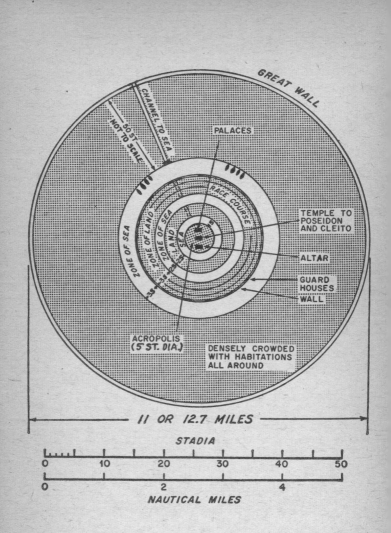

GREAT WALL

CHANNEL TO SEA
50 ST. NOT TO SCALE

PALACES

ZONE OF SEA

ZONE OF LAND

ZONE OF SEA

ZONE OF LAND

SEA

RACE COURSE

TEMPLE TO POSEIDON AND CLEITO

ALTAR

GUARD HOUSES

WALL

ACROPOLIS (5 ST. DIA.)

DENSELY CROWDED WITH HABITATIONS ALL AROUND

11 OR 12.7 MILES

STADIA
0   10   20   30   40   50

0   2   4
NAUTICAL MILES

FIGURE 1. Metropolis of Atlantis drawn from Plato's description in *Critias*.

Prologue

Atlantis, the greatest legend of the sea, has reverberated in men's minds for over 2,000 years and through the pages of as many volumes. The story, told by Plato, has been given countless interpretations, all deriving from the assumption that somehow it masked a physically real and living place that had once, in truth, existed. Not only historians, but poets, novelists, geologists, and oceanographers have speculated upon the location of the lost continent of Atlantis. But always men have felt that somewhere Atlantis did in fact exist, that as surely as Heinrich Schliemann, against all odds, discovered Troy, so would Atlantis someday be found.

It is my belief—and this book will spell out the reasons for that belief—that Atlantis did actually, physically exist, not in the Atlantic Ocean, on the grand scale of legend, or in the North Sea, the Bahamas, the East Indies, South America, Spain, the Indian Ocean, or other parts of the world which have been mentioned as its location—but in a lesser, more familiar dimension, in a sea utterly familiar to Plato. It is my belief that Atlantis lay in the Aegean itself, on one of the islands of the Cyclades, and in a position and under circumstances that would have certainly insured that its destruction, which did in fact occur, would be remembered through time to the classical Greek era, and through Plato to us.

The Troy of King Priam described in Homer's *Iliad* as having a great palace of polished stone and a population of some fifty thousand is now agreed to be a glorified and exaggerated account of the sixth or seventh real town within the mound of Hissarlik in northwestern Turkey. Homer wrote of many real people and events, compressing them in time and space in the manner of legend. I believe that the story of Atlantis went through the same sort of evolution as the legend of Troy, always growing in the telling. But there was a difference. The reality from which the myth of Atlantis sprang was so cataclysmic and so far-reaching in its physical effects that a multitude of myths and legends was fostered, each, because of difficulties of communication in very ancient times, coming to have an independent life of its own in all the civilizations it affected.

And now, in support of that contention, modern science has found incontrovertible evidence of a real catastrophe worthy of Plato's description of the fantastic disappearance of Atlantis, a discovery that removes it from the realm of fiction and exaggeration and makes the facts of the story completely intelligible. . . .

The Greek philosopher Plato is the source of the Atlantis legend that has so puzzled the world. About 360 B.C., toward the end of his life, he wrote two works, *Timaeus* and *Critias*, which modern editions usually place between his great dialogues on social order *The Republic* and *The Laws*. It is *Timaeus* and *Critias* specifically that contain the story of Atlantis as we know it. The first of these dialogues introduces the story of Atlantis and describes the island briefly and in general terms; the second, which has come down to us incomplete, provides detailed descriptions of Atlantean people, places and practices.

According to Plato, the account of Atlantis, "a tale which, though strange, is certainly true," was first told to Solon, the great Athenian lawmaker, by priests of Saïs, an Egyptian city having close religious and cultural ties with Athens. Solon then told the story to a relative, Dropides, who passed it on to his son, Critias the elder, who later told it to his grandson, another Critias, an Athenian statesman of Plato's time. It is this Critias who, as a speaker in the two Platonic dialogues, talks about

Atlantis. Though this chain of communication seems complicated, the account was probably recorded in writing on two
different occasions and, in any case, the art of accurate oral
transmission was highly developed in ancient times. To this very
day there are persons in Greece who can recite the entire
Odyssey and *Iliad* of Homer.

The story told to Solon by the Egyptian priests concerns the
founding of Athens in very ancient times by the goddess Athena.
The citizens of this early Athens are praised as "the fairest and
noblest race of men which ever lived," and the city itself is
hailed as "first in war and in every way the best governed of all
cities." When Solon asks to hear more about these noble early
Athenians, the priests tell him the following story:

> Many great and wonderful deeds are recorded of your state in
> our histories. But one of them exceeds all the rest in greatness
> and valour. For these histories tell of a mighty power which un-
> provoked made an expedition against the whole of Europe and
> Asia, and to which your city put an end. This power came forth
> out of the Atlantic Ocean, for in those days the Atlantic was
> navigable; and there was an island situated in front of the straits
> which are by you called the pillars of Heracles; the island was
> larger than Libya and Asia put together, and was the way to
> other islands, and from these you might pass to the whole of
> the opposite continent which surrounded the true ocean; for this
> sea which is within the Straits of Heracles is only a harbour,
> having a narrow entrance, but that other is a real sea, and the
> surrounding land may be most truly called a boundless conti-
> nent. Now in this island of Atlantis there was a great and won-
> derful empire which had rule over the whole island and several
> others, and over parts of the continent, and, furthermore, the
> men of Atlantis had subjected the parts of Libya within the
> columns of Heracles as far as Egypt, and of Europe as far as
> Tyrrhenia. This vast power, gathered into one, endeavoured to
> subdue at a blow our country and yours and the whole of the
> region within the straits; and then, Solon, your country shone
> forth, in the excellence of her virtue and strength, among all
> mankind. She was pre-eminent in courage and military skill, and
> was the leader of the Hellenes. And when the rest fell off from

her, being compelled to stand alone, after having undergone the very extremity of danger, she defeated and triumphed over the invaders, and preserved from slavery those who were not yet subjugated, and generously liberated all the rest of us who dwell within the pillars. But afterwards there occurred violent earthquakes and floods; and in a single day and night of misfortune all your warlike men in a body sank into the earth, and the island of Atlantis in like manner disappeared in the depths of the sea. For which reason the sea in those parts is impassable and impenetrable, because there is a shoal of mud in the way; and this was caused by the subsidence of the island.

These crucial and, until now, mystifying events conclude the brief account of Atlantis in *Timaeus*. From references earlier in the dialogue, we are given to understand that the events took place 9,000 years before Solon's time (638–559 B.C.) and were recorded by the priests of Saïs 1,000 years after that. This reference to 9,000 years is repeated when the tale of Atlantis is taken up again in *Critias*.

Here the account of Atlantis is taken back to the time when the whole earth was portioned out among the gods.

And Poseidon, receiving for his lot the island of Atlantis, begat children by a mortal woman, and settled them in a part of the island, which I will describe. Looking towards the sea, but in the centre of the whole island, there was a plain which is said to have been the fairest of all plains and very fertile. Near the plain again, and also in the centre of the island at a distance of about fifty stadia, there was a mountain not very high on any side. In this mountain there dwelt one of the earth-born primeval men of that country, whose name was Evenor, and he had a wife named Leucippe, and they had an only daughter who was called Cleito. The maiden had already reached womanhood, when her father and mother died; Poseidon fell in love with her and had intercourse with her, and breaking the ground, inclosed the hill in which she dwelt all round, making alternate zones of sea and land larger and smaller, encircling one another; there were two of land and three of water, which he turned as with a lathe, each having its circumference equidistant every way from the centre, so that no man could get to the island, for ships and voyages were not as yet. He himself, being a god, found no difficulty in making special arrangements for the centre island, bringing up two springs of water from beneath the earth, one of warm water and the other of cold, and making every variety of food to spring up abundantly from the soil. He also begat and brought up five pairs of twin male children; and dividing the island of Atlantis into ten portions, he gave to the first-born of the eldest pair his mother's dwelling and the surrounding allotment, which was the largest and best, and made him king over the rest; the others he made princes, and gave them rule over many men, and a large territory. And he named them all; the eldest, who was the first king, he named Atlas, and after him the whole island and the ocean were called Atlantic.

Plato goes on to describe the vast wealth of the descendants of Atlas—the greatness of their empire and the extent of its natural resources and its imports—all of which made them richer and more plentifully supplied than any potentates before or since. Thus blessed with resources, they constructed temples, palaces, harbors, and docks, which are described in detail.

First of all they bridged over the zones of sea which surrounded the ancient metropolis, making a road to and from the royal palace. And at the very beginning they built the palace in the habitation of the god and of their ancestors, which they continued to ornament in successive generations, every king surpassing the one who went before him to the utmost of his power, until they made the building a marvel to behold for size and for beauty. And beginning from the sea they bored a canal of three hundred feet in width and one hundred feet in depth and fifty stadia in length, which they carried through to the outermost zone, making a passage from the sea up to this, which became a harbour, and leaving an opening sufficient to enable the largest vessels to find ingress. Moreover, they divided at the bridges the zones of land which parted the zones of sea, leaving room for a single trireme to pass out of one zone into another, and they covered over the channels so as to leave a way underneath for the ships; for the banks were raised considerably above the water. Now the largest of the zones into which a passage was cut from the sea was three stadia in breadth, and the zone of land which came next of equal breadth; but the next two zones, the one of water, the other of land, were two stadia, and the one which surrounded the central island was a stadium only in width. The island in which the palace was situated had a diameter of five stadia. All this including the zones and the bridge, which was the sixth part of a stadium in width, they surrounded by a stone wall on every side, placing towers and gates on the bridges where the sea passed in. The stone which was used in the work they quarried from underneath the centre island, and from underneath the zones, on the outer as well as the inner side. One kind was white, another black, and a third red, and as they quarried, they at the same time hollowed out double docks, having roofs formed out of the native rock. Some of their buildings were simple, but in others they put together different stones, varying the colour to please the eye, and to be a natural source of delight. The entire circuit of the wall, which went round the outermost zone, they covered with a coating of brass, and the circuit of the next wall they coated with tin, and the third, which encompassed the citadel, flashed with the red light of orichalcum. . . .*

There follows a description of the palaces and temples, all magnificent structures, particularly Poseidon's temple. The account continues:

In the next place, they had fountains, one of cold and another of hot water, in gracious plenty flowing; and they were wonderfully adapted for use by reason of the pleasantness and excellence of their waters. They constructed buildings about them and planted suitable trees; also they made cisterns, some open to the heavens, others roofed over, to be used in winter as warm baths; there were the kings' baths, and the baths of private persons, which were kept apart; and there were separate baths for women, and for horses and cattle, and to each of them they gave as much adornment as was suitable. Of the water which ran off they carried some to the grove of Poseidon, where were

* A yellow metallic substance considered precious by the ancient Greeks, probably a type of brass.

growing all manner of trees of wonderful height and beauty, owing to the excellence of the soil, while the remainder was conveyed by aqueducts along the bridges to the outer circles; and there were many temples built and dedicated to many gods; also gardens and places of exercise, some for men, and others for horses in both of the two islands formed by the zones; and in the centre of the larger of the two there was set apart a race-course of a stadium in width, and in length allowed to extend all round the island, for horses to race in.

After describing guardhouses and the crowded docks, Plato goes on:

Leaving the palace and passing out across the three harbours, you came to a wall which began at the sea and went all round: this was everywhere distant fifty stadia from the largest zone or harbour, and enclosed the whole, the ends meeting at the mouth of the channel which led to the sea. The entire area was densely crowded with habitations; and the canal and the largest of the harbours were full of vessels and merchants coming from all parts, who, from their numbers, kept up a multitudinous sound of human voices, and din and clatter of all sorts night and day.

I have described the city and the environs of the ancient palace nearly in the words of Solon, and now I must endeavour to represent to you the nature and arrangement of the rest of the land. The whole country was said by him to be very lofty and precipitous on the side of the sea, but the country immediately about and surrounding the city was a level plain, itself surrounded by mountains which descended towards the sea; it was smooth and even, and of an oblong shape, extending in one direction three thousand stadia, but across the centre inland it was two thousand stadia. This part of the island looked towards the south, and was sheltered from the north. The surrounding mountains were celebrated for their number and size and beauty, far beyond any which still exist, having in them also many wealthy villages of country folk, and rivers, and lakes, and meadows supplying food enough for every animal, wild or tame, and much wood of various sorts, abundant for each and every kind of work.

I will now describe the plain, as it was fashioned by nature and by the labours of many generations of kings through long ages. It was for the most part rectangular and oblong, and where falling out of the straight line followed the circular ditch. The depth, and width, and length of this ditch were incredible, and gave the impression that a work of such extent, in addition to so many others, could never have been artificial. Nevertheless I must say what I was told. It was excavated to the depth of a hundred feet, and its breadth was a stadium everywhere; it was carried round the whole of the plain, and was ten thousand stadia in length. It received the streams which came down from the mountains, and winding round the plain and meeting at the city, was there let off into the sea. Further inland, likewise, straight canals of a hundred feet in width were cut from it through the plain, and again let off into the ditch leading to the sea: these canals were at intervals of a hundred stadia, and by them they brought down the wood from the mountains to the city, and conveyed the fruits of the earth in ships, cutting transverse passages from one canal into another, and to the city. Twice in the year they gathered the fruits of the earth—in winter having the benefit of the rains of heaven, and in summer the water which the land supplied by introducing streams from the canals.

Plato then tells of the population, the armed forces, with their 10,000 chariots and 1,200 ships, the laws of Atlantis and their administration. In discussing "the vast power which the god settled in the lost island of Atlantis," Plato says the virtues of the people of Atlantis remained great as long as the divine element lasted in them. But, he says:

> when the divine portion began to fade away, and became diluted too often and too much with the mortal admixture, and the human nature got the upper hand, they then, being unable to bear their fortune, behaved unseemly, and to him who had an eye to see, grew visibly debased, for they were losing the fairest of their precious gifts; but to those who had no eye to see the true happiness, they appeared glorious and blessed at the very time when they were full of avarice and unrighteous power.

Zeus, "perceiving that an honorable race was in a woeful plight, and wanting to inflict punishment on them, that they might be chastened and improve," called all the gods together to address them. On this note, intimating the overthrow of Atlantis, the text of *Critias* as we have it breaks off in the middle of a sentence.

This account by Plato is the only authoritative picture we have of Atlantis. The extent to which we can now read it as a credible *historical* record will be made clear by this book. Nearly three years have gone into the writing of this book, years that included extensive research and two scientific expeditions to the Aegean. These expeditions produced more than their share of political intrigue, some personal danger, and an international dispute of page-one proportions. But they also resulted in exciting and dramatic discoveries, all of which will be covered in detail in the pages that follow.

But, in addition to learning of these discoveries, the reader will be introduced to something just as intriguing—a new way of looking at history. The theory that led me to search for Atlantis—*and find it*—casts a whole new light on the interpretation of mythic events. Perhaps the most startling discovery I made was not Atlantis itself, but the realization that Atlantis has lain exposed for centuries, for all to see, if they but knew what to look for.

Book I

CHAPTER 1

TO know Greece thoroughly is impossible, but to fall in love with it is completely natural. We forever seek to know ourselves through man's creations and nowhere are these more eloquent. Every facet of Greece reveals an unrealized aspect of our own being, and in no other country are so many diverse elements drawn together into a cultural unity.

A land of barren hills eroded by the ravages of millennia of cultivation and time itself is the modern traveler's first impression. He streaks, encapsulated, over the dark Aegean and down out of a cloudless sky to be released from an airport and thrust into the sea of faces, talk, commotion, and solid realism that is Greece.

But in the heat of a summer afternoon, the people are quiet, some sleeping, some merely subdued. I first entered Athens at this time of day on Saturday, July 22, 1965, with my wife, Mary, and our three children. The blinding heat, 114 degrees F., and the stark whiteness of everything about us was a shock, an inauspicious beginning for a physically active adventure. But we had felt that we knew the country long before we saw it, and indeed soon felt at home, as Americans inevitably do in Greece.

That evening, when Athens had come alive again, we joined our friends, Dr. Christos Stergis and his family, with whom we planned to travel through Greece. Chris, a space scientist working with the U.S. Air Force, introduced us to a Greek colleague of his, Professor Michael Anastasiades, physicist at the University of Athens Astrophysical Observatory. For a time, inevitably, the conversation concerned outer space. Since my own specialty is oceanography and oceanographic engineering, and since we were all seated on the terrace of a restaurant overlooking the Saronic Gulf, my attention wandered to the scene below. There lights of the night fishing fleet lined the horizon as the local fishermen attracted their catch with large stern-mounted gas lamps that penetrate the water. I reflected on the hard life of a fisherman in the Aegean.

The sea and the people who live on it have always fascinated me. I myself have always lived on or next to the sea. As an engineer at the Woods Hole Oceanographic Institution my work has been constantly related to the sea and its mysteries. For four years I had been working with great intensity on the most exciting project of my career, the design and construction of *Alvin*, the deep-sea research submarine which less than a year later, in early 1966, was to recover a hydrogen bomb lost off the coast of Spain. Before that I had developed a device for probing beneath the sea bottom.

At last, discerning a lull in the conversation, I thought I would ask about oceanography in Greece. Dr. Anastasiades' face lit up with interest. He explained that the person closest to oceanography whom he knew was Angelos Galanopoulos, a seismologist. "But you must see Dr. Galanopoulos," he insisted. Galanopoulos' seismological research had led him to a new theory. Had I ever heard of it? "He has placed the lost continent of Atlantis in the Aegean." Atlantis. All sorts of images and things remembered flooded into my mind. "Yes," I heard Anastasiades say, "just think of it, Atlantis, within an hour's flight or a day's sea voyage from Athens; and there you are, back before the days of the Homeric epics and the birth of the gods of Mt. Olympus." But it was not until I met Galanopoulos on the following Monday, and heard the details of his marvelously ingenious theory, that the magic of Atlantis began to envelop me.

I was delayed in reaching the offices of the Seismological Observatory, high on the Acropolis hill near the Pnyx, ancient place of the Athenian assembly. The street demonstrations of 1965 against the removal of the Premier, George Papandreou, by King Constantine were in progress. Thousands of noisy, excited people crowded the main streets. One had been killed the day before. Nevertheless, everybody, demonstrators and the police who were trying to maintain order alike, seemed reasonably good-natured. Driving was out of the question, so I picked my way through the crowds and up the winding road to the Acropolis. Political unrest is a way of life in Greece, a reality I was later to face up to myself in my quest for the secrets of Atlantis.

At our first meeting, Dr. Galanopoulos, in the Greek tradition, was extremely cordial and friendly. A short, round-faced, heavyset man in his middle fifties, he seems always to exhibit good-humored cheer. His spacious office reflected his personality. It was light, sunny and decorated with flowers from the garden surrounding the building. The hilltop building itself I thought was one of the most beautifully situated in all of Athens.

Dr. Galanopoulos asked me about some of my recent adventures in oceanography. I told him of how we had developed *Alvin* and of my hope that we might possibly bring her to the eastern Mediterranean. We discussed the fact that many oceanographers think of this deep and salty sea as a model ocean. It has, in miniature, many of the characteristics of the great oceans of the world—wide, sweeping currents, upwellings and downthrusts of water, and evidence of the evolutionary changes in animal and plant life. But, as a seismologist, Galanopoulos' principal interest in the Mediterranean was in its vulcanism, earthquakes and seismic sea waves.

He had gathered historical and current data on these geologic events. I realized that this research must have led him to the topic of Atlantis, which topic I was most interested in hearing him talk about. To encourage him, I mentioned the Aegean Sea. I told him it is considered a mysterious source of water circulation lying between the Black Sea and the greater Mediterranean. "Interesting," said Galanopoulos, and smiled. "A fit

Euboea

Thebes

Helike

Corinth
Mycenae

Athens

Pylos

Cyclades

Cape
Tainaron

Cape Maleas

Kithera

Anti Kithera

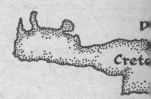

Crete

■ Volcanic Origin

Statute Miles
0   50

Kilometers
0   75

Figure 2. The Aegean Sea, showing islands of volcanic origin.

location for Atlantis, would you not say, this archetypal ocean?"

Here was my opportunity, and I asked him directly about his theory of the lost civilization of Atlantis. His round face beamed, and for the next two hours we talked of nothing else. Galanopoulos was impressive and convincing, and I found myself captivated by his thesis. His enthusiasm set me on fire, and as much of his scientific argument as I could understand, on brief exposure, seemed sound. Many months would elapse before I felt in command of all the subtleties.

Galanopoulos identifies the culture of Atlantis with a known civilization of the ancient world—the people of Crete and the Aegean known as the Minoans. For more than half a century, since the excavations of Arthur Evans in Crete, the Minoans have been recognized as one of the richest, most powerful, most advanced, and most colorful peoples of the ancient world. Despite this parallel to the Atlanteans described by Plato, before Galanopoulos only a few almost-forgotten theorists had remarked on the relationship, and then only superficially.

We tend to identify the Minoans with Crete exclusively, but, as Galanopoulos reminded me, their island empire extended throughout the Aegean Sea, including the group of islands known as the Cyclades and parts of mainland Greece. Dr. Galanopoulos believes that one of these Cycladic islands, Thera, also known as Santorini, was as important to the Minoans as Crete, 60 miles to the south. And it is Thera, a volcanic island with a long history of eruptions, one as recent as 1950, that he assigns as the site of "lost" Atlantis.

As a seismologist, Galanopoulos was well aware that the Thera volcano has long been of interest to geologists. Records of eruptions are to be found in the writings of classical Greek historians, where one can be dated at 197 B.C. Others have occurred since that time, at an average rate of one every fifty years, and even more frequently in this century. The two most gigantic eruptions occurred long before any Greek historians were around to record them—the first at least 25,000 years ago, and the other about 1500–1400 B.C.

Galanopoulos interprets Plato's story as descriptive of two islands, the larger being what Plato called the "royal state" and the smaller the "metropolis," or capital city and religious center. He believes that Plato's description has Thera as the center of Minoan life and Crete as its larger adjunct. This reverses the archaeological findings and is not at all in accord with historic fact as we know it. That is, the evidence suggests that Thera was a Minoan outpost, albeit a very important one religiously, economically, and militarily, and Crete, with its famous palace of Knossos, the cultural and population center. But Galanopoulos has an explanation for this peculiar reversal. Plato, he says, living a thousand years after the fact, would more likely have come in contact with the memory of the cataclysmic explosion at Thera rather than with any memory of the actual geographic disposition of Minoan civilization. As for direct knowledge of the Minoan civilization, it is important to remember that Plato had none.

Dr. Galanopoulos says that Plato's description of the "metropolis" clearly indicates a small volcanic island which had been free of major eruptions for thousands of years. From the description of the external form and plan of the metropolis is it evident that this island was Thera, known to geologists as Stronghyli, or Round Island, in its pre-eruption entirety.

Central to Dr. Galanopoulos' theory and to his interpretation of the disappearance of Atlantis is the enormous catastrophe that destroyed this civilization in a night and a day. The presumed impossibility of such a catastrophe having taken place contributed for centuries to the notion that Atlantis was a myth rather than a fact. According to Dr. Galanopoulos, the catastrophe described by Plato was in fact the eruption, or series of eruptions, in the fifteenth century B.C., of the Minoan island of Thera. The eruptions were accompanied by a massive collapse of the high central portion of the island, some 10 or 11 miles across, in such a way as to form a sea-filled trough, or caldera, 1,300 feet deep. According to Dr. Galanopoulos, this steep height that had collapsed into the sea had been densely peopled, and on its slopes white marble palaces and other considerable structures had glowed in the sunny haze of the Aegean summer.

The acropolis, he believes, would have been on a small hill on the central volcanic cone, largest among several satellite cones. Conceivably, traces of the harbors or the canal described by Plato might be found in the depths of the caldera of Thera. What a subject for investigation by *Alvin!* I thought. Any such evidence, whether discovered by the sub or by other means, would provide the strongest substantiation of Dr. Galanopoulos' theory. He was most anxious to verify the existence of remnants of a circular harbor, as described by Plato. Investigation of the subbottom could reveal geological formations corresponding to the metropolis' harbor. Underwater investigation of the caldera, he also felt, would substantiate the enormity of the Thera eruption and its consequent effects throughout the eastern Mediterranean area. He had great interest, too, in seeing an archaeological expedition dig on the island itself. The discovery of major Minoan ruins would further support his theory.

From the "metropolis" he turned his attention to the "royal state," and his idea of its external form and land plan. Galanopoulos believes it had exactly the characteristics of the Neogene basin of central Crete, of which the great plain of Messara is a part. Here were built the elegant Minoan palaces of Knossos, Mallia, Phaistos, and Hagia Triada. The plain described by Plato lay "towards the sea, but in the centre of the whole island." He tells us it "is said to have been the fairest of all plains and very fertile." In describing it in detail, Plato provided actual measurements. These figures led Dr. Galanopoulos to the most ingenious feature of his theory.

This plain, says Plato, "was smooth and even, and of an oblong shape, extending in one direction three thousand stadia, but across the centre inland it was two thousand stadia" (approximately 340 by 230 miles). The Greek stadium is the length of a racecourse, 600 Greek feet. Recently, it was learned that the length of the foot used in Minoan Crete was almost exactly equal to the present-day English foot, an unexpected convenience.

The size of the plain described in *Critias* is much too large for the plain of Messara in Crete, larger than all Greece, in fact. To explain this discrepancy, Dr. Galanopoulos came up with a startling and original concept. When he had attempted to fit Atlantis into the framework of Minoan history, he told me, he found that all numerical references in the thousands seemed quite implausible, while those involving sums under one thousand were always entirely reasonable. He noted, for example, that whereas the diameter of the circular outlines of both the metropolis and Thera are identical, that is, approximately 11 miles, the dimensions of the royal state seem to be too large by a factor of ten. There is a consistency here, he feels. An error of tenfold crept in, he believes, as the story grew in its telling through the 1,000 years between its provenance and Plato's era.

Atlantis as described by Plato, Galanopoulos says, must have been a Bronze Age civilization. The Bronze Age in Europe and the Near East is dated from 3000 to 1000 B.C., but Plato dates the destruction of Atlantis at 9,000 years before the time of Solon—590 B.C. Plato certainly did not describe a Mesolithic culture, as this date, taken literally, implies. So, there must be an error in date. Let us again assume for the moment that there is a tenfold error, as in the case of the distances. The date of the destruction then comes out 900 + 590 = 1490 B.C., which is very close to our best estimate of the beginning of the catastrophic Thera eruptions.

Is it really possible that a tenfold error of this kind exists? One case would hardly prove the theory. To make it more believable, there must be a consistent error throughout Plato's story and in a substantial number of instances. Dr. Galanopoulos assured me that this is indeed the case. Upon my return home, I was able to verify his claim to the letter. The tenfold error, if it is that, is at any rate completely consistent.

In addition to the detailed dimensions of the "metropolis" and the "royal state," a ditch or river is described surrounding

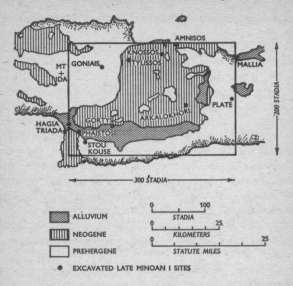

FIGURE 3. Geological map of central Crete with Plato's royal state of Atlantis superimposed. (Geology after Galanopoulos, 1960.)

the plain of the "royal state," 10,000 stadia long. This would be 1,100 miles. The periphery of the plain of Messara is about 110 miles, again one-tenth of Plato's figure.

The plain was divided into 60,000 lots of land, each about one square mile in area. The leader of the residents of each lot was required to furnish, for the war between Athens and Atlantis, one-sixth of a war chariot, two horses and riders, one light chariot, a foot soldier with shield, a charioteer, two heavy armed men, two archers, two slingers, three stone shooters, three javelin men, and four sailors to man the ships, which were 1,200 in number. If the number 60,000 were correct, this vast military machine would have numbered 1,200,000 men, far too many for Minoan Crete, or for any other political entity of that period in history. Minoan Crete in the sixteenth and fifteenth centuries B.C. had an estimated population of only 500,000 to

800,000. Again the error occurs in the 60,000 lots and probably in the 1,200 ships but not in the smaller numbers, Dr. Galanopoulos pointed out to me. He feels, however, that one-tenth of those figures—6,000 lots, 120 ships, and 120,000 men—come very close to all best possible estimates.

Dr. Galanopoulos has an explanation for the tenfold discrepancy: in the translation of the Egyptian scripts by Solon, the symbol representing 100 was unquestionably rendered as 1,000. An example of this same sort of confusion in modern times is the contrast between the American billion, which is a thousand million, and the English billion, which is a million million.

Error was inherent in the transmission of the Atlantean legend to Plato. In referring to two written versions, one in the Egyptian sacred writings and the other by Solon in Greek, Plato states: "You must not be surprised if you should hear Hellenic names given to foreigners. I will tell you the reason for this: Solon, who was intending to use the tale for his poem, made an investigation into the meanings of the names, and found that the early Egyptians in writing them down had translated them into their own language, and he recovered the meaning of the several names and retranslated them, and copied them out again in our language."

So there was a Greek written version of at least part of the story of Atlantis which Plato may have seen. If Solon wrote the poem he intended to, then perhaps Plato saw that. Now the records are lost, if, indeed, they ever existed. If we can believe Solon's contention that the names of the kings of Atlantis were originally Greek in character, certainly a close-to-home location for the mysterious island is indicated.

For the date to fit Galanopoulos' scheme, as he explains, the error must have been made when Solon obtained the story in Egypt. It was said to have been kept in the sacred records, records written in hieroglyphs on stone or on papyrus. These hieroglyphs are themselves not easily confused, which would suggest that the error either arose with Solon or had already crystallized before the Egyptian recording which Solon encoun-

V.T.A.—B

tered. We do not know what the documentation seen by Solon could have been like. If the Egyptians obtained the story from a Cretan refugee who was sufficiently educated, it might have been written in the Aegean Linear A or B script. In this writing system the symbols for 100, 1,000 and 10,000 are very similar and could be easily confused. Another possibility is that the Minoan refugee trail passed through Ugarit in modern Syria, a commercial and literary center of Hittite, Babylonian, and, later, Phoenician influence. The story Solon knew could have followed this trail.

In Solon's time, Greek numerals were imprecise and easily mistaken, but we cannot be sure just where the tenfold error developed. The circumstantial evidence that it did, however, becomes more impressive the deeper we dig into Aegean prehistory. If the tenfold error was indeed made in translation, it would explain why figures below 1,000 stand correct. The length of the canal from the center of the metropolis to the sea is 50 stadia, 5½ miles, which gives the palace and surrounding town an 11-mile diameter—precisely that of Thera.

Dr. Galanopoulos suggests that Plato, misled by the tenfold error, put Atlantis in the Atlantic Ocean beyond Gibraltar (the Pillars of Herakles of Plato's time) simply because it would not fit anywhere else. He did not know of the Thera eruption and his only notion of prehistoric times was through the Greek myths. He was evidently not bothered by the lack of logic in placing Atlantis so far from Athens. Once again, the catastrophic aspect of the story was clearly what held him.

Dr. Galanopoulos says that it is clear that in the Egyptian writings there is no mention of the Pillars of Herakles and that for the Egyptians Atlantis was located in the Aegean Sea. He pointed out that in *Timaeus* the priests are made to say: "This sea . . . within the Straits of Heracles is only a harbour, having a narrow entrance, but that other is a real sea, and the surrounding land may be most truly called a boundless continent."

It is known, he added, that most of Herakles' or Hercules' feats were performed in the Peloponnesus, and had no connec-

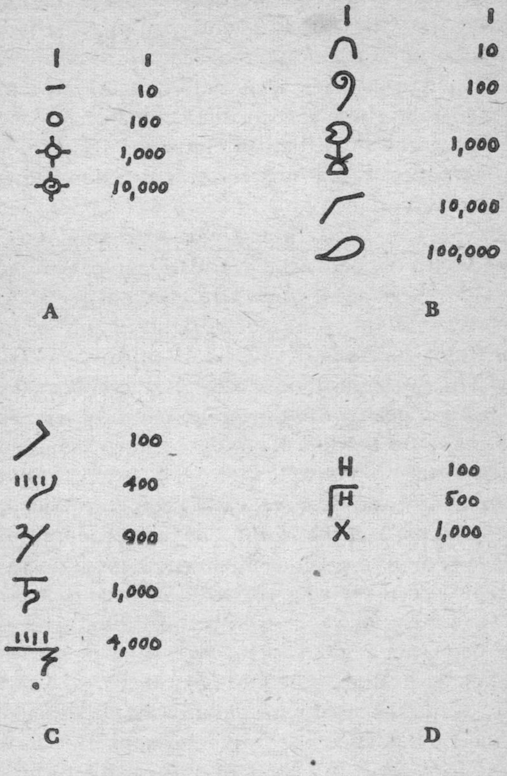

A

B

C

D

FIGURE 4 a. Cretan Linear script (1500 B.C.).
   b. Egyptian hieroglyphs (3000 B.C.–A.D. 500).
   c. Egyptian hieratic.
   d. Greek Attic script.

tion with Gibraltar. Also, he believes that the Pillars of Herakles actually referred to Cape Malea and Cape Tainaron (Cape
Matapan) on the Peloponnesus, and not to Gibraltar at all.
The mention of the Pillars by Plato may again be a reiteration
of a misinterpretation originating with Solon. Plato's priests at
one point say: "and there was an island situated in front of the
straits which you call the Pillars of Herakles." This implies that
the pillars were introduced into the story by Solon and were not
in the original Egyptian record.

Progressing to a more scientifically based argument to support
his Thera-Atlantis connection, Dr. Galanopoulos pointed out to
me that in the Aegean, or anywhere else, only small tracts of
land have ever suddenly sunk out of sight, as did, for example,
the city of Helice in the Gulf of Corinth during the earthquake
of 373 B.C. The disappearance of a large land area of thousands
of square miles is geologically possible, but only very slowly, so
slowly that it would be difficult to detect any change even in a
human generation. Conversely, the rise of the oceans due to the
melting of polar ice is only 3 feet each 1,000 years. Such changes
take place in all parts of the world, but they produce no percep-
tible damage and, because of their slowness, go unnoticed.

Discouraging to those who would have Atlantis in the mid-
Atlantic, Galanopoulos says, are oceanographic data that are
constantly being augmented as research ships of many nations
sample the ocean bottom. The mid-Atlantic ridge, on which lie
the Azores, often associated with Atlantis, has been dated radio-
logically and no evidence was found for sunken islands in the
last 72,000 years. The thickness of the earth's rocky crust is
greater under the continents than under the oceans. At a location beneath the mid-Atlantic ridge near the Azores, the earth's
crust has been found to be much thinner than that under the
continents. This indicates that an Atlantean continent in this
area is all but impossible.

Given its location at the center of the ancient world, the
collapse of Thera was a disaster comparable to nuclear war
today. Hundreds of thousands of persons could have lost their

lives. Cities, ports, and villages on many islands and on the mainland of Greece and Turkey could have been washed away or inundated by torrential rains triggered by the spew of ash. What remained would have been toppled and pounded to rubble by tidal waves. Fleets of ships would have foundered or been hurled miles inland. Cities in the highlands, at least those close to Thera, would have been rocked and torn by earthquakes. And all the while, volcanic ash would have blackened the heavens, turning day into night, with thunder crashing, lightning searing the sky, and the seas becoming clogged with mud.

A disaster of such magnitude must surely have left its impact upon the folk memory of the peoples of the entire eastern Mediterranean area. Indeed, Dr. Galanopoulos firmly believes that the story of Atlantis is but one of a family of related myths. The Greek legend of the deluge of Deucalion, he feels, also has its origin in the eruption and collapse of Thera. The deluge of Deucalion is the Greek counterpart of the Biblical flood and Utnapishtim's Babylonian inundation in the *Epic of Gilgamesh*. In addition, Dr. Galanopoulos relates other Greek myths or legends and the Biblical account of the Exodus to the cataclysmic eruption of Thera.

I have outlined here Dr. Galanopoulos' theory as he presented it to me that day in his office. The many details of this theory and of Plato's account, and their significance, took me months to master. They were, of course, all familiar to Galanopoulos, and as he spoke he would digress to point up the fascinating ramifications of some small item. For example, the twin brother of Atlas, the first king, was Eumelos, who, it was said, ruled the portion of Atlantis nearest the Strait of Herakles. If this strait was really at the southeastern tip of the Peloponnesus, as Galanopoulos believes, and not as far off as Gibraltar, then the nearest Minoan island, Melos, may have been the domain of King Eumelos. Geologically similar to Thera, Melos is a collapsed volcano, but with no recorded mention of eruption. On Thera there is a stone bearing the archaic Greek inscription

FIGURE 5. The Mediterranean Sea from Tunisia to the Levant.

Eumelos. It is probably, says Galanopoulos, the name of an early post-eruption settler, who may have been a descendant of the ancient king.

At one point he gazed out of his observatory window in the direction of the Acropolis and quoted Plato on the subject of ancient Athens at the time of its war with Atlantis. "In the first place the Acropolis was not as now. For the fact is that a single night of excessive rain washed away the earth and laid bare the rock; at the same time there were earthquakes, and then occurred the extraordinary inundation, which was the third before the great destruction of Deucalion. . . . Where the Acropolis now is there was a fountain, which was choked by the earthquake, and has left only the few small streams which still exist in the vicinity. . . ." He followed this, still gazing from the window, with the remark, "Attica, you know, is seldom subject to severe earthquakes and flooding. Only an event as catastrophic as the Thera collapse could have this effect on the Acropolis. And there remains, of course, evidence of a spring on the Acropolis which was dried up by earthquake in about 1500 B.C. Also it is interesting that Plato mentions three floods, because when the volcanic island of Krakatoa, between Java and Sumatra, collapsed in 1883, there were three great seismic sea waves. Thus, by analogy, several waves could be expected from the collapse of Thera, which became styled in the myth of Deucalion as three."

It seems to me, in retrospect, as if more than chance was involved in my meeting with Galanopoulos. But, questions of fate and destiny aside, it certainly occurred at a time peculiarly suited to our future relationship. We were both, unwittingly, ready for an adventure. For me it was time to think beyond *Alvin*, now operational and nearing the end of her shakedown period. Atlantis was a subject bound to appeal to any oceanographer with a bit of romance in his makeup. Looking back, knowing all I do now, I can well imagine how personally moving, how exciting, it must have been for Dr. Galanopoulos to discuss his theory with me, to see how he was infecting me with his own enthusiasm. The possibility I represented even then, however remotely, of organizing an expedition to prove his theory must have fired him all the more.

Excavations had been conducted on Thera in the nineteenth century, before Evans revealed the glories of the ancient Minoan civilization. Thus the finding of Minoan relics meant relatively little, and digging on the island was sporadic. After some field-work at the close of the century, Thera appeared to be a forgotten island. But it was not entirely neglected.

During the sixty-six years in which archaeological interest in the island lapsed, great quantities of volcanic ash were being mined and exported for use in making cement. Frequently during this period antiquities had turned up, and some of them had found their way to the small museum on the island, while others vanished among collectors. In 1956, in the course of one of these quarrying operations, a Minoan house appeared quite accidentally. On this occasion Dr. Galanopoulos obtained a piece of wood from a tree buried in the pumice, submitted it to radiocarbon dating and found it to be about 3,500 years old. This placed the newly discovered relics at the peak of the Minoan period.

Was it possible to reconstruct what Thera looked like before the collapse? Would modern oceanographic techniques help to do this? I was suddenly forcibly convinced they would. In a burst of enthusiasm I could not have foreseen two hours earlier, I told Dr. Galanopoulos that I would try to bring back the necessary scientists and equipment. Perhaps I was spurred by the recurring image of this project as a "natural" for the *Alvin*. But, even then, I was aware that proving Dr. Galanopoulos' theory involved archaeological examination of the island as well as underwater exploration of the caldera. Nevertheless, he had fired me with a determination to try to find the evidence I felt must be there to prove that Atlantis and Thera were one.

On this note we parted, and I returned to everyday modern Athens to see along noisy Panepistimeou Street army trucks carrying off the demonstrators. Taking care not to be hauled

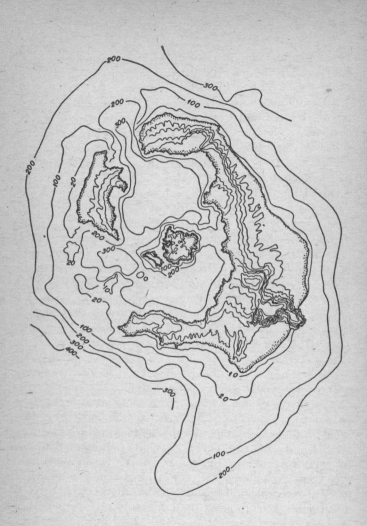

FIGURE 6. Thera, showing sea depth and land elevation contours. Soundings in meters. (After Reck, 1936.)

off as an agitator myself, I found my hotel, where our two-family group planned the details of our long-anticipated auto trip north into Greek Macedonia.

After my visit with Galanopoulos, we were sorely tempted (or I was) to change our plans to include a tour of the Aegean Islands, but we had a commitment to travel north, and decided to abandon the islands for that summer. As it turned out, our visit to the mountain village of Paleogratsinon, where my physicist friend Christos Stergis was born, only fed my growing excitement about Atlantis, and provided an extra spark needed to push me ahead on my studies of the Mediterranean lands in prehistory.

The people of the northern mountains of Greece may well be the earliest Greeks, direct descendants of the Mycenaeans of prehistory, the Athenians of the story of Atlantis. There are, at least, striking similarities between their textile patterns and Mycenaean pottery designs—black and white rectangles, dog-tooth staircases and saw edges, the primitive interplay of images and figures. These may well have sprung from the same source.

Once back in Athens, I began at once to acquaint myself with the Atlantean theme, an effort I was to continue diligently upon my return to America. An English translation of Plato was available in Athens, as were well-known works of Atlantis lore. I soon learned not only that Plato's dialogues offer the only account of the legend in literature in which the name Atlantis is used, but that most of the many published interpretations of the Atlantis myth are pseudoscientific from the start, and the facts they contain are more credibly presented in more widely accepted works of science and history.

I realized that these accounts could be a pernicious distraction, diverting me from the purpose of my research. I sought to confirm a particular theory locating Atlantis in the Aegean, and my source must be the history of this region. The other material could only catch me up in the web in which so many others have become entangled. Such was my mood on entering the arena of Atlantis lore.

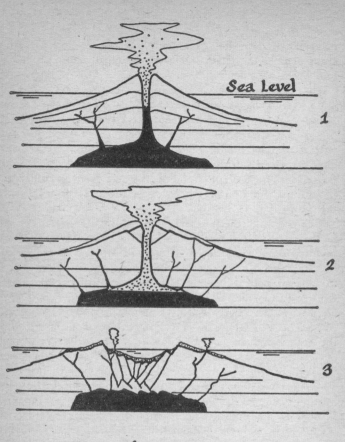

Sea Level

1

2

3

■ Liquid Magma

▨ Ash and Pumice

FIGURE 7. Volcanic eruption and collapse, typical behavior of a Theran cone.
(1) Eruption.
(2) Eruption and partial voiding of magma chamber below.
(3) Collapse of unsupported cone into empty magma chamber, creating great water-filled caldera.

CHAPTER 2

THE many volumes written on Atlantis have one feature in common—lack of a convincing explanation for its sudden catastrophic destruction. Theories are rampant and include even the sudden and irregular behavior of heavenly bodies, from meteorite showers to comets. These are theoretically possible occurrences, but they have not been tied close enough in time or place to the destruction of Atlantis to be credible. The establishment as fact, with a confidence unprecedented in Atlantis lore, of just such a catastrophic event provides the explanation. That event was the eruption and collapse of the volcano of Thera.

Sudden natural catastrophes—volcanic eruptions and collapses, earthquakes, floods from the sea or by excessive rain—have occurred all through man's lifetime on earth. There have also been slower forces—glaciation, change of climate, change in sea level, gradual earth movements—altering his environment. Sudden cataclysms are known to have destroyed cities and affected populated areas adversely. Gradual changes have also made them uninhabitable, causing large-scale migrations of people. Both types of natural force have figured in the theorizing about Atlantis' destruction.

We have ample documentation of the effects of sudden natural catastrophes in populated areas. In November, 1775, Lisbon was victim to a coastal submarine shock that engulfed 60,000 persons. Mt. Pelée on the West Indian island of Martinique erupted in 1902, killing 30,000 people. And these are but two of the more famous instances. The slower natural forces of destruction have affected whole cultures. Their effects, while less dramatic, have been just as devastating.

As the gigantic glaciers advanced and receded, people moved similarly, following the environment to which they had become accustomed and at the same time slowly adapting to the new. As the Sahara desert of North Africa encroached on the once-verdant terrain, beginning about 2000 B.C., peoples moved to the coasts, to the south and to the east, where Egypt with its advanced civilization was in flower. We are now learning that changes of climate were probably responsible for migrations of peoples of the Mediterranean shortly after the time of the Thera eruption, migrations that, heretofore, had not been satisfactorily explained. Legends grew from all these changes in man's environment. Then myth compounded myth when attempts were made to associate Plato's Atlantis with events throughout the world far from Greece, and golden temples were invented to fit Plato's story.

Of the many theories that attempt to locate Atlantis beyond the Aegean, that of Paul Borchardt, in 1927, is perhaps the most reasonable. He, like Galanopoulos, recognized the description of two distinct regions in Plato's story. He placed the lesser island of Atlantis, the seat of the king, distinguished by Plato from Atlantis in a wider sense, a few miles inland of the Gulf of Gabès in Tunisia in the region of "shotts," from the Arabic word *chot*, a saline lake, which geologists think was a former water area connected with the Mediterranean. He identifies the Platonic Atlantis—really two regions—with the whole of coastal North Africa, physically cut off from the rest of the continent. He puts Plato's Atlantis Sea in the inland gulf connected to the Mediterranean by a narrow strait such as Plato described, and the engulfment is supposed to have been the sinking of a small island by earthquake.

He has seen similarities between the names given to the ten kings of Atlantis and existing Berber tribal names of Tunisia. Also, a complex of irrigation canals, as described by Plato, was likely, and some other features of Plato's account do fit the realm of possibility. While evidence is sparse, it is possible, and the timing could be right, that the people from Tunisia, forced to migrate east by the encroaching sands of the Sahara or by earthquake, may have influenced the story of Atlantis recorded in Egypt, and some details such as names and canal descriptions may have been blended into the story basically built on the Minoans and the Thera disaster.

Rather less plausible is a recent theory put forward by Dr. Jürgen Spanuth, a Lutheran pastor and amateur archaeologist, who is convinced that the island of Atlantis is to be found under the North Sea near the island of Heligoland, about 30 miles off the coast of Germany. He claims that an island sank rapidly during the Bronze Age. Regrettably, marine coastal research shows that it was precisely during the Bronze Age that the North Sea was in a period of exceptionally quiet development and no evidence for the submergence of a land mass can be found. In addition, underwater photographs of stone slabs claimed to be man-made pavement have been examined by geologists and appraised as completely natural formations.

My concern, however, is not with the disproof of Dr. Spanuth's or any other theory of a vanished civilization, but with the claim that these are the root of Plato's Atlantis. The study of ancient history is in a period of ferment and new researches are needed.

Indeed, we are constantly finding evidence that prehistoric peoples traveled farther than anyone had ever suspected. Great Britain certainly, and probably Spanuth's northern Germany, were visited by the Minoans of the second millennium B.C., and I am willing to believe that Europeans crossed the Atlantic Ocean to both North and South America well before the Christian era. Cyrus Gordon of Brandeis University has recently found convincing evidence of a Phoenician voyage around Africa in the sixth century B.C. in which the travelers were blown off course and crossed the Atlantic to land on the coast of Brazil.

Another unlikely location of Plato's Atlantis is off the rocky shoreline of Ansedonia, 70 miles north of Rome. Italian archaeologist Constantino Cattoi sees evidence there of giant rock sculptures which he believes were made by the people of Atlantis. He claims that the massive sculptured lions guarded a city that now lies under water.

In the Marquesas Trench southwest of Peru, giant man-made columns are said to have been photographed deep beneath the sea as evidence of Atlantis. These may be solidified lava flows such as are found in Fingal's Cave on the Scottish island of Staffa, where long hexagonal columns appear. If so, it would not be the first time that nature's sculptures were mistaken for antiquities.

In support of an Atlantic Ocean site for Atlantis, Lewis Spence has turned to a popular notion of natural history, the annual march of the lemmings to the sea. These small rodents of migratory habit reputedly swim far out into the Atlantic from the Norwegian coast. Then, on reaching a spot to which the migratory instinct has supposedly taken them, they are supposed to circle around as if in search of land, and, failing, sink exhausted into the depths. Spence has also pointed out that large flocks of birds do indeed annually migrate to a part of the Atlantic where no land is now visible, and after fluttering about in dismay for some time, fall spent into the sea. These and other similar occurrences depend presumably on some deepseated biological instinct not yet understood and, if the idea has any validity, it would be correlatable with oceanographic data. In any case, such a theory may locate former islands inhabited by lemmings and birds, but not Atlanteans.

These are a few notions from current Atlantis lore. But no book on the legendary empire would be complete without a recitation of some of the more colorful ideas that have come down to us under the cloak of science and history or as proposed by mystics.

Charles Brasseur de Bourbourg, an erratic French scholar, was intrigued by the imaginative translation of Mayan script by

Diego de Landa in the sixteenth century and conceived, in 1864, via this script, an account of a volcanic catastrophe that destroyed a land he called "Mu."

Le Plongeon, shortly afterward, developed the romantic story of the Queen of Mu. Atlantis, a large island in the Atlantic Ocean, was identified with Mu. After the land had sunk beneath the sea, the queen fled to Egypt, where, as the god Isis, she founded a civilization. At the same time, other Muvians or Atlanteans went to Yucatán and became the Mayas.

Ignatius Donnelly, whose *Atlantis, The Antediluvian World* was first published in 1882 and is still in print in a revised edition, started Atlantis as a popular cult. He expanded on the tale of Mu and built a splendid prehistoric civilization upon an island in the Atlantic Ocean. He drew on many legends and historical records, interpreting them to support his theory.

In 1912 Paul Schliemann, grandson of Heinrich Schliemann, discoverer of Troy, entered the arena with a story involving a bronze vase, supposedly found in Troy, inscribed "From the King Cronos of Atlantis." Otherwise, he followed the revelations of Donnelly and Le Plongeon.

From the shaky ground provided by these few investigators, the lore takes off into occultism, where Atlantis has become so surrounded by flights of fancy that many reputable scholars, understandably, have become wary of associating with it in any way. A rather primitive but large stone structure, named Nan Matol, on the island of Temuen, in the Caroline Islands of the Pacific Ocean, is the focus of the "cult of Lemuria." In the 1860's, the theory of a former continent or land bridge in the Indian Ocean connecting India and South Africa was proposed seriously by geologists and biologists. Philip Sclater, an English zoologist, coined the name Lemuria after the lemurs, the primitive monkeys of Madagascar, an island supposedly part of the "bridge" that also included the Seychelles. This idea was picked up by Elena Blavatsky, who founded the Theosophist cult. She included Atlantis as well as Lemuria in her Cosmos and promoted a thriving medicine show until her death, in 1891, after which her followers were unable to maintain public interest. Other occultists revived the theory and moved Lemuria into the central Pacific, where geologically it is most unlikely, and associated it with Nan Matol.

More recently, the mystic Edgar Cayce, who would place Atlantis in the western Atlantic Ocean with a twenty-first-century culture, prophesied that Poseidia, as he had named the largest island of the Atlantean empire, was due to rise again in 1968 or 1969. Perhaps Cayce was prophesying metaphorically and did not mean that the island would actually rise but that it would be identified. At any rate, let us hope so.

Dr. Galanopoulos had expressed a profound idea, which now came to my mind. It was that eastern Mediterranean earthquakes and floods have always been purely local events. In each inlet where the floodwaters rose, an independent legend would be born and grow. This must be true the world over. Must every legend of a sunken island be a variation of the Atlantean theme? He did not think so.

He had gone on to say that in the Aegean, destruction from an earthquake has never been found outside the circle formed by a 250-mile radius from the epicenter, and that the circle is generally much smaller. An event like the Thera collapse could affect both Crete and the Greek mainland and give rise to a legend in which both participated in a single catastrophe. But the legend would have to have a localized provenance. The simultaneous destruction of the "Athenians" and "Atlanteans" could be traced to a single local point of origin —the eruption of Thera.

Plato's *Timaeus* is the first Greek account of a divine creation, an attempt to bring together a rational explanation of nature and the theology of Plato's Greece. It was one of the few works of classical antiquity to survive as a contemporary written document through to the Middle Ages. Because of this we can have some confidence that what we read today is what Plato actually wrote. It is comforting to find the story of Atlantis so well founded in its literary source.

If we do take Plato's story of Atlantis at face value, we are repeatedly reminded in it that it is a tale that came to him through others from Egypt. There is no strong reason for believing that Plato himself dreamed it up and much reason for believing that he did not. For something over 2,000 years, scholars have endlessly debated whether Atlantis sprang entirely from Plato's imagination, or should be viewed as a twice-told tale.

W. A. Heidel, for example, the American scholar who so eloquently denies the reality of Atlantis, claims that Plato and certain other men of the fourth century B.C. thought that the Egyptian priests were introduced into the tale not because they were held in awe by the Greeks of that day, which in fact they were not, but by way of mockery. There is a passage in *Timaeus* in which Plato says that the Egyptian priests claimed that Athens was older than Egypt by 1,000 years and that the institutions of Egypt were derived from an ancient Athens. Heidel believes that here Plato is merely spoofing the Greek tradition, and that elsewhere the same spirit holds true.

However, a very famous predecessor of Plato, Herodotus (485–425 B.C.), expressed a strong conviction that Greek institutions were derived from Egypt, which would suggest an emphasis quite opposite to Heidel's. Herodotus has been known by epithets ranging from "father of lies" to "father of history." But scholars today agree that the *History* of Herodotus was in fact a remarkable inquiry into events of his own time and of centuries previous. His personal observations, in a great many instances, have proved accurate time and time again. Whether Plato "reported" or created his history out of whole cloth we can never know from internal evidence; but that it can be founded in fact is at least plausible, on the grounds that Greeks are typically realists and that, in general, all legends of this nature have their roots in actuality.

What have scholars other than Galanopoulos had to say about an Aegean location for Atlantis? He was not, I discovered, the first to identify Thera, Crete, and the Minoan civilization in general with the "lost continent" of Atlantis. The idea had been at least incidentally brought forward on a number of occasions in earlier years.

First of all came the French geologist Ferdinand Fouqué, whose excavations revealed that Thera had been the scene, sometime in the Bronze Age, 3000 to 1000 B.C., of a tremendous siege of volcanic activity, the result of which was a subsidence into the sea of the entire mountainous center of the island. This series of eruptions, as described by Fouqué, unquestionably had been of a magnitude great enough to fill the whole island region with dense clouds of ash and sulphurous gases. Fouqué's attention had been drawn to Thera when mining operations for pumice, to be used in making cement for the construction of the Suez Canal, disclosed evidence of the life that had existed on the island before the vast eruptions of long ago. Houses were revealed that had been sheared off as the rocky base of the central portion of the island gave way—an event that had to await Fouqué's laborious examination to be authenticated. An even earlier scientist, another Frenchman, l'Abbé Pègues, had speculated that Thera might have suffered volcanic collapse. However, it was Fouqué who laid a systematic foundation for this belief.

To still another Frenchman must go the honor of linking the Thera Bronze Age eruption with the legendary Atlantis. This was Auguste Nicaise, who gave a lecture on this idea in 1885. Significantly, the Nicaise lecture occurred two years after the great eruption and collapse of the island of Krakatoa in Sunda Strait between Sumatra and Java. We now know that the Thera eruption was similar in its behavior to that of Krakatoa, only Thera was some five times greater. After Nicaise, it was Crete, only 60 miles from Thera, which often was identified with Atlantis. This natural shift of emphasis to an island that must have been drastically affected by volcanic events on Thera persisted for some decades.

On January 19, 1909, the London *Times* carried an anonymous article that said that Minoan Crete and Plato's Atlantis were one and the same. A year later, the Reverend James Baikie suggested in *The Sea Kings of Crete* that the legend was a memory of the sudden destruction of the Cretan civilization and had been handed down by the Egyptian priests to Plato. Thirty years later, the British archaeologist J. K. Frost gave his endorsement to the theory that the Minoan culture of Crete and Atlantis were one and the same, and admitted that he had been the author of the anonymous article in 1909.

Baikie, back in 1910, explaining his theory that the sudden destruction of civilization on Crete was the memory on which Plato based his dialogues, wrote: "Doubtless to the men of the latter part of the Eighteenth Dynasty [in Egypt] the sudden blotting out of Minoan trade and influence by the overthrow of Knossos seemed as strange and mysterious as though Crete had actually been swallowed up by the sea. The island never regained its lost supremacy, and gradually sank into insignificance which is its characteristic throughout the classical period. . . ."

The Reverend Baikie had additional reasons for locating Atlantis in the Aegean. "The only difficulty in the way of accepting the [Cretan] identification," he wrote, "is that it is stated that the lost Atlantis lay beyond the Pillars of Herakles; but doubtless this statement is due to Solon's misinterpretation of what was said by his Egyptian informant, or to the Saite priest's endeavor to accommodate his ancient tradition to the wider geographical knowledge of his own time. The old Egyptian conception of the universe held that the heavens were supported on four pillars, which were actual mountains; and probably the original story placed the lost island beyond these pillars as a metaphorical way of stating that it was very far distant, as indeed it was to voyagers in those early days. But by Solon's time the limits of navigation were extended far beyond those of the early seafarers. The Phoenician traders had pushed at least as far west as Spain; Necho's fleet had circumnavigated Africa; and so 'the island farthest west,' which naturally meant Crete to the Egyptian of the Eighteenth Dynasty who first re-

corded the catastrophe of the Minoan empire, had to be thrust
out beyond the Straits of Gibraltar to satisfy the wider ideas of
the men of Solon's and Necho's time."

In 1939 Dr. Spyridon Marinatos, who was to join our research
team as director of the Thera excavation in 1967, after some
years of rumination, published his theory that the eruption
and collapse of Thera were responsible for the destruction of all
the coastal Minoan palaces and towns on Crete in about 1500
B.C. Then, in 1950, Professor Marinatos wrote, "The Egyptians
unquestionably had heard about the sinking of an island, which
was Thera, but this island, small and insignificant, was unknown
to them. This event they transferred to the neighboring Crete,
an island which was dreadfully struck and with which they had
lost contact suddenly. The knowledge of the loss of tens of
thousands of souls was standardized into the legend of the
drowning of an army. With the lack of coherence and logic
which characterizes myths surely not even Plato felt the incon-

FIGURE 8a. Late Minoan oc-
topus jar, Heraklion museum.

FIGURE 8b. Libation jug from
the Katsabas tombs, Crete. C.
1500 B.C.

sistency that at the same time Atlantis sank in the Atlantic and the army of the Athenians sank in Athens."

Galanopoulos' ingenious theory of 1960 was, in part, a consolidation and extension of ideas going back many decades. Other writers registered similar, if more tentative, opinions; among them highly respected archaeologists.

J. D. S. Pendlebury, former curator at Knossos for the British School at Athens, in 1939, in *The Archaeology of Crete*, wrote this of the Minoans: "The impression we get is of an ordered state with a highly centralized bureaucracy, the whole being ruled from the royal city of Knossos, where, as all Greek legends agree, was the seat of Minos, lord of Crete and many overseas dominions. How deep an impression this empire made has been fascinatingly brought forward by J. K. Frost, who pointed out the extraordinary resemblance between Plato's Atlantis, as described in the *Critias*, and Minoan Crete. Even more interesting is Leaf's suggestion that the Phaiacia of the *Odyssey* is no less than a picture of the Minoan realm transferred to fairyland, while Miss Lorimer has shown that many of the early elements in the Homeric poems are a reflection of the golden days of Late Minoan I–II."

In 1962 R. W. Hutchinson, lecturer in classical archaeology at Cambridge University, wrote in his *Prehistoric Crete:* "It has been suggested that Plato's account of Atlantis, that island with its wonderful culture, its cult of Poseidon, and the emphasis on roads and water supplies, might be a reference, derived from folklore, to the lost island culture of Crete, and even that the reference to Solon deriving his information from Egypt might refer to information about Minoan Crete preserved in Egyptian records. It is clear, however, that Plato himself did not identify Atlantis with Crete, and if he used folklore referring to Minoan Crete he was quite unconscious of any connection between them."

It has long been known that between 1450 and 1400 B.C. the Minoan settlements on Crete were destroyed simultaneously by a large-scale disaster. Archaeologists have claimed that the disaster was caused by invasion, insurrection, or earthquake. Arthur Evans consistently maintained that the disaster was the result of natural causes.

In 1939, Dr. Marinatos' theory that the eruption and collapse of Thera, in addition to concurrent quakes, were responsible for the general Cretan destruction was so sensational that it was largely ignored by scholars. Through the years, however, it has gained a measure of acceptance. Marinatos has no doubts concerning the destructive potential of Thera, a potential of far greater magnitude than any earthquake. In his 1939 paper he wrote, "A normal earthquake is wholly insufficient to explain so great a disaster. In all the many earthquakes known to us, there has never been such a widespread destruction at one and the same moment."

Professor Galanopoulos confirms the truth of this assertion. Nowhere in the world is there such an accumulation of data on earthquakes as in Greece. In the past 200 years alone, over 2,000 severe earthquakes have been recorded—that is, quakes registering over 4¾ on the Richter scale. Activity is concentrated mainly in the large geological fault zone bordering the western and southern coasts of Greece. The southerly zone of high activity is in a rectangle of which the islands of Crete, Rhodes, Nisyros, and Thera form the corners, so that we know well the effects of normal earthquakes in this area. Of the varied geological deposits on Crete, by and large sedimentary, the central, newly formed basin containing the palace of Knossos and the southern palaces of Phaistos and Hagia Triada is most prone to tremors, which have always been local in their effects. During 1450–1400 B.C., the whole of eastern Crete was overcome during a few decades or less. What the ash and the waves did not destroy, the earthquakes before and after did.

The eruption and collapse of Thera is the greatest natural catastrophe that has occurred in historical times. Where Thera now lies, there was originally a limestone mountain whose three peaks of bright marble pierced the surface of the sea. The highest was 2,000 feet, the present Mt. Hagias Elias, the others

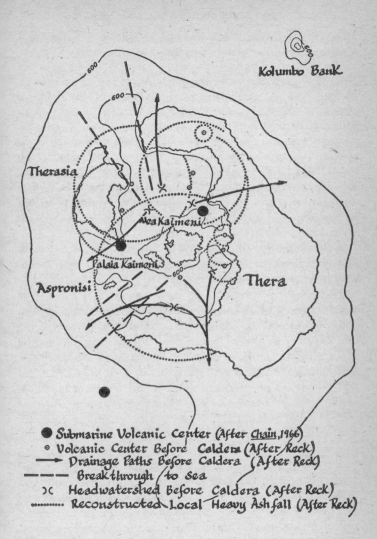

FIGURE 9. Location of pre-eruption volcanic vents, watersheds and drainage paths of Thera before 1500 B.C. Soundings in feet. (After Reck, 1936.)

Monolithos and Platinamos. They are connected by a stony submarine ridge to the island of Anaphi, 15 miles to the east.

Many thousand, though probably less than a million, years ago, a fracture occurred in the earth's crust running southwest to northeast, and submarine volcanoes began to build in the bottom of the sea. In the vicinity of Thera perhaps a dozen volcanoes erupted fitfully over the centuries, causing the water to steam and boil and the fish to die. Today the descendants of these fish have adapted to the sulphurous environment and are without color. These volcanoes thrust themselves above the sea and formed the circular island of Thera, named in its pre-eruption state, as we have said, Stronghyli, or Round Island, by modern geologists to distinguish it from its subsequent remnants.

To the southwest, the volcanic islands of Kristiana appeared, and to the northeast, the island of Anihdros. On Stronghyli, considerable mountains were formed.

Then, about 25,000 years ago, came a spectacular eruption of ash and pumice which covered the entire eastern Mediterranean with volcanic debris. After a tremendous final paroxysm, the central part of Stronghyli, the original Thera, collapsed into the sea leaving a ringlike island. We do not know in any detail what this looked like. Perhaps it was uninhabited. Then for many thousands of years the volcanoes built up again and much of the collapsed center was filled in. After a time, most of the island became volcanically dormant. The lava flows weathered, creating a fertile brown, red, and black soil. By the second millennium, there was probably more rainfall than the spare 15 inches a year found today. And the humus held the rainwater much better than the present-day surface of dry, porous volcanic ash. However, cisterns were probably used to collect and save fresh water, for only on the limestone peaks are natural springs and storage cavities found. A prehistoric culture gradually developed on the island.

The birth of Thera, both geologically and as a site of human habitation, has been recorded, though we have tended to ignore this, in the myth of the Argonauts.

Jason, sailing homeward from his search for the Golden Fleece, approached Crete from the island of Karpathos. A great bronze giant, Talos, threw rocks at the *Argo* as she tried to sail into the harbor of Dicte in eastern Crete. Medea, the sorceress, used her magic to slay the giant, and the crew spent two nights ashore before setting sail to the northward, headed for the mainland.

"The next night," Apollonius tells us, "caught them well out in the wide Cretan Sea, and they were frightened, for they had run into that sort of night that people call the pall of doom. No star, no moonlight, pierced the funereal dark. Black chaos had descended on them from the sky, or had this darkness risen from the nethermost abyss? They could not tell whether they were drifting through Hades or still on the water. All they could do was commit their course to the sea, with no idea where it would take them." Apollonius goes on to say that Jason then appealed to Phoebus, who sent Leto with a bow to shoot light into the darkness. "The bow shot beams of dazzling light into the dark all around." An island was seen and they landed. This island they called Anaphe (Revelation) because Apollo had revealed it to them.

Apollonius then tells how Euphemus, of the *Argo*'s crew, had been told in a dream to throw into the sea near Anaphe the clod of dirt given to him in Libya by Triton. In the dream, the clod became a virginal woman with whom Euphemus lay, then threw into the sea; however, she later reappeared in time to welcome his descendants. The dream was recounted to Jason, who thereupon was reminded of an oracle of Apollo and he prophesied a new island grown from the clod. Euphemus then threw the clod into the depths and there grew the island called Calliste. Euphemus' descendants lived first in Lemnos, then in Sparta, then settled on Calliste under Theras, who named the island Thera. This happened long after Euphemus' days were over.

"No star, no moonlight, pierced the funereal dark. Black chaos had descended on them. . . ." Very early in my ruminations on Thera it struck me that the Argonauts could have witnessed an eruption of Thera, with its blackness and lightning and volcanic bombs showering down on Crete, perhaps before the collapse, when it was truly "calliste" or "most beautiful among others." Today an island, Nea Kaimeni, is growing up from the sea in the crater of Thera. Geologically, there is good reason to believe that similar growth also took place before the great eruption, and this is what the Argonauts may have seen.

In about 1500 B.C., the island, by this time a Minoan outpost, suffered a protracted catastrophe. Ashy eruptions lasting for decades progressively covered the island with debris. The showers of ash rained down in two major phases, the first leaving a uniform covering of small pumice stone from 10 to 15 feet thick, the second depositing fine powdery ash of greatly varying thickness up to 150 feet. We are not sure whether or not the people as a whole fled the island in time to avoid being buried, but at least one person did not. In the brief excavations of 1867, one man's skeleton was found embedded in ash.

Another tremendous and similar volcanic eruption took place much later halfway around the world when Krakatoa in Sunda Strait between Sumatra and Java erupted in 1883. This event is richly documented. A tremendous roar was heard over 2,000 miles away and the vibrations of the atmosphere broke windows and cracked walls 150 miles from their source. Dark night was experienced for some 24 hours within a circle of 200 miles' diameter during the last and most violent ash eruptions, at which time the island could be seen by no one. Only the lightning flashes accompanying the spasms were visible. Ash was airborne for 1,000 miles out into the Indian Ocean.

And this, generally acknowledged the most catastrophic natural upheaval of recent times, had only one-fifth the destructive energy of the Thera cataclysm!

As to its effect on Crete, the "royal state" of Atlantis, we must recall that eruptions on Thera probably started in 1500 B.C., but it was not until perhaps thirty years later that the paroxysmal fall of ash came that turned day into night. The long buildup probably had little effect on the Cretans, but the final outburst would have deafened and terrified them beyond description, and the rain of mud and ashes would have killed them, their animals, and their crops.

Indeed, as in the eruption of Krakatoa, ash from Thera must have fallen all over the Near East, on Egypt as far away as the Sudan, on Arabia and Turkey. But analogy is not proof. It was Dr. Galanopoulos who adduced oceanographic data providing the demonstrable proof needed to move the theories ahead. The Swedish research ship *Albatross*, in 1948, extracted cores of sea-bottom sediment over a wide area of the deep eastern Mediterranean, and the *Vema* of the Lamont Geological Observatory of Columbia University took more in 1956–1958. Seven of the Swedish cores and fourteen of the Lamont cores showed volcanic ash stratified between small shells forming a sediment known as globigerina ooze. From what is known of the evolutionary change and sequence of these small animals, called foraminifera, and from radiocarbon dating, the ash could be dated. By measuring the optical properties of the ash, which is in fact powdered glass, it was traced to Thera.

The core having the thickest ash layer, 7 feet, was taken 100 miles to the southeast of Thera, at that time the closest to the island that an oceanographic vessel had ever approached. Final results were sensational. Some cores showed two layers, one datable to less than 5,000 years ago, and the other to somewhat more than 25,000 years ago. Here was solid data showing that explosions at Thera were of a dimension sufficient to visit great calamity upon the entire eastern Mediterranean.

So, between 1450 and 1400 B.C., the greater part of the island of Thera collapsed into the cavernous abyss left by the eruption of cubic miles of ash and pumice, leaving behind the three remnants we know today. Thera, Therasia, and Aspronisi are disposed concentrically about a central bay some 32 square miles in area, with a maximum depth of 1,300 feet. This enormous

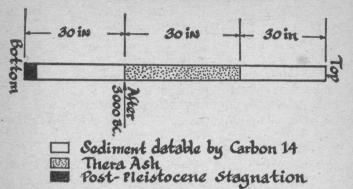

FIGURE 10. A typical deep-sea subbottom core taken from the Aegean, showing dating of the Thera eruption.

hole is the most imposing marine caldera, or collapsed volcano, in the world.

The collapse also created tremendous sea waves, which radiated in all directions as far, certainly, as the coasts of Africa and the Levant. Nearby mainland Greece experienced flooding of coastal lowlands of the Argolid, at the head of which lay the citadel of Mycenae.

Dr. Marinatos, in his 1939 paper, wrote, "I think there is little reason to doubt that the devastation of the coast sites of Minoan Crete was caused by the waves from the eruptions of Thera. We read of similar phenomena on the occasion of later eruptions of the same volcano, which in every case were less violent than the one in 1500 B.C. Philostratus, for example, reports that during the eruption of A.D. 60, when a new island was formed in the center, the sea receded about 3/4 mile from the south coast of Crete.... In the eruption of A.D. 1650 in Thera itself the waves came two miles inland and swept away old walls and chapels, foundations and all."

The Minoan port of Amnisos—known on the basis of archaeological evidence to have been destroyed between 1500 and 1400 B.C. by a natural convulsion—lies on the north coast of

Crete not far from Knossos. It is due south of Thera, protected by the small island of Dia from the prevailing northerly seas. The royal villa of Amnisos was excavated by Marinatos, who found beautiful wall paintings of lilies on stucco, from which the building takes its name, Villa of the Frescoes. One painting of a formal garden was interpreted by Marinatos in 1956 as symbolizing a kingdom of two islands, one large and the other small, which governed the Minoan sea empire. Later, Galanopoulos became convinced that the kingdom symbolized by the fresco was Atlantis and that the large island was Crete, or the royal state, and the smaller Thera, the metropolis of Atlantis.

Marinatos also notes that during the destruction, the walls and corners of the Amnisos villa had fallen in an unusual way that could not be attributed to an earthquake. The massive stone blocks of the west wall were pushed *outward,* and some of those of the south wall parallel to the sea were missing. He concludes that this could have resulted only from great waves crashing upon the building and then carrying the blocks away in their powerful backwash. He also observed evidence of intense fire in the largely wooden building. The presence of fire recalls again a most informative parallel to the Thera eruption, the eruption and collapse of Krakatoa.

The mountain of Krakatoa is a volcano, geologically similar to Thera, but smaller. The island itself was uninhabited. But extensive destruction ensued largely because of the seismic sea waves created by the subsidence of the mountain's mass following the eruption. The events at Krakatoa, well documented in Dutch and British reports, tell us that the ash turned day into night, causing the residents of the coastal towns to light their lamps. Then came three successive waves, 50 feet high and 80 miles long at their origin. Each broke with devastating effect upon the low-lying villages, destroying houses, upsetting lamps, and setting fire to the ruins. Ships were thrown far inland, and 36,000 lives were lost. Volcanic ash colored the world's sunsets for years thereafter.

Dr. Marinatos points out that Thera lies only 60 miles north

of Crete and considers it "certain, therefore, that the inhabitants of Crete in 1500 B.C. lived through the same moments of
terror as did the inhabitants of Java and Sumatra in 1883." He
thinks, however, that only the northern coastal settlements were
destroyed by waves, among them—in addition to Amnisos—Nirou Khani, Mallia, and Gournia. At Nirou Khani large cere-
monial double axes lay where they had fallen. At Gournia,
carpenters' and coppersmiths' shops were left intact.

The only warning of the approaching sea waves came as air
blasts generated by the collapse of the central mountains of
Thera. They reached Crete within a few minutes, cracking the
walls of buildings and perhaps throwing people to the ground.
The seismic sea waves followed insidiously, rushing unseen
across the sea of Crete to crash upon the shores thirty minutes
after their birth at Thera. We can estimate conservatively that
the sea climbed to heights of 300 feet or more on Crete and
coastal Greece and Turkey. Waterborne pumice stone has been
found on the island of Anaphe, near Thera, at an elevation of
750 feet.

We can be sure that the sea flooded deep into coastal valleys radiating from the Aegean shores. A contour drawn at 300
feet above sea level runs over 100 miles up the Yamanlar and
Büyük Menderes rivers of Turkey and up the Argolid of the
Peloponnesus to the citadel of Mycenae, seat of the mainland
power soon to overcome the Aegean islanders. On the plain of
Messara, the "royal state" of Atlantis, the contour is 10 miles
inland. The palace of Knossos lies on high land 3 miles inland
on the side of a deep valley, not so high but that the waters
would have lapped at the base of the hill and inundated outlying farm buildings.

Near Krakatoa, in 1883, a ship lay in Sunda Strait while the
volcanic island was collapsing into the sea. She rose and fell to
three great waves, so gradual in their effect at sea that her crew
hardly noticed them. In three major stages during twelve hours
the island disintegrated, in less time than the sinking of Atlantis in a day and a night. Thera, like Krakatoa, unquestion-

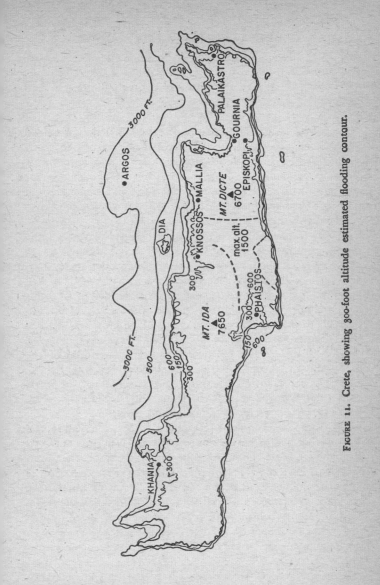

FIGURE 11. Crete, showing 300-foot altitude estimated flooding contour.

ably collapsed in stages, creating several immense seismic waves. We cannot help but visualize the effects of the Thera collapse, five times greater than that of Krakatoa, as nothing less than cataclysmic.

According to Dr. Galanopoulos, the story of Deucalion's flood is a folk memory of the flood waves that plagued the coasts of the Mediterranean following the tremendous eruption at Thera, or Stronghyli, as he prefers to call it. He concludes that an event of such extraordinary magnitude and violence could scarcely have been forgotten and inevitably would echo down through the generations.

In this myth, Zeus is said to have become angry with the rowdy and irreverent sons of Lycaon. When he paid them a visit disguised as a poor traveler they served him a disgusting stew, a mixture of entrails of sheep and goats and one of their own brothers. Divining the horrid recipe, Zeus decided to forgo his meal and grimly returned to Olympus, whence he loosed a terrible flood, intended to drown mankind, so great was his disgust with the sons of Lycaon. The Titan Prometheus, however, warned his son, Deucalion, of impending general disaster; the latter built an ark and rode out the storm with his wife, Pyrrha. A terrible south wind sprang up, "the rain fell and the rivers roared down to the sea which, rising with astonishing speed, washed away every city of the coast and plain; until the entire world was flooded but for a few mountain peaks, and all mortal creatures seemed to have been lost, except Deucalion and Pyrrha. The ark floated about for nine days until, at last, the waters subsided." Deucalion, reassured by a dove sent out to find land, disembarked and went to the shrine at Themis to pray for the restoration of mankind. "Veil your heads and throw the bones of your mother behind you," came the answer. Deciding that this meant the bones of Mother Earth, they threw stones over their shoulders and where they landed men and women sprang up.

Thus the flood of Deucalion, a natural event, was certainly

caused by some massive tectonic commotion. This earth- and sea-shaking catastrophe has been at least roughly dated. From several sources, the Deucalion flood can be set approximately between 1529 and 1382 B.C. That these dates straddle those of the cataclysmic activity of Thera, as based on archaeological evidence, lends credence to the relation of the Deucalion flood to Thera.

The caldera of Thera has a surface area of 32 square miles and is some 1,300 feet deep, with a volume about five times that of the Krakatoa caldera. Based on the volume of collapsed land, a Hungarian scientist, P. Hedervaris, has estimated that the heat energy released during the Thera eruption must have been four and one-half times that of Krakatoa. The total energy unleashed during the Krakatoa eruption has been estimated as 430 times more powerful than the explosion of an Eniwetok H-bomb. It has been estimated that the energy of the seismic waves emanating from Thera was about four times greater than that following the powerful earthquake in Chile in May, 1960, effects of which were felt on the coastline of Japan.

The tsunami that followed an earthquake on the Aegean island of Amorgos in 1956 reached to the coast of Palestine, an earthquake that also caused extensive damage on the island of Thera. Following a large-scale earthquake in the eastern Mediterranean in A.D. 365, a wave carried a ship two miles inland from the Peloponnesian coast, and raised the ships in the harbor at Alexandria, Egypt, above the houses and onto the coastal road.

Among the high points reached on land by the sea as a result of earthquake-caused tsunamis is one in the year 1737 on Cape Lopatka, on Russia's Kamchatka Peninsula, a height of 220 feet. In 1936, following a slump in the Norwegian lake of Loen, a wave 240 feet in height was generated. In 1958, during an earthquake in Alaska in Lituya Bay, water was raised to the unprecedented height of more than 1,200 feet by the flood wave. Such a wave striking Crete might have passed completely over

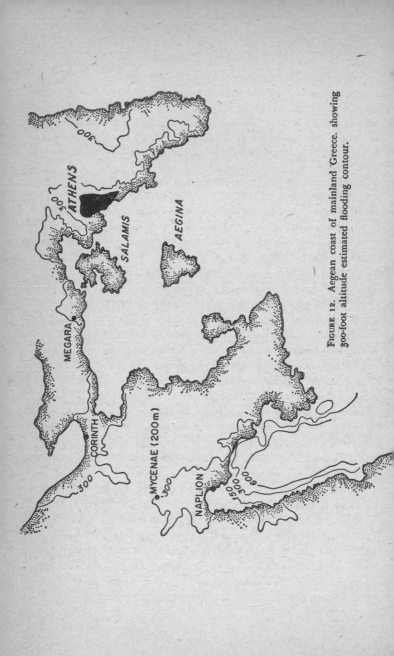

FIGURE 12. Aegean coast of mainland Greece, showing 300-foot altitude estimated flooding contour.

Figure 13. Aegean coast of Turkey, showing 300-foot altitude estimated flooding contour deep into river valleys.

the island. A slump in Italy in 1783 caused a flood wave that penetrated 3 miles inland at Salle.

And all these larger events, it must be borne in mind, were trivial compared with the Thera cataclysm. It is not difficult to imagine the coasts of the whole eastern Mediterranean being inundated—in effect the whole known world of the people of the region.

The accounts of the deluge of Deucalion, the Old Testament flood of Noah recorded in Genesis, and the Babylonian inundation under Utnapishtim are remarkably similar, though they may not all be memories of the same event. While Deucalion's flood can be related to the Thera collapse, Utnapishtim's legend, so archaeologists claim, is dated to the third millennium B.C., well before the Thera catastrophe, and indeed occurred in the Fertile Crescent, land of ancient Babylonia and Sumer, not in the Aegean.

The Old Testament's Book of Jeremiah, written in the sixth century B.C., reports (47:2, 4), "... Behold, waters rise up out of the north, and shall be an overflowing flood, and shall overflow the land. ... Because of the day that cometh to spoil all the Philistines ... the remnant of the country of Caphtor." The Philistines are considered by many Biblical scholars to be Minoan migrants from Crete, or Caphtor, as the Semites called it. We can speculate that they were refugees dislodged by the Thera catastrophe who had fled Crete and settled in Palestine in time to experience the flooding from the north, which was felt as far as the African coast.

The closing chapter in the life of the Minoans who remained on Crete includes probable widespread local earthquakes over a decade or two, during which all the settlements were destroyed. After this, people from mainland Greece settled in numbers and a Mycenaean colony replaced the glorious Minoan empire of previous centuries.

But there are a number of other inferences implicit in the Galanopoulos and related theories. The Thera catastrophe, Galanopoulos believes, was responsible for no less an event than the Biblical plagues brought on the Egyptians because Pharaoh would not release the Israelites from bondage. And he even goes so far as to state that the subsequent destruction of the Egyptian army during the flight of the Israelites was caused by mammoth sea waves that, generated by the collapse of Thera, then traveled 500 miles south to the exposed African shore. After my visit, Galanopoulos had sent me his monographs on these aspects of the subject, and I found that a plague-by-plague account of the Israelites in bondage was most revealing. Biblical scholars allow enough latitude in their dating of these events for a nice chronological agreement to be quite possible.

The plagues are given in Exodus, 7 through 12. There were twelve plagues,* which to avoid confusion I have numbered in chronological order for easy reference:

1.	Serpents	7.	Blains and Boils
2.	Water turned to blood	8.	Pestilence
3.	Frogs	9.	Hail, thunder and fire
4.	Lice	10.	Locusts
5.	Flies	11.	Darkness
6.	Murrain of animals	12.	Death of the firstborn

Between the fifth and sixth plagues, the people of Goshen divided and the Egyptians and Israelites lived in separate areas.

As noted, the first plague, serpents, is not included in the age-old account memorialized in the Jewish Passover service; the second plague, we are told, turned all of the waters red. The first of the two major phases of the Thera eruption was the deposition of rose-colored pumice. Observations made at Batavia (now Djakarta), on Java, 100 miles from Krakatoa, give us a clear picture of the sequence of events following the ash eruption as observed from some distance away. At 7 A.M. the sky was clear. It then began to darken and become yellow. There was

---

* Traditionally there are ten plagues, which do not include two of those listed in the Bible—number one, serpents, and number eight, pestilence. It is interesting to note that the plagues in the Greek myth of Cephalus parallel those in the Biblical account.

a fall of fine watery particles followed by a few grains of dust. By 11 A.M., there was a regular heavy dust rain followed by complete darkness. The heavy rain continued until 3 P.M., and in the latter phases the dust fell in small rounded accretions resembling hail and we know that complete darkness for a matter of several hours occurred at distances of more than 150 miles from Krakatoa. The red waters could have been caused by both airborne and waterborne pumice.

The plague of frogs could have resulted from a pumice fall which would be somewhat destructive to the way of life and, as the Bible states, cause frogs to come up out of the waters and die on the shores, away from their natural environment. During the eruption of Tambora, in Indonesia, and its accompanying earthquakes in 1815, for example, Sir Stamford Raffles wrote of an ash fall that gradually built up to a depth of 8 inches. He said that the ashes were observed to cling to various plants, and only because these plants were shaken as the ash fell in a following rain did they survive. Despite this timely rainfall, the crops were considerably injured, a large part of the paddy was totally destroyed and horses and cattle perished from want of forage for a month after the eruption. We can speculate that the destruction of the crops was followed by a similar deficiency of food, that the animals starved and died, and that the poor hygienic conditions resulted in pestilence, smallpox (represented by the plague of boils), and the plagues of lice and flies. Malaria was no doubt rampant. The plague of locusts would have destroyed every last stalk of plant life.

A brief paroxysmal eruption is rather convincingly described by plagues nine and eleven, during which hail fell—hail severe enough to kill crops and animals—mingled with thunder and fire that ran along the ground, and complete darkness. We know that not only was the eruption of Krakatoa accompanied by spectacular lightning displays covering the entire sky but that the mud rain that covered the rigging and decks of ships in the vicinity of the volcano was phosphorescent and gave in the intense darkness the impression of a blaze of fire, which the crews attempted to extinguish. We know, too, that at a distance of 100 miles from Krakatoa, complete darkness obtained for most of a day.

The reference to the killing of the firstborn would represent widespread death due to deprivation of the land. The statement that the Israelites were saved could mean that an infectious disease spread through the Egyptian population but did not reach the Israelites because they were a separate community by this time. Mention of the firstborn, rather than children in general, could also be explained by the special consideration given them by the Israelites, the Canaanites, the Egyptians, and the Libyans. All the plagues occurred before Pharaoh would allow the Israelites to leave Egypt. This implies a strong Egyptian king whose power was so reduced and his people so weakened by the volcanic disaster that he could no longer prevent them from leaving. Such a pharaoh could have been Thutmose III (1505–

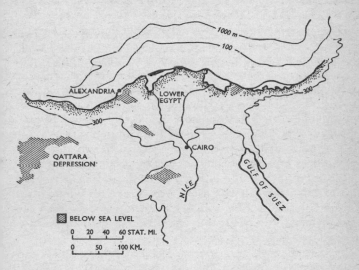

FIGURE 14. Mediterranean coast of Africa, Nile Delta and Sinai with land and sea contours. Elevations in feet.

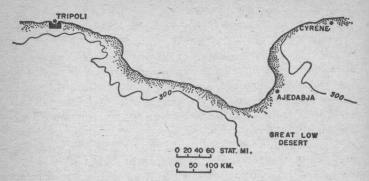

FIGURE 15. Mediterranean coast of Africa from Tripoli to Cyrene, showing 300-foot contour on land where possible flooding took place from Thera collapse.

1450 B.C.). It is possible, alternatively, that the plagues and the Exodus lasted longer than the reign of a single pharaoh and Amenhotep II and III were involved.

The correspondence between the Biblical plagues and the effects of a Thera-size eruption made a deep impression on me; even the order of events was correct. I felt that I simply must date the plagues more precisely to the time of the eruption. Since the dual problem of dating the eruption itself and correlating the Biblical material came to occupy a great deal more of my time than I had anticipated, and the Biblical passages referring to or influenced by the Thera eruption turned out to be unexpectedly extensive, I have relegated to two appendices in this book the total accumulation of supporting evidence. But two conclusions could be drawn from all the data. A large number of datable events and dated records serve to pinpoint the Thera eruption in time with reasonable certitude. And a surprising number of passages in the Bible can be interpreted as descriptions of that cataclysm.

Perhaps the most suggestive correlation of the events of exodus with the eruption of Thera comes from the Bible itself. In the Book of Amos (9:7), there occurs this statement by the

Lord: "Have I not brought up Israel out of the land of Egypt?
And the Philistines from Caphtor, and the Syrians from Kir?"
The implication of this juxtaposition seems undeniable. The
Minoans were driven from Crete at the same time that the
Israelites made their exodus from Egypt.

The more I explored Dr. Galanopoulos' theory and its implications, the more impressed I grew. But even more impressive was the extent to which evidence in support of the theory
lay before everyone's eyes, waiting to be read in the proper
light. I could not wait to translate theory into fact, and mount
an expedition that would take us to the very heart of Thera—
and Atlantis.

Book II

FIGURE 16a. Possible reconstruction of Thera before the great collapse of the fifteenth century B.C.

FIGURE 16b. Aerial view of Thera today.

CHAPTER 3

TOWARD the close of 1965, I had enough confidence in my grasp of the subject to set about interesting my professional colleagues at Woods Hole in a modern attack on the enigma of Atlantis. About this time, too, I began to write an article on Thera-Atlantis that later attracted a good deal of notice not only among my oceanographic colleagues but among the general public, so much so that, to my genuine amazement, it eventually was translated into forty languages.

As chairman of the Journal Club Committee at Woods Hole, a group that organizes and sponsors lectures on oceanographic subjects, I was responsible for filling the program of evening speakers. When I could not find a suitable candidate for January 3, always a difficult time, I decided to fill the gap myself.

Less than a week before, I received a copy of "Santorini Tephra," a paper by Ninkovitch and Heezen of Lamont Geological Observatory. Some of the historical and geological research that I had pursued on the inspiration of Dr. Galanopoulos had also been pursued, quite independently, by these authors. Additional geological detail was presented and many of our conclusions were the same, though the authors were cautiously noncommittal on the subject of Atlantis.

Armed with this additional valuable information, I switched from my originally limited subject, the geology and vulcanism of Thera (Santorini), to a discussion of Galanopoulos' theory of Atlantis. I decided to use this occasion to announce publicly my conviction that here was a theory about the lost civilization that had a sound scientific basis. In taking this step, laying my professional reputation on the line, I knew that I faced certain ridicule in some quarters, but I hoped that in spite of this enough enthusiasm would be generated among Woods Hole scientists to result in follow-up sea research to eventually vindicate my position.

The talk was attended by a capacity audience and lively discussion followed. One oceanographer who had studied Plato fervently in his youth insisted that the story of Atlantis was pure myth, but the excitement of the geological aspects of the anticipated research made him one of the first to wish to participate. Others felt that what I had said at least made sense, and I felt that some of my enthusiasm had rubbed off. Bolstered by this encouragement by my oceanographic colleagues, there was now no turning back.

I wrote an article, based on the talk, for the general public called "A Mighty Bronze Age Volcanic Explosion," for the April, 1966, journal *Oceanus*. Now my planning became more detailed.

What would be my goal for the summer of 1966? Mainly, I wanted to determine the pre-eruption shape of Thera, to see if it could be shown to conform to Plato's description of the metropolis. This, of course, is what I had promised Dr. Galanopoulos. This would require a large ship and powerful seismic gear that could penetrate thousands of feet below the bottom. I would need to pinpoint submarine vulcanism to tell me where the former volcanic peaks were. An oceangoing magnetometer, which measures the local magnetic field of the earth, was called for because lava from beneath the earth's crust is more magnetic than the crustal rocks through which it has been extruded. I also wanted to see if more could be learned about the people who lived on this island before 1500 B.C. If Thera really was the metropolis of Atlantis, as Galanopoulos claimed, it must have been heavily populated, featuring palaces and settlements of great wealth.

In 1867 the French geologist Fouqué had excavated a few structures considered by archaeologists to be farmhouses, part of a simple Minoan outpost. I was not so sure about the "simplicity" of this settlement. Two gold rings had been found, as well as a beautiful intact fresco and pottery of a high quality. I wanted to find the excavations of Fouqué, perhaps the house of the brightly colored, flowered fresco, which had been lost to view many years ago and not rediscovered since. I must search on the land and in the shallow waters surrounding the exterior of the island for Minoan ruins. Captain Graves' Royal Navy chart of 1848, the basis for subsequent navigational charts, had identified five locations where underwater ruins were to be found. I wondered if these ruins were Minoan and if it would be possible to excavate them. Dr. Galanopoulos told me of two large underwater structures on the southeast coast labeled "ancient moles," or stone breakwaters. These might be the remains of a Minoan harbor or a later port, or simply natural formations. Basically, the island was virgin archaeological territory.

In February, 1966, prepublication copies of my article were circulated to a few people who I hoped would take an interest in the forthcoming venture and whose talents would be most valuable. One, I felt, who would surely be excited was Edward F. K. Zarudzki, called "Rudy" by his friends and associates. A geophysicist who had joined the Woods Hole staff only recently, he was familiar with the Lamont core work and had a keen interest in Mediterranean vulcanism. Also, while in Italy, he had participated in the development of a new optical instrument that allowed for examination of ancient Etruscan tombs without excavating them. In addition, Rudy's career had taken him all over the world in search of oil, the principal task of the modern industrial geophysicist.

He was an accomplished linguist with a flair for international relations, and was not only interested—with some reservations about Atlantis that I was pleased to see he was later to lose—but was in the throes of planning a cruise to the eastern Mediterranean for one of Woods Hole's large research ships, the 2,000-ton RV *Chain,* a capable former U.S. Navy salvage tug, which had acquired her prosaic name while in the service.

I also felt certain that Dr. Harold Edgerton, professor of electrical engineering at MIT, my alma mater, would find the project irresistible. Well known for his research in optics and underwater sound, Edgerton, known affectionately as "Doc" to his many friends and associates around the world, was also no neophyte in archaeological ventures. I had known him for some time through our common interest in underwater devices such as *Alvin*.

Doc had developed an instrument that he modestly described as his "mud pinger." This was in fact a sophisticated sonar device, developed for archaeological search, which had been used successfully, albeit briefly and in prototype, to locate ancient wrecks and buildings beneath the sea bottom. To be really useful, such an instrument has to be small, easily transportable, self-contained for use in out-of-the-way places not having standard power sources and handy repair shops, and reliable. Doc's pinger was all these things.

So the makings of an expedition came into sight. If I could work out problems of scheduling, money, and other logistic details, and persuade Rudy and Doc to travel to Thera, the search for Atlantis would be off to a good start.

An oceanographic cruise from the United States to the Mediterranean and beyond is scheduled at least one year in advance. Research Vessel *Chain* of Woods Hole was due to spend six months at sea during which she would sail through the Strait of Gibraltar (the Pillars of Herakles), zigzag between the European and African shores as she made her way east, then through the Aegean and the Bosporus into the Black Sea. She was to steam back through the Aegean and south, past Cyprus and the Levantine coast, to the Suez Canal. From there she was to sail the length of the Red Sea, putting in at the British protectorate of Aden, on the southern tip of Saudi Arabia, her farthest port of call.

Such was her outgoing itinerary. Her mission was primarily geophysical, to study the sediments and rocks of the earth's crust beneath the sea. This skeletal purpose, as the year of planning and fund raising progressed, was gradually augmented by many other scientific projects. Financed by the U.S. Navy and the National Science Foundation, the operation of the ship for the six-month period would cost a great deal of money, over $500,000. While the major missions typically pay the freight, it is usual for many small investigations to be included in the program, which must remain flexible throughout the cruise.

I hoped to fit Atlantis somewhere into this scheme.

Often it is possible to perform several studies at once, towing parallel strings of instruments astern. If equipment breaks down, backup projects must be on hand to prevent loss of valuable time, for the ship's operating cost of $3,000 per day pertains to 365 days a year, wherever she is and whatever may be her deployment. She is truly the oceanographer's floating laboratory, and an expensive one. As cruise time nears, the competition for ship time intensifies as each scheduled scientist tries to justify, to those holding the purse strings, the maximum time and money for his particular interest.

Rudy Zarudzki and I originally wanted a week of the ship's time at Thera, with deep-sea cores to be taken over a wide area surrounding the island. It seemed, in the larger geophysical view, that there was more interest in cores from the Mediterranean south of Crete than in the Aegean, so we had to be satisfied with less than we had hoped for. The geophysicist looking at the large-scale geological phenomena over many millions of years considers the Thera eruption a mere crustal anomaly and, in geological time, a modern event. The scientific concept stands in stark contrast with the human view, a thought that was to recur again and again in my attack on the riddle of Atlantis. My ambition was to encompass both viewpoints and perhaps draw them together.

As spring approached, the Black Sea was cut from the schedule because of increasingly strong interest in the Red Sea, where mysterious hot spots—segregated volumes of water with relatively high temperature—had been discovered deep in the ocean. With this development, we feared for our Aegean sea time, but the tectonics of this area are so spectacular that a look at the vast east-west Aegean fault with modern deep-sea acoustic and magnetic instruments for the first time was a matter of multi-disciplinary scientific interest. Thus a good look at the Aegean remained a part of the schedule.

Dr. Galanopoulos helped out at this point, if unknowingly. Our relationship, after correspondence over several months, had flowered into a real friendship and we exchanged much information on our mutual interest, Atlantis. As a matter of fact, I was gradually to appreciate in some depth his mastery of the vulcanology not merely of Thera but of the whole eastern Mediterranean. In the deepest part of the Mediterranean, a great hole in the ocean bottom just off the southwestern Peloponnesus, 15,000 feet in depth, the German geologist M. Pfannenstiel had claimed that two undersea volcanoes existed. Galanopoulos' records of earthquakes showed no activity centered here, and so ran counter to Pfannenstiel's assertion. I passed this information along to Zarudzki, who became keenly interested and was able to include a run over these locations. Later, Galanopoulos was proved correct, which only further reinforced my feeling that he was on the right track in regard to Atlantis.

From that area in the Ionian Sea, a course through the Gulf of Corinth and a stop in Athens could be anticipated, permitting us to join the ship. A stop at Thera, if only for a short time, was then practically assured.

Poring over nautical charts, Rudy and I wondered if the *Chain* could enter the bay of Thera and maneuver inside the gigantic cauldron, towing her cumbersome array of electronic tentacles. The "sparker" and line hydrophone for listening to the reflected sound signals were the most powerful in the world but required a depth of 60 feet and 150 yards of towline astern. The magnetometer on a cable 250 yards in length made quite a clumsy and grotesque tow when it came to navigating in close quarters.

We finally decided that the *Chain* and tow could enter and operate in the bay, but that only a limited area could be covered in the time available and that she certainly would have difficulty approaching the shores. Clearly, a smaller vessel with more compact gear would be required for working close to the interior cliffs and in the shallows off the exposed beaches of the island's exterior rim. We had hoped the *Chain* could leave one of her launches with a small party and return after two weeks or so to pick it up. Convenient for us but, for the ship to adjust her complex schedule to return to Thera, impossible. In the end my survey party with gear had to be put ashore at Thera to fend for itself.

Rudy and I brought Harold Edgerton up to date on the *Chain* cruise plan. The ship was due to leave Woods Hole on July 10 and would arrive at Athens on August 21, after some exercises in the Atlantic. Doc was enthusiastic. He had made plans to use his mud pinger searching for antiquities in the Sea of Galilee and on the Mediterranean coast of Israel during most of August. This enterprise was to be undertaken under the auspices of the Undersea Exploration Society of Israel, headed by the dynamic Elisha Linder, whom I was to meet later and whose work on Phoenician and Philistine harbors is so important to our knowledge of the period following the Thera eruption.

That both the Phoenicians and the Philistines were in part Minoan refugees or former Atlanteans is a theory that I was beginning to find more and more intriguing. For example, Professor Cyrus Gordon, a philologist of Brandeis University, believes, on the basis of language characteristics, that the Minoans originated in the Semitic lands and Africa and that, after they left the Aegean, they became the Phoenicians, the preeminent seafarers of the first millennium B.C. The Philistines, on the other hand, have been labeled landlubbers by historians because they built their settlements inland from the shores of Palestine and Sinai. Could it be that the Thera catastrophe had put a very real fear of waterfront dwellings into them?

In any event, if I could arrange for a small boat at Thera,

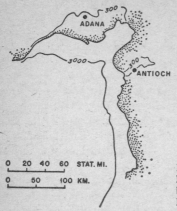

FIGURE 17. North Syria, showing land and sea contours where possible flooding took place during collapse of Thera.

preferably two, and living accommodations, Doc and his companion, Dr. Wolfson, would join us in Athens on August 24 to be transported with their equipment on board the *Chain* to Thera for a two-week survey of the island. I was elated. Already, top people in oceanography were eager to participate and committed. And we could look forward also to having a medical doctor on hand.

I heard from my old friend and colleague at Woods Hole Dr. Hartley Hoskins, now a professor of geology at the University of Chicago. An extremely capable and energetic young man, he is full of the love of adventure, and I was pleased that he wished to join us in Greece. He already planned to operate an Edgerton mud pinger for the summer, loaned by Doc to the Council of Underwater Archaeology headed by John Huston (now deceased) of San Francisco.

Hartley and I had found our way into archaeology at the same time, without knowing of the other's interest. Huston and Hoskins were to try the equipment at several European sites—in Holland, in Italy and in Greece. I corresponded with Hartley and John and it was agreed that Hartley would join us on board the *Chain* when it arrived in Athens on August 21. However,

John Huston was not able to come, as he had commitments in America, but he kindly offered to pay living expenses for Hartley, who has a legendary appetite. He also proposed to loan us some walkie-talkie radios and other small equipment, which were to prove extremely useful.

Through my letters, Galanopoulos had been kept informed of developments. He awaited our arrival eagerly and would, of course, be pleased to be part of the expedition, which I now could rightly call a joint Greek-American expedition to Atlantis. Six of us—Rudy Zarudzki, Doc Edgerton, Hartley Hoskins, Dr. Wolfson, Dr. Galanopoulos, and I—would embark at Athens on August 24 on board the *Chain*, which would spend a couple of days at Thera doing the deep seismic work under the direction of Zarudzki. After that we would leave the ship for further land and sea surveys of Thera under my leadership.

With the publication of the *Oceanus* article, which was written in a popular style and picked up by the International News Services, I received many letters from interested persons the world over. Among them was one from Edward Loring, sent from Thera itself. Mr. Loring announced that he was "the American resident" on the island; for three summers he had made his home there and had conceived a deep interest in the island's history and archaeology. He knew of the Minoan theory of Atlantis and, indeed, supported it. After an exchange of letters, he put himself at the disposal of the expedition, offering to help with local arrangements. I knew practically nothing of Loring's personal background except that he was an expatriate American with a house in Venice, but I concluded that he was intelligent and capable and possessed valuable local knowledge and contacts. I accepted his help.

As spring wore on, I realized I also had to enlist the help of the archaeologists. I wrote to Professor Marinatos, enclosing my article and others, and inviting him to participate in the Thera survey. As luck would have it, Dr. Marinatos was lecturing in Australia and did not reply to my letter until the fall of 1966, when the first phase of our fieldwork had been completed.

I knew that archaeological permission would be difficult to acquire from the Greek authorities, traditionally jealous of such favors, as we have known since Schliemann's day. For that reason I tried to keep the expedition primarily an oceanographic one, as indeed in essence it was. We did not expect to excavate antiquities, merely to search for them by remote sensing instruments and by visual inspection.

Since Dr. Galanopoulos was part of our group, I expected I would not have to concern myself with Greek government permission beyond what was needed for the *Chain* to operate in Greek territorial waters. However, when he wrote asking if I had obtained permission from the archaeological authorities, I realized that I had neglected an important formality and that something less than free communication existed between the archaeologists and the scientific community at large. Ships from Woods Hole have frequently worked in European territorial waters and cooperated closely with marine and hydrographic authorities, but never had we been required to deal with archaeological officialdom. Now it appeared as if we were about to cross the line separating coastal oceanography and archaeology.

On the recommendation of Dr. Cornelius Vermeule, curator of the Classical Department of the Museum of Fine Arts in Boston, I approached Dr. Henry S. Robinson, director of the American School of Classical Studies in Athens, with a frank and accurate prospectus of the work I wished to perform. I asked him if any part of it would require permission from the Greek archaeological authorities. He wrote back that my program was, in his view, distinctly archaeological. He had discussed it, he said, with John Kontis, then Director General of the Greek Archaeological Service, who had willingly agreed to issue a permit to me and to the *Chain*, provided we did not touch antiquities and an observer from the American School was present during our small-boat and land survey of Thera. We would not be permitted to use scuba equipment except to retrieve lost underwater gear or take geological samples. At the time, this rather restrictive reaction did not please me greatly, but later I was to appreciate that both Dr. Robinson and Mr. Kontis were being very cooperative indeed in allowing people without archaeological credentials to roam free on a potentially promising site. Contributing to that surprisingly ready acceptance of our project may have been the lack of interest among those in the Athens archaeological community in Thera as an excavation site.

In the meantime, Loring had responded enthusiastically and efficiently to my requests for logistic aid. Though the only boat large enough for our needs, a fishing boat called a caïque (*kaiki*, in Greek) about 35 feet in length, was on dry land and in need of a new engine, Loring convinced the owner that our two-week charter was so important to the economy and prestige of his island that he installed an old English oil engine, painted his boat and launched her in time to meet the *Chain* as she sailed into the caldera. In addition, Loring engaged a 25-footer, called a *varca*, owned by the leading fisherman of Kamari, and indeed the most daring seaman on Thera, Manolis Kafouros— Kafouros means pirate.

As for living accommodations, Loring insisted that his house could handle all our needs, even the anticipated eight or nine persons, and I was not one to look a gift horse in the mouth. I committed myself personally to pick up the bill for the Thera arrangements, having no other source of funds to tap. Afterward, Harold Edgerton, thank heavens, split the cost of boat hire and accommodations with me, excluding the cost of food, which was shared by all.

The time neared for the departure of the *Chain* from Woods Hole. Rudy Zarudzki, who was assigned as chief scientist for a part of the voyage, had hoped that he would be relieved at Athens and so could join us on Thera for our two-week intensive survey. Alas, much to his chagrin, he found that he must stay aboard until the ship made port in Rhodes three weeks later, after traveling to the south of Crete. Thus Rudy, who had been so keen, in the end was denied direct participation in what was to be a fascinating adventure. But he would have compensations. He would be running a sophisticated survey of a little-known part of the Aegean sea floor and would be manning the great seismic "sparker," or electric spark sound source, which creates underwater electric explosions, and he would see the records of the deep-ocean subbottom as the ship passed through and around Thera. Also he is a scuba diver and, had he gone along, would have found the denial of diving permission most frustrating.

Frustrations and small setbacks are bound to occur in any large undertaking. The important thing was that we had assembled a crew and obtained a base of operations and, most important, that we were going to have the impressive technical aid of the Research Vessel *Chain* in our search for Atlantis.

CHAPTER 4

JULY 10 came and the *Chain* departed, but Atlantis remained far off while I pulled together the many loose ends of our enterprise, now a relatively solid scientific expedition. In fact, in order that my plans be taken seriously, I found it necessary in my letters and conversations to suppress my enthusiasm for Galanopoulos' Atlantis theory in favor of a purely geological study of Thera; Atlantis was still, in the minds of most persons, solely the domain of mystics, romantics, and pseudoscientists. Of this I was constantly being reminded by my colleagues, most of whom at this stage were still either unconvinced or not terribly interested in my oceanic divagations.

The *Chain* was due to make port in Piraeus, after cruising the length of the Gulf of Corinth and the Corinth canal, on August 21. I was scheduled to arrive in Athens by plane from the United States the same day after a stop in Rome, where, by prearrangement, I met with Harriet and Lee Pomerance, also on their way to Athens. The Pomerances, of Great Neck, New York, were about to join Dr. Nicholas Platon, University of Thessaloniki archaeologist, at Kato Zakros on the eastern tip of Crete. For several years now, they have furnished part of the support for the excavation of a major Minoan palace discovered there in 1962, and spend some weeks each summer working on the site.

The excavation of the waterfront complex at Kato Zakros, destroyed at the same time as all of Crete, in 1450–1400 B.C., offers a unique opportunity to assess the widespread effects of the Thera catastrophe. Kato Zakros, on the east coast of Crete, close enough to have felt severe effects from the eruption, is a site in an early enough state of excavation for the evidence to be recognized—evidence of seismic sea waves, water-washed pumice, earthquakes, and fire.

The Pomerances and I exchanged views on how Kato Zakros had been affected by the ash fall and seismic waves. In time I was to become convinced that Kato Zakros was one of the "hundred cities of Crete" and thus a part of the Atlantean empire.

We also discussed in some detail the climate and trading logistics of the Minoan island empire, and the Cyclades, stepping-stone islands linking Crete with mainland Greece. Melos and Thera, two islands in the Cyclades, could be expected to relate closely to the Cretan homeland during Minoan times. They have special qualities that make them stand apart from their companion Cyclades, and they may have had great importance in the Minoan or Atlantean scheme of things.

I was struck by this line of thought in my conversations with the Pomerances because Plato's metropolis was described as a fertile land, with even a lush agriculture, a far cry from the Cycladic islands of today. Plato wrote, in *Critias*: "There was provision for animals of every kind, both for those which live in lakes and marshes and rivers, ... and again, the cultivated fruit of the earth, both the dry edible fruit and other species of food ... all these that sacred island lying beneath the sun brought forth fair and wondrous in infinite abundance. ... The water which ran off they carried, some to the grove of Poseidon, where were growing all manner of trees of wonderful height and beauty, owing to the excellence of the soil."

In spite of the picture of lush vegetation, there is much concern about fresh water in the *Critias*, implying that it was in short supply. This paradox of fertility and aridity exists today on Thera. I believe that, very likely, the Aegean climate was not much different in ancient times from what it is today. Changing wind patterns no doubt have affected the occurrence and amount of rainfall but the temperature average may have been nearly the same. In Minoan times Thera, at least, was intact, a volcanic island with a typically rich soil, developed after eruptions 25,000 years before, and extremely fertile. This to me suggested that the island probably was a significant producer within the Minoan economy and, as such, an important population center.

Both Thera and Melos are volcanic, and on Thera there is a well-preserved rich earth layer of Minoan times under the thick ash, the product of millennia of weathering of the lava. Both these islands, I suggested to Pomerance, may have been more fertile than their neighbors in the Cyclades in ancient times. Crete today, as in antiquity, has sufficient rainfall to support a prosperous agricultural community.

Thera today, with its deep ash covering—unique among the Aegean islands except for Nisyros—is once again a fertile island, at least compared with the others around it, though still sterile compared with Minoan times. Did Thera in the pre-eruption era have lush vegetation and, if so, how was it supported with such small rainfall? I intended to seek answers to these questions on the island.

In Athens, the Pomerances and I parted and I set about locating the *Chain*. I knew she would land in Piraeus, and sure enough, eventually I found her after a tour of the waterfront. The 210-foot ship lay stern-to off the quay, riding to a bow anchor, Mediterranean style. Her bright blue hull was in marked contrast with the many yachts resting at the pier like so many white seabirds with wings folded.

It was 7 P.M. on the *Chain*'s first day in port. I found the vessel quiet, and no one but the deck watch seemed to be on board. On the way to the chief scientist's quarters, I stopped to read the bulletin board. On it was listed the schedule for the ship's scientists and crew during her three days in Athens. Never before, to my knowledge, had one of our ships met with such a welcome.

All the scientific and archaeological organizations in Athens were represented in a program of receptions and meetings elaborately organized by Warren Dunn, scientific officer of the U.S. Embassy. There had been considerable worldwide publicity about our trip before our arrival in Greece, but we had hardly expected to excite so much professional interest and popular attention. The following day, Tuesday morning, a conference was scheduled on board ship to which representatives of all of the schools of archaeology in Athens were invited to hear Dr. Galanopoulos and me explain our work.

Suddenly, I noticed an item posted on the bulletin board: "Reception, given by Professor Galanopoulos for the scientific party of the *Chain*, August 21, 7 P.M." My mail, including the schedule of events, had not caught up with me, and I found myself late for the first item on the program. In half an hour I was at Dr. Galanopoulos', a spacious apartment in the center of Athens, a few blocks' walk from Constitution Square.

Entering the living room was like a homecoming. First, the warmest of greetings by Dr. Galanopoulos and his charming wife and then by my many colleagues at Woods Hole, whom I had last seen two months before. Dr. Hartley Hoskins was there. During the previous weeks, he had served capably and with his legendary enthusiasm as our ambassador in Greece, adding a personal touch to the numerous diplomatic matters attendant to our trip. Seeing Dr. Galanopoulos after our year of correspondence was a moving experience for both of us. I had left Greece fascinated by his story of the Thera eruption and his theory of Atlantis in the Aegean and hoping that I could return with a scientific party to explore this further. For him it had also been merely a hope. But now that he was to see it culminate in reality marked a high point in his life, as it did in mine.

The next morning, Dr. Galanopoulos and I met with the archaeologists, and what was scheduled as a one-hour discussion lasted for three hours. The ship's small library, where we had gathered, was bursting at the seams with interested listeners, themselves drawn into the talk. Even in that time, we could not hope to cover the ground represented by the many astute questions put to us. Few of the archaeologists had given much thought to the implications of the Thera eruption. Many of them, specialists in other periods of history, were quickly caught up in the excitement of the occasion. And there were skeptics. While none sought to place Atlantis in any other part of the world, some preferred to believe that Plato had created a myth. This conference and others like it, I felt, would at least encourage exploration of the historical implications of the Minoan eruption of Thera.

This meeting was followed by two evening receptions on board the *Chain* and visits to archaeological sites at Corinth, the Greek Naval Hydrographic Office, and the Greek Institute of Oceanography. Our research vessel had come to the Mediterranean to perform an oceanographic study under auspices of the Office of Naval Research. Hunting for Atlantis was not officially on the itinerary. However, everyone seemed to be under the impression that the main purpose of the *Chain*'s visit to the Aegean was to discover Atlantis.

One of our missions on the expedition to Thera was to apply oceanographic scientific methods to archaeology. Therefore we were particularly pleased when Hartley Hoskins arranged with Professors Oscar Broneer and Robert Scranton, to take us on a tour of the excavations at the vast site of ancient Corinth. The Isthmus of Corinth, lying to the west of Athens, was once the most concentrated center of population in Greece and Corinth its largest city.

Of particular interest to us were the underwater excavations being made in its port at Kenchreai with its extensive submerged harborworks. The sea level has risen relative to the land and the submerged structures are under survey by a number of modern techniques, serving for my purposes as a proving ground for equipment we were to use on Thera. Dr. Robert Scranton of the University of Chicago directs the work here and Dr. Hartley Hoskins applied his acoustic techniques both on land and underwater in association with the late John Huston. Dr. Edgerton searched underwater here as well, finding indications of possible ancient shipwrecks underneath the submerged moles and within the harbor enclosed by them. These will be excavated in the future. For land search for underground buildings, a seismograph, a proton magnetometer and a resistance measuring instrument were tried, all with some success.

Our group spent a night on the summit of the striking mountaintop fortress of Acrocorinth, which overlooks the entire isthmus. At dawn I looked down on the sea toward the Saronic Gulf, which figures in a scene described in Euripides' play *Hippolytus,* written about 428 B.C. At this point in the play, Theseus, the famous slayer of the Minotaur and now ruler of Athens, is enraged at his son Hippolytus. The unfortunate young man has been falsely accused by Phaedra, his stepmother, of trying to seduce her. Theseus, believing Phaedra, has rejected his son and banished him. A messenger describes the beginning of Hippolytus' journey into exile.

> And straightaway he took into his hands the goad
> and laid it on the horses while we men ran on
> close to the chariot's reins in escort to our lord,
> on the straight road to Argos and Epidaurus.
> Now, when we reached the open country just beyond
> the frontier of this land, there is a stretch of shore
> that lies already facing the Saronic Gulf.
> Here from the ground a roar like Zeus' thunderclap
> came sounding heavy round us, terrible to hear.
> The horses raised their heads and pricked their ears right up
> into the air, and on us fell a lively fear,
> wondering what the sound could be. And when we looked
> along the foaming shores, we saw a monstrous wave
> towering up to the sky, so big it took away
> the view of Sciron's promontory from my eyes.
> It hid the Isthmus and Asclepius' rock.
> Next, swelling up and surging onward, with, all around,
> a mass of foam, and with the roaring of the sea,
> it neared the shore where stood the four-horse chariot.
> And in the very surge and breaking of the flood,
> the wave threw up a bull, a fierce and monstrous thing,
> and with his bellowing the land was wholly filled,

and fearfully re-echoed. As for us who saw
the sight, it seemed too much for eyes to look upon.
Immediately a dreadful panic seized the steeds. . . .

Hippolytus drowned, it is said, in the great wave. The messenger, probably standing on the highlands of the Peloponnesus west of the isthmus, watched from his safe vantage the high wall of foaming sea crash upon the Corinthian shore. The Isthmus, where it is now cut by a canal, is 210 feet high and 3½ miles wide. The funneling effect of the long and narrow Saronic Gulf would in fact have built up a tremendous surge from the seismic waves; it is entirely possible that the sea passed clear over into the Gulf of Corinth on the north. In any case, the description is amazingly evocative. The fifteenth- or fourteenth-century B.C. date generally given to Theseus conforms with the Thera explosions and their side effects. The bull very well could be derivative from the familiar Minoan bull symbol—that is, the personification of the deep rumbling of an earthquake. No other waves since have given rise to such an account.

Just how powerful the Thera tsunamis were remained a tantalizing question and one that the forthcoming expedition could answer. The difficulty in trying to reconstruct the tsunamis —my object being to visualize the wave or waves generated by the collapse at Thera—lies in a dearth of reliable information about similar events, the great differences between even approximately similar situations, and, of course, the sparse data on the Thera collapse itself. The tsunamis caused by coastal landslides or submarine faults or slumps have been many and disastrous in their effects. In broadest historical span they have occurred fairly frequently, but in terms of the last fifty years, during which period modern scientific facilities have been available to study them, we have had very few examples. They generally occur without warning, so that even with today's sophisticated instruments, they cannot be anticipated beforehand to insure absolutely adequate recordings.

Nevertheless, we can learn something from some of the more recent catastrophes. On July 10, 1958, in Lituya Bay, Alaska, a rockslide occurred, the largest ever reliably measured. Lituya Bay is T-shaped, the crossing of the T flanked by high mountains and glaciers. On the north side of the bay, an immense body of rock slid into the water, expending tremendous energy in its fall—about 3.5×10^{14} foot-pounds. As the rock slid into the sea a single massive wave was formed, which surged up the mountain on the opposite side of the bay to an elevation of at least 1,200 feet above sea level. Thereafter a wave about 200 feet high moved out down the bay into the sea. The height of the wave was evidenced by destruction on the shore and mountainsides, where trees 50 feet in height were broken like matchsticks. D. Miller, a seismologist, calculated in 1960 that the energy of motion in the violently turbulent wave was about 2 percent of the energy expended as the mountain crashed down to the sea, and this has been confirmed in a few other cases where it has been possible to calculate the forces involved. Here, then, is a means for calculating the size of the Thera tsunamis.

Miller made a scale model to reproduce the wave and showed that the force of the water was sufficient to snap these great trees, in fact 10 times greater than necessary. As the towering wave rushed sidewise along the flank of the mountain it leveled trees before it, leaving them, upon its retreat, lying neatly arranged in horizontal windrows as far as an elevation of 700 feet.

The energy of the Thera collapse, as measured by Galanopoulos, was 2,000 times greater than that of the Lituya Bay slide. If we accept the 2 percent of the land collapse energy as contributing to sea waves, the 7×10^{17} foot-pounds figure for collapse energy at Thera is convertible to three ocean waves each having a height of 700 feet at Thera and a length of 80 miles. Or, in another form, we can picture three great waves each having a height at sea of 200 feet just before crashing on the Cretan shore, sweeping all humanity before them and rushing miles inland to climb hundreds of feet up the mountainside before exhausting their gigantic energies.

How rapidly could the cubic-mile masses of rock torn out of Thera have fallen into the sea? Again modern parallels are available. Landslides in the fjords of Norway have caused loss of life and destruction. In using landslides as analogues, we have the advantage that the geometry of the situation is more accessible than in the case of a slide out of sight under the sea. At Tafjord, at a point where the fjord is 0.6 miles wide and 600 feet deep, a large-scale landslide occurred in 1934. About one million cubic yards of an overhang fell, with the top of the slide 2,300 feet above sea level. The sea wave created was from 90 to 180 feet high, decreasing to 30 feet several miles away. The slide reached a speed of over 325 feet per second, so that the enormous block torn from the mountain fell the 2,300 feet into the sea in about 15 seconds. On Thera, on that dreadful day, we can envisage great sections of the island crumbling into the ocean over perhaps a 24-hour period, twice the duration of the Krakatoa collapse, each landslide complete in about 30 seconds.

Whereas the central portion of Thera had collapsed, most of the outer coast remained relatively undisturbed; that is, land slumping was local and probably did not exceed 50 feet. Several ruins of buildings were reported to have been seen in this shallow water, where visibility ranges to over 100 feet. The thick ash blanket that covered the land would have been washed away from these ruins, leaving them exposed or covered with but a small depth of volcanic debris, or so we hoped. In *Critias,* as we have noted, Plato wrote of the outer reaches of the metropolis: "Passing out across the three harbours, you came to a wall which began at the sea and went all round: this was everywhere distant fifty stadia from the largest zone or harbor. ... The entire area was densely crowded with habitations." It was my hope that Edgerton's pinger would enable us to discover some of these densely crowded habitations and perhaps the great wall.

On Thursday, August 24, Harold Edgerton was scheduled to fly in from Israel with his boxes of electronic apparatus, his mud pinger. Hartley Hoskins, who had been working through the summer at various sites in Europe, had with him one re-corder and two sound projectors, each for a different type of bottom. These were of the type that can be carried on a small boat and operated by automobile storage batteries. Edgerton had been working during August using a larger recorder and equipment (powered by a portable gasoline-driven generator) capable of greater power and penetration of the bottom. Our plan included taking both sets to Thera, where both Hartley and Doc would be available to operate them with the help of the rest of us, using two boats concurrently.

On Thursday, we had an anxiously awaited phone call from Doc Edgerton at the Athens airport. He was delayed by cus-toms in getting his instruments into Greece. It seemed that the Greek government wished to assure itself that the equipment, once permitted into the country, would also leave or, in lieu of leaving, certain taxes would be paid. This sort of thing per-petually plagues the internationally traveling scientist with his mysterious black boxes of uncertain monetary value. However, after a short time Edgerton appeared on the dock in Piraeus with a truckful of gear ready to go.

The nucleus of the group that was to disembark on Thera and stay for two weeks was on board—Dr. Galanopoulos, Harold Edgerton, Hartley Hoskins and I. Dr. Wolfson was unable to come. Arrangements on Thera were being handled by Edward Loring, whom we had not yet met. We had placed considerable responsibility in his hands and the nature of our reception at Thera remained uncertain until we set foot on shore. John Pike, master of the *Chain*, and I each had copies of a letter from the U.S. Embassy assuring island authorities that we had permission from some half-dozen Greek governmental agencies for our en-terprise. But whether this document, in English, would cut any ice 150 miles from Athens was not at all certain.

Euaggelos Aneirousis, deputy of the Greek parliament repre-senting the island of Thera, took keen interest in our work and toured the ship before departure. He spoke no English and since none of the *Chain*'s scientific party spoke Greek, it was hard to communicate the nature of our work, even with an interpreter. However, he assured us that we would be received hospitably on the island, and his help in this regard indeed turned out to be crucial in setting the local officials at ease. Our permit from the Greek Archaeological Service was to be brought by Jane and Bill Biers, archaeologists of the American School of Classical Studies in Athens, who were to join us a few days later, even though it meant a regrettable interruption of their honeymoon. Bill had been appointed by Robinson to represent the school as observer.

During the course of Thursday, August 24, two young Englishmen appeared on board, rucksacks on their backs. They were Cambridge University students who had been swimming and diving around ancient harborworks on the coast of Africa for the entire summer and were anxious to come with us, primarily to put their experience to work on any underwater sites. Lee Pomerance had suggested that they look me up. There had been no proscription against diving without scuba gear, and we did anticipate taking geological samples in shallow water and having to retrieve lost gear. The boys had been diving up to 40 feet, and they would be willing and useful members of our group thus did David Davidson and Robert Yorke join us to complete our complement.

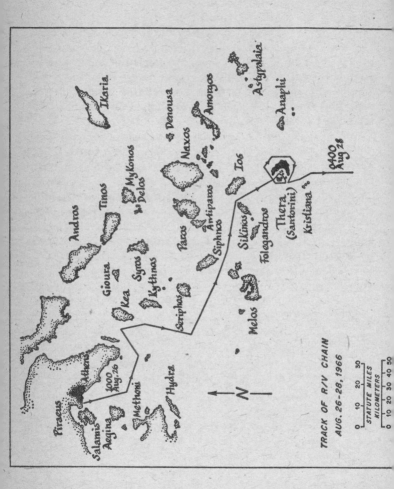

FIGURE 18. The Cyclades, showing track of the *Chain*, August 27 and 28, 1966.

CHAPTER 5

AT 9:30 A.M. the next morning, the *Chain* weighed anchor. The sea was flat beneath the sultry haze which persisted all the way to Thera. The ship is a floating oceanographic laboratory with few peers as to number and sophistication of oceanographic instruments, which she carries routinely during her cruises throughout the world's oceans. And now she was on a truly pioneering study of the Aegean, the first ship to take such an array of instruments into the sea of legend.

My excitement grew as we approached Thera for the first time, a dream coming true. I felt that I knew the island well from my reading, and had constructed mental pictures of what it would look like when we finally arrived. Meanwhile the members of the scientific party went about their duties as usual, looking tolerantly upon Galanopoulos and me as a bit possessed. To some extent they were caught up in our enthusiasm, and at least wanted to know more about Galanopoulos' theory.

The *Chain* steamed out of the harbor of Piraeus, past a number of cruise ships, and soon the mainland faded astern. It was time for the *Chain* to let out her gear, streaming from cables like electronic tentacles. The simultaneous setting of these three long wires astern of the ship in such a way that they do not become entangled is a complicated process. It involves about a dozen highly trained members of the scientific crew, and must be done with the ship traveling at slow speed. The instruments being let out are extremely delicate, and the cables by which they are towed are long and prone to fouling unless handled with great care. In rough weather, safety precautions must be taken to keep the crew members from being injured or swept overboard. In addition, some last-minute adjustments or repairs always need to be made before letting the gear into the water.

Now the sea was calm; even so, the wide stern deck, covered with gear, was a bustle of activity. All the while instructions were being shouted back and forth. A rip was discovered in the plastic covering on a package of electronics, kept in a bath of oil to prevent corrosion and short-circuiting by the seawater. It had to be repaired. A cable had to be flaked out on deck to avoid kinking when it was later payed out over a sheave on the stern.

The scientific resources of this cruise were directed to learning about the earth's crust beneath the bottom of the sea. Volcanic cones and rocky precipices more rugged than the surrounding land characterize the underwater mountain range which lies beneath the Aegean. The sea here drops from a depth of a few hundred feet down to 6,000 feet in a matter of several miles. For this purpose we carried five basic instrument systems. First, a sonar system was carried to measure depth. Three instrument systems, the seismic profiler, the magnetometer and the gravimeter, gave continuous measurements of the nature of the earth's crust beneath the bottom. Finally, a gravity coring system enabled samples of the bottom to be retrieved on board ship to be analyzed after the return to the laboratory at Woods Hole.

Not only was this equipment being employed in the Aegean Sea for the first time, but this marked the *Chain*'s first passage into the interior of a collapsed volcano. We hoped to learn enough about the geological structure beneath the bottom to reconstruct what this volcano looked like before it collapsed. This was indeed a big order, and one without precedent. Furthermore, this was the first time that modern science was utilizing such tremendous resources in the search for Atlantis.

The seismic profiler was the most elaborate of the instrument systems, consisting of four parts. Towed astern were two of these, the sparker and hydrophone. The third component, the analyzer-recorder, was a mass of electrical equipment covering one wall of the scientific control center, a large compartment topside. The control center, located forward in the superstructure, was so remote from the busy scene of crew members streaming cable off the stern that the two areas of activity had to keep in touch by telephone. Equally remote was the fourth component, the power source of the sparker, a bank of enormous electrical condensers weighing almost ten tons, deep in the hold. This system used by the *Chain*, a vessel almost the length of a city block, was repeated in diminutive form by our six-man group when we left the ship at Thera to work from two chartered fishing boats. The components were different, but the system the same.

The sparker (so named because it produces a gigantic electrical underwater spark), one of the components towed behind the ship, consists of a pair of electrodes that are the ends of two very heavy concentric cables. For most of their approximately 200-foot length, the cables are heavily insulated; the last few inches of exposed cable, supplemented by massive copper lugs, are the electrodes between which passes the spark. Towed from a boom that extends some 50 feet out from the side of the ship to port, the spark originates from a point off to the side and slightly aft of the stern. The electrical potential between the two electrodes is 10,000 volts. Their spark is created when the condensers in the hold of the ship are suddenly discharged of their pent-up electricity and vaporize a volume of water under the surface surrounding the electrodes. This vapor-filled cavity then is forced to collapse by the pressure of the surrounding water. The explosive sound accompanying the formation and collapse of the cavity passes out into the water in all directions. The initial part of this is the pulse that we use to study the earth beneath the ocean bottom.

The sound emanating from a point underwater at 100 feet

from the ship can be heard distinctly on deck. But below the waterline aboard ship the explosion is much louder. This sound repeated every ten or twenty seconds, all night long, takes some getting used to and usually interferes with one's sleep for the first night or two. It certainly did this first night out for several of us who had come aboard in Athens. The spark itself is a startling sight at night, a bright flash of light covering a 100-foot circle on the surface of the sea. The scientific party of the *Chain*, most of whom had now spent some seven weeks at sea, were well used to the sparker and the rigging of all the equipment needed with it. They had towed the gear for thousands of miles, only stowing it on board when the ship made port or came to a stop at sea for a time to take a core, for example, or to dredge the bottom.

The acoustic pulse, our best means for sensing, measuring and communicating in the sea, rushes deep below the surface in all directions at the rate of approximately one mile per second. When the pulse reaches the sea bottom some of its energy creates a new pulse which is reflected immediately back to the surface. The time taken from the initial explosion to the sensing of this reflected pulse by the hydrophone, the receiving instrument also towed behind the ship near the surface, provides us with a means of measuring the ocean depth. This is the same principle by which sonar operates.

But measuring the depth of the bottom is not the primary function of this system. In fact, as noted earlier, there is another sonar system on board for just that purpose. Most of the energy in the sparker pulse goes deep into the earth's crust, for a half mile or more, in the form of a transmitted pulse, which moves considerably faster than the pulse in water. This is reflected back to the surface whenever it strikes a discontinuity in the crustal rocks, a change from one type of rock to another. The type of rock can be identified by the speed at which the pulse travels through it. In addition, the depth of the discontinuity is measured by the time lapse between the spark explosion and the hydrophone's receipt of the reflected pulse. This

time lapse, usually a few seconds, can be measured with great
precision.

This then was the system which would tell us where and how
large were the vertical faults in the earth's crust beneath the
bottom of the central basin or caldera of the island of Thera.
It could also tell us where the underwater volcanic vents were
located. And it might tell us whether previous eruptions and
collapses occurred in geological time going back millions of
years, and, if so, how many. It could, we hoped, find remnants
of the harbors of Atlantis described by Plato.

Dr. Galanopoulos was familiar with instruments used in the
detection and measurement of earthquakes, but the oceanographic gear carried by the *Chain* was unfamiliar to him, as
it was to Professor Hajikakadis, a biologist from the Athens
Oceanographic Institute, invited aboard the *Chain* to learn
about the latest methods available in his field. The Greek scientists, though expert in the classical phases of their disciplines,
have not had the benefit of the modern technology used by
some of the more affluent nations of the world. Both Professors
Galanopoulos and Hajikakadis were eager to learn and quick
to appreciate the potential of the *Chain*'s resources.

The hydrophone is towed some 200 yards behind the ship
so that it will pick up only the pertinent pulses and none of the
noises created by the ship's engines and propellers, which could
confuse the record. The device used on the *Chain* on this occasion was designed at Woods Hole. It is an array of sensitive
elements strung out in a 100-foot line enclosed in a black oil-
filled plastic tube known as "the snake." This arrangement
makes it more sensitive to pulses coming up from the bottom
than to extraneous ones that might come from other directions.
Even dense schools of fish can cause discernible pulses, and the
interpretation of the printed record requires considerable art.
The streaming process was one in which we all participated, because the snake must be laid out in a straight line and gradually
fed over the stern by hand without bumping or bending it. A
line of men holds up the snake during this procedure, much as

the attendants in a zoo might carry a long, slippery and thrashing python.

In the hydrophone the pulse is converted to an electrical voltage which passes through wires to the analyzer-recorder aboard ship in the scientific control center. Here the signal is amplified and ultimately recorded. The paper recording, which spews out of the machine in duplicate on continuous strips each about 15 inches wide, contains a diagrammatic picture of a vertical cross section through the sea and below it into the earth's crust. As the ship travels through the sea at about 6 knots, the paper record is printed out at the rate of about one inch per mile, so that, in the course of her cruise from the United States, the *Chain* produced literally hundreds of feet of record. This paper would be taken home, photographed, enlarged, studied and restudied, and eventually would form the basis of the major conclusions of the cruise. A continuous time reference running along the bottom of the recording correlates this seismic profile with the ship's position, a vital piece of data. Near land, in the Aegean for instance, navigation can be extremely precise by positioning with reference to the land. But in the open sea, where navigation is by astronomical observation or radio waves, position may be a matter of miles in error, making it very difficult to draw an accurate map of the ocean subbottom. The potential of the seismic profiling system at Thera was tremendous. Not only was position relative to land known extremely accurately, but geological features above water were clearly visible in cross section in the cliffs of the collapsed interior. The information in these cliff sections could help in interpreting the record of the seismic profiler. I felt that the capability of the seismic profiler could be determined in such an environment as Thera better than anywhere else in the ocean.

The diagram that appears on the paper strip emanating from the recorder (see Plate 3) consists of three elements—a straight line representing sea level, an irregular line representing the sea bottom, and a complex pattern of lines and shaded areas representing the subbottom geological strata. Sharp discontinuities between different types of rock appear as sharp lines.

After the seismic profiler was streamed and operating, the magnetometer, a small highly sophisticated instrument, was let out on a separate and smaller wire. This device measures the strength of the earth's magnetic field by the behavior of very small radioactive particles in a liquid. The location of a volcanic plug or vent can be pinpointed geographically, though not as to depth, by the strong magnetism that is always associated with this type of geological structure. This capability I thought would be particularly valuable on Thera, where I hoped to prove that the island was formerly not a single central cone, but a complex of volcanic vents, more nearly approximating Plato's Atlantean harbors. The reading obtained from the magnetometer is printed out on the same roll of paper that records the seismic profile. It appears as a single irregular line across the top of the recording.

From a broad oceanographic view, the magnetic data, in addition to localizing volcanic activity, tells us of the relative movements of portions of the earth's crust over many millions of years. It is possible to determine past magnetic orientation of geological samples, mainly lava, and to compare this with the magnetic orientation of the present day. It has been found on this basis that Italy was once on the same longitude as the Himalayan mountains, millions of years ago. The currently popular continental drift theory has the American continents pressed closely against Europe and Africa with no Atlantic Ocean between. This idea has been picked up by some people looking for a source of the Atlantean legend, but this geophysical movement took place slowly over millions of years, and the Atlantic has been as we know it for millions of years also, long before Atlantis existed.

In addition to the deep seismic profile, and magnetics, the force of gravity was also measured continuously by an instrument mounted on gimbals deep within the ship near its center of motion, so that the pitching, rolling and heaving of the ship at sea would cause as little error as possible. The gravimeter is, in fact, one of man's most precise instruments, measuring fluctuations as small as one part in a million. The invention of such a precise instrument was one of the major steps forward in recent oceanographic technology, and an important part of this device is the electronic computer installed on board ship to reduce the data to a form which can be interpreted. The gravimeter tells us primarily the thickness of the earth's crust, which did not vary as we crossed the Aegean Sea. It was found that the crust under the Aegean is thinner than under the European continent but not as thin as beneath the open oceans. This tells us that the Aegean Sea has been there for a long time, probably millions of years. It has been thought that a land bridge once crossed the Aegean where the Cyclades and Dodecanese islands now lie, and also through Crete. If so, it ceased to exist long before man appeared in the region.

The final key instrument system on board the *Chain* was the coring system. This does not give continuous measurements, as do the others, and to operate it the ship must stop. A 30-to-40-foot-long steel tube, with a plastic liner inside, is dropped over the side of the ship and propelled downward by a heavy weight attached on top. It drops with the tube remaining vertical to the bottom of the sea and digs deeply into the sediments, provided they are soft enough to allow penetration. There is a wire attached to the coring tube so that it can be retrieved. The tube, which is closed automatically at the bottom after the core has been taken, is brought back to the ship where the plastic liner filled with the sediment sample is removed from its steel outer casing. The core is used by geologists who wish to know the sediment composition and by biologists who wish to know what animals are living in the sediment. Our group working from fishing boats on Thera also carried a gravity corer duplicating in miniature that used by the *Chain*.

With all the gear streamed astern and operating, which was accomplished within an hour because everything went well, the ship settled down to a routine. In the nerve center, Rudy Zarudzki gave directions for speed and course and three members of the scientific party stood watch around the clock, in four-hour shifts.

Our course in the Aegean led us on a zigzag path among the islands. We sought to cross the edge of the volcanic arc that sweeps across this sea from Attica in the west through Melos and Thera to the island of Kos, reaching the coast of Turkey near ancient Halicarnassus, birthplace of the historian Herodotus. Passing to the west of the Cycladic island of Serifos, we crossed a great fault in the bottom of the sea. This was probably the edge of the volcanic arc which Zarudzki sought, and appeared on the seismic record as a great vertical displacement of the geological strata deep below the bottom.

Through the night we traveled among the islands of the western Cyclades, here and there passing close to a lonely lighthouse on a barren limestone crag. When morning came, we found ourselves north of Sikinos. The sea was calm and the summer haze obscured more distant islands. Passing close to Sikinos, rugged and mountainous, we saw white villages dotting the upper slopes. There was no sign of a harbor. To the northeast was Ios, one of the most enchanting Greek islands; and we could make out the town, the lighthouse, and a well-protected harbor. And then, passing between Ios and Sikinos, we could see at last, some 18 miles away and gradually emerging from the haze, Thera—the island that could be "lost" Atlantis.

We slowly approached the island, which was in sight a full three hours before we reached it. I searched the hills and cliffs for familiar landmarks which I knew from the maps and descriptions I had read so many times. The black profile of Thera gradually gave way, as we drew nearer, to white-topped cliffs, white vineyards tinged with green, villages of clustered gleaming white buildings. I could make out the 150-foot-thick blanket of volcanic ash covering the island, and the great bay or caldera in the center with the black cone of Nea Kaimeni thrust above the sea. It was low but dominated the expanse of water cradled within the cliffs. Our route through the northern channel may have been the channel or canal to the sea described by Plato. It had been drawn in that position by Galanopoulos from the description in *Critias*. But the channel was a good mile wide, a great mass of land having collapsed into the sea, so that the canal of Plato, if it had been here, was now obliterated.

Our excitement was intense. Dr. Galanopoulos was the only one on board who had seen the island previously and his anticipation matched my own. The impressive volcanic remnant materialized full force and provided a striking sight as we headed into the caldera. It was framed by the northern peaks of Thera on the left and the sawtooth profile of Therasia, the western islet, on the right. At the entrance into the immense bay nearly vertical cliffs rise on both sides. It was the most awesome marinescape that I had ever seen.

On the east, the town of Ia gave an impression of decay but its pumice quarries at least were active, with ships waiting below the cliff to be loaded. We were later to find that a large portion of this town, the second largest on the island, had fallen into the sea as the cliff face crumbled under it a mere ten years ago, when the worst earthquake in 300 years was felt by the island group.

On the right, sparsely inhabited Therasia loomed before us with its long-abandoned pumice quarries that had cut a great step in the cliff during the Middle Ages, when Venetian noblemen ruled the island. In quarrying, the top layer of ash, 150 feet thick, is bulldozed away from the face and over the cliff, down chutes into waiting ships, and taken for use in making an underwater cement with remarkable bonding qualities. This material, used for over 2,000 years, is now being marketed for use in building reinforced concrete ships.

We drew opposite the capital town of Phira on the eastern cliff of the caldera. The town was a cluster of buildings on top of a 1,200-foot cliff. Built into the ash blanket on the steep slope, they appeared to sit one above the other. Steps zigzagged up the cliff, as I had remembered from pictures. The bay is

about 9 miles in the north-south direction and about 7 miles in
the east-west. All around us the black cliffs, so steep that the ancient lava flows and pumice falls were clearly outlined, formed
the sides of this great bowl. The water, 1,300 feet to the bottom,
was deeper than the cliffs were high.

I tore myself away from the magnificent view to duck into
the ship's control center to examine the seismic record being
tapped away. The moment we had all waited for so long was
here. The ship maintained her straight course right up to a
spot near the center of the bay already partway up the flank
of the active volcano of Nea Kaimeni.

From time to time throughout the day I returned to the control center to watch the paper record spill out of the machine.
At nightfall, the *Chain* left the caldera by the west channel to
turn north and circumnavigate the island. The seismic record
showed the presence of stratified debris beneath the caldera
bottom, which confirmed that the final phase of the Thera
cataclysm was a collapse of the central part of the island into
the sea rather than a monstrous central explosion. This had
been tentatively concluded from the visible geology of the island
formation and ocean depth soundings, but had never been
proven before the *Chain*'s voyage. Numerous submarine volcanic vents were disclosed in the contours recorded by the ma-
chines. These unseen vents, revealed by the *Chain*, when considered along with others whose remains are visible above sea level,
give us a picture of a complex volcanic island having at least
twelve to fourteen vents.

A major feature appeared on the south coast, where a monstrous exterior collapse caldera was discovered, created in the
fifteenth century B.C. at the same time as the interior disintegration. Formerly, the now-collapsed land had undoubtedly given
protection to the southern beaches facing Crete, the natural lee
side of the island, most of the year. The Minoan fleet had probably berthed here, pulled up on the beach, the larger vessels
perhaps moored inside the caldera, smaller then than it is today.

The irregular terrain accompanying these many volcanic

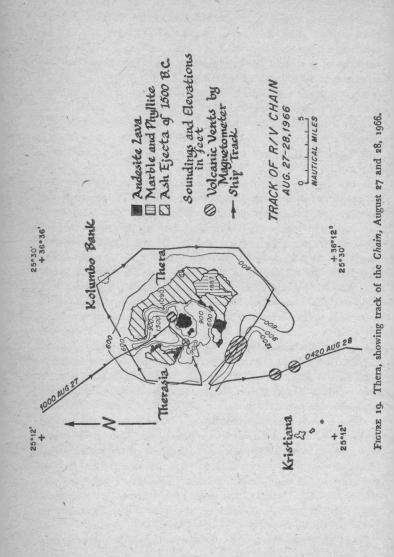

FIGURE 19. Thera, showing track of the *Chain*, August 27 and 28, 1966.

cones was confirmed by the radial seismic profile in the caldera, which revealed a deep basin in the northern part that could well have been below sea level before the collapse. Probably the island in its earlier Stronghyli shape had internal bays winding about volcanic cones, even as it does today. We know from cores that the 1500 B.C. collapse was at least the second such event in Thera's geological history, so that central cones growing up out of the bay would be expected to have existed before the collapse, even as new and probably similar ones do today. Prior to 1500 B.C., however, there was more land than there is in modern times and the bay was smaller. In Figure 16a the island has been reconstructed, using all of the information now available, as it might have appeared before the great collapse.

Plato described the metropolis as an island 11 miles in diameter with three concentric ringlike harbors near the center surrounding concentric zones of land. Galanopoulos has superimposed a map drawn from Plato's description upon the actual outlines of Thera today. Here is a similarity of surface outline reinforced by the hidden bottom topography, which shows subtle depressions following approximately the circular surface contours of the central island.

Plato's description of the metropolis has it that Poseidon, "as he was a god," created the circular harbors and brought two springs, one cold and one hot, to the central island. But the canal from the sea was dug by mortal Atlanteans, albeit descended from gods. The concentric harbors, then, can reasonably be imagined as natural, with a man-made channel cut through to them from the sea. The banks of the "zones," or "ring" islands, were raised, in Plato's concept, considerably above water and the stone used in building was quarried from beneath the center island and from underneath, from the outer and inner sides of the zones of land. "One kind [of stone] was white, another black, and a third red, and as they quarried, they at the same time hollowed out double docks, having roofs formed out of the native rock," he wrote.

As in Minoan times, the Therans today quarry white pumice stone and marble, and red and black lava rock from the interior, exterior, and underpart of their island, and live in caverns excavated from the stone. This is a truly impressive confirmation of detail in Plato's tale of Atlantis.

The scheme of harbors described by Plato, taken literally, is not believable. As Dr. Galanopoulos pointed out to me at our first meeting, the lunar tides in the Aegean are very small. With no lunar tide to drain and refresh it, elementary hydraulics tells us that the Atlanteans would have found it impossible to prevent the stagnation and fouling of their channel. I think that we can assume that Plato's detail has been either confused with some other story or merely exaggerated. Let us be content with the notion that some rambling waterways surrounded the ancient volcanic cones of Thera. This physical feature in itself was unique and would provide the basis for Plato's account of harbors of fantastic complexity.

To this extent, at least, our expedition, after only one day at Thera, had suggested a correlation between Thera and the metropolis of Atlantis. We could project with some accuracy the probable arrangement of land and sea areas at Thera in Minoan times. The arrangement coincided with the geometry of Plato's metropolis. Previously it had been assumed that pre-eruption Thera had been a solid, reasonably circular land mass. We had demonstrated that very likely it had internal bays winding about volcanic cones, as it does today. I saw in this the basis for Plato's overelaborated harbor scheme.

During the time that *Chain* stayed in the caldera, a small party went ashore on the active volcano of Nea Kaimeni with the gravity meter, measured the earth's field, and marked the station with a concrete surveyor's monument for the benefit of scientists of the future and the mystification of tourists. Another small boat party, led by Hartley Hoskins, surveyed the west channel exit of the caldera with Edgerton's pinger operated from a rubber boat. The objective here was to see if there was enough water to pass the ship and her large tow. The finding was barely positive but, unfortunately, the seismic profiler was not operated until the ship had almost left the caldera. Thus we did not obtain a second tracing of the caldera subbottom, which might have helped define Plato's circular harbors.

Shortly after the *Chain* came to rest off the town of Phira, capital of Thera, a caïque was seen putting out to us. This was the prelude to our long-awaited rendezvous with Edward Loring and a look at the boat that we were to use for the next two weeks surveying the waters of the interior and exterior coasts. All our gear, some 1,700 pounds of it, was piled on the deck of the *Chain* in anticipation of this moment. The caïque chugged toward us, then, with some uncertainty and a great deal of smoke, came to a halt off our starboard side. I put off in the rubber boat to meet her and give instructions for coming alongside. We were about to leave a floating laboratory of twentieth-century technology for a centuries-old island of tangled myths and history.

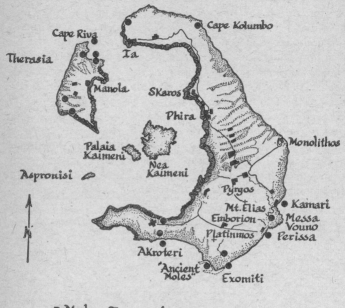

FIGURE 20. Thera, showing archaeological sites and modern villages.

CHAPTER 6

THE bright blue hull of the *Chain* seemed small when seen from a rubber boat in the vast central bay of this collapsed volcano and surrounded by precipitous cliffs. She lay unanchored in 1,000 feet of water. Any misgivings we had about leaving the security of the *Chain* were quickly overborne by the anticipation of getting on with our mission.

If Thera were the Atlantean metropolis of Plato, it should have had temples, palaces and a busy harbor, and have been thickly peopled. Would we be able to find evidence of any of this? The central portion containing the abode of King Atlas, from whom came the name Atlantis, was surely lost beyond recovery—not only beneath the sea, but beneath the new volcano, Nea Kaimeni, grown up since the great collapse. Yet there was a possibility that this was not entirely so, because by a freak of nature, according to the German geologist Hans Reck, a large piece of pumice stone, which could have come only from the 1500 B.C. eruption, lay on top of Nea Kaimeni. He concluded that this gigantic rock had been lifted from the bottom of the sea, 1,600 feet below, to the summit of the new volcano by eruptive activity—virtually lifted up the volcanic tube by the rising magma as on an elevator. Assuming Reck to be correct, was it too much to hope that a palace column might have experienced a similar excursion? Temples are unknown in Minoan Crete; votive offerings were made in caves and in the palaces. If Galanopoulos was right, and this was the religious center of Atlantis, could there be temples on Thera? These and countless other thoughts churned in my mind as I now came to grips with the physical problem of Thera.

We came alongside the caïque and Edward Loring introduced himself and his fiancée, Anna Brychaeas. Loring was a man of twenty-nine, younger than I had expected him to be. Slender and of a little more than medium height, he was casually dressed and had about him an appropriately Byronic air of intensity and adventure. Anna was an Athenian beauty. We exchanged greetings with the captain of the caïque and his crew.

Loring told me that, since it was 1:30 P.M., the town officials would not permit us to land. We must wait until five o'clock, when they had finished their afternoon naps and could receive us properly. Apparently the officials had only the vaguest idea of our mission on their island, though Loring had at least succeeded in impressing them with our importance. Because of garbled telephone communications with the mainland they had been waiting some twenty-four hours for us. But we could not hold up the ship, so I quickly decided that we must risk courting official ire and load our gear on the caïque and go ashore, improvising excuses later for our lack of protocol.

The caïque came alongside the *Chain* and our 1,700 pounds of boxes, bags, bottles, and the like were unloaded. Galanopoulos, Edgerton, Hoskins, Yorke, Davidson, and I joined the four originally aboard the fishing boat and we put off for shore. As we neared the pier at Phira, at the foot of the tremendous cliff of tortured volcanic rock topped by the sharply contrasting white buildings of the island's capital, we saw, to our surprise, the harbormaster in his neat white uniform waiting to greet us. He was a big man, of dour Turkish aspect. The reception, at first, was cool. With no fluency at all in Greek, I left the talking to Loring and Galanopoulos and shortly the latter and the harbormaster disappeared into the nearby café to continue their discussions over glasses of ouzo. Dr. Galanopoulos was widely known as a distinguished scientist, and his mere presence appeared to solve our problem of entry for the time being. No one asked to see our papers, nor was any other formality necessary in spite of the fact that our archaeological permission would not be in hand until the archaeologists from the American School arrived some days later.

The port of Phira is a narrow concrete quay attached to the cliff face at sea level. A few buildings—café, chapel, power station—are built into the cliff. We faced a climb up some 550 steps, 1,100 feet, to the capital town above, where we would stay. This required our locating a safe storage room on the quay for our equipment, and we found one at $1.50 per week— a little stable behind the café, which proved to be adequate enough despite occasional donkey intrusion.

After a time, the customs officer made his appearance. He looked exactly like the harbormaster, white uniform and all, and all through our stay I always confused the two. He wished to visit the *Chain,* which was accomplished by sending off our handy caïque (supplied with a gift from us to the parched complement of the *Chain* of five 9-kilogram bottles of the world-famous Santorini wine) with him and Loring as interpreter. They were able to speak with Rudy Zarudzki and John Pike, who fortunately had come equipped with the aforementioned letter from the U.S. Embassy. This document let it be known that proper Greek authorities had approved the presence of the *Chain* in Greek territorial waters. Fortunately the customs officer was satisfied with this official-looking piece of paper—it was in English, which he could not read—and after having been given a tour of the ship and a good stiff drink, he came ashore quite content. Later that day he received a cable from Mr. Anerousis in Athens, also vouching for our integrity, so we were accepted by officialdom, at least for the present.

After storing the mud pingers, corers, batteries, sample bottles, and the like in the donkey stable, and leaving the remainder of our nautical gear, including 200 pounds of canned food, on board the caïque, we commenced our first of some dozen ascents of the cliff to Phira. Loring instructed us to tell the donkey driver, Georgos, to take us to *"to spiti Amerikanos."* His house was well known, it seemed. The poor donkeys have learned a few facts of survival under the arduous conditions of their existence. A smart animal will travel at the head of a train, knowing that only those in the rear will be beaten by the driver. He has learned, too, that it is less painful to be beaten regularly than to exert himself without being beaten. So to the driver's cry of "*delux, delux, thaaay*"—an exhortation unique to Theran donkey drivers, which means "get going"—we toiled up the steps to the top. An intelligent donkey also knows that it is easier to take a hairpin turn in the trail on the outside, and each of us found himself perched on his animal, perilously overhanging the low retaining wall, looking down nearly vertically 1,000 feet to the sea.

We all arrived at Loring's house intact, however, and while we were soon to become quite accustomed to the ascent ritual, none of us ever summoned the nerve to ride down the often damp, slippery, black lava cobblestones. Loring's house was built on a 45-degree slope, dug into the pumice at the top of the cliff. It was a typical Thera dwelling, of arched construction for earthquake protection. It was, in fact—as Fouqué had described and we were to see for ourselves some time later—very similar to the Minoan homes of 1500 B.C. Loring gave all of us pleasant quarters that included hot running water, a rare amenity in this ashy place.

Soon after we had settled in, Dr. Galanopoulos was called upon to visit the chief of police, who is the custodian of antiquities and other valuables on the island. The two spent some time together, but no problems resulted and we saw little of him—a situation that was to change quite radically when we returned to Thera in 1967

The customs officer eventually, days after our arrival, took an interest in our equipment and insisted on seeing our papers. Stories of the mysterious strangers and their witchcraft must have reached him. We became used to this ritual, which was apparently based on our inability to communicate our mission to the simple farmers. Our complex array of electronic equipment was inventoried on a number of imposing-looking documents that Harold Edgerton had made a point of securing in Athens. Though the customs officer called us to his office on three occasions to view these documents, he never took the trouble actually to read them or to inspect the equipment. The people of Thera, I was to learn, are very superstitious, as well they might be living in this extraordinary and mysterious place. Thera is traditionally the home of Greek vampires, *vrykolakas*, wretched beings neither dead nor alive, corpses from which the spirit has fled. It is said that they fly through the air carrying others with them.

Our first evening on the island found us comfortable and even somewhat relaxed, cheered by pleasant surroundings, good companions, and fine drink. Beneath us the lights of a departing cruise ship glided slowly to the north. The sharp, rapidly changing tones of *bouzouki* came down to us from the Taverna Loukas above.

Later, alone on my veranda perched on the edge of the black abyss, I mused on my surroundings. On the sacred island of Delos to the north, legendary birthplace of Apollo, was said to be the birthplace of the world. On Thera, beneath my feet, came the end of the preclassical world.

The next day was August 28, a Sunday. Inspired by the vigorous Hartley Hoskins, we arose at 5 A.M. He climbed up and down many stairs awakening our sleepy group, for the rooms of Loring's house are arranged vertically on the cliff face. We had made earnest plans to start our first pinging foray as early as possible, but not until 7:30 did our caïque get under way—and then with a newcomer to our party whom I had telegraphed from Athens. Ernest Lehman is a teacher at the American dependents' school at Iraklion, and I had been in touch with him in the United States. He had hoped to join us at Thera, and, as it turned out, he arrived—improbably enough on an itinerant pumice boat from Crete—precisely on time and was able to contribute valuable assistance in manning the caïque. In addition, Ernie spoke Greek and, after two years of living on Crete, knew the people.

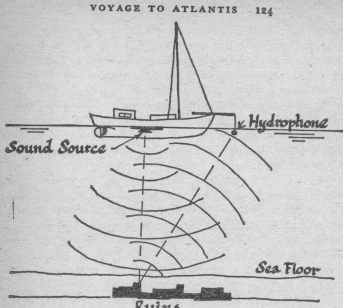

FIGURE 21. Caïque with Edgerton sediment profiler in action.

The first pinging traverse was to be made out to the central volcano, followed by a few zigzags between Nea Kaimeni and the main island of Thera to check out our equipment and procedure. We planned thereafter to head for Point Akroteri, a distance of five miles, to examine the shallows between Akroteri and Aspronisi (White Island). These are regions where underwater ruins have been reported. Fouqué had theorized that a pottery factory was located there, and the water was shallow over a large area. It was the shallowness of the water that made examination with Doc's pinger feasible.

Doc had looked acoustically at the subbottom at several sites in Israel. His equipment is new to archaeology and its value much depends on the correlation of known features with the record produced by the instrument. One type of wiggle on the recorder trace might mean a stone wall, another a wreck, and so on. On the ancient moles of the harbor of Caesarea, such a correlation was made, where the bottom was cored and excavated at the same time that it was examined by acoustic eyes. Hoskins has done similar work at Kenchreai.

There is an important difference between the two distinct types of acoustic instruments used in our work that summer. We were about to work with the low-power portable "sediment profiler" developed by Edgerton for use in a small boat for work primarily in shallow water. The amount of bottom penetration is quite small, up to 40 feet, but the minimum-size identifiable target is also quite small, about 6 inches. The device is suitable for looking at ancient building structures and wrecks as well as statuary and ceramics. The 210-foot *Chain,* on the other hand, carried a "deep seismic profiler." Its very powerful sound source, which penetrates through the bottom for a half mile or more, cannot identify an object less than 40 feet in size. This makes the device suitable for geological probing only.

Shortly after leaving the dock, our first run revealed that vibration of the boat was too much for the recorder, which was mounted in the cabin below. We returned to the pier and provided the recorder with a soft mounting, which solved the jiggling problem. But, on starting the engine again, we learned that it had a personality that would put even Edgerton's good humor to the test. With the engine stone cold, it took about fifteen minutes to start; when warm, a mere five minutes. The preheating ritual involved lighting two blowtorches, permanently mounted, one on top of each cylinder head.

The engine was an ancient English two-cylinder, 20 hp oil job, which at top speed raced at 500 rpm. After preheating, it was hand-cranked into action by the captain, who had to crawl into his after deckhouse and then forward of the engine into a cramped and stinking space to perform his sweaty task. Eventually the engine would start after many great puffs of smoke had enveloped the boat and we had crowded into the companionway to make certain that the captain in his engine cubby had not been cremated by the blowtorches. There was no fire extinguisher aboard and life preservers are a conceit unknown on most Greek fishing craft.

There were two fuel injection valves to this astonishing engine, one for each cylinder, these valves having been intended by the builder to vary the speed. The captain had jammed them both wide open so that our speed had only two values, wide open on one cylinder or two cylinders. Neither speed was right for our pinging traverses, so progress was made either by sail when the wind was right, or under power by fits and starts with billowing smoke and ominously anguished noises from the engine.

At last we started our first track in earnest, 240° on the com-

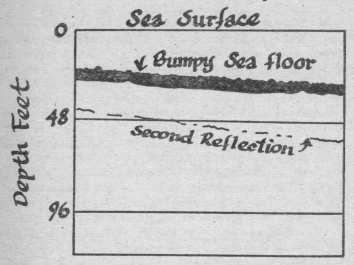

FIGURE 22. Edgerton mud pinger traverse northwest of Therasia and parallel to the shore. The little bumps on the sea floor having a weaker second reflection than the smoother portion are large basaltic blocks, some the size of an automobile, thrown up during the great eruption. The sea floor is a continuation of the ash layer which covers most of Therasia. (Linearized record after Edgerton 6 kc mud pinger record, September 2, 1966, 1332–1341B. From H. Edgerton and H. Hoskins.)

pass, more or less west-southwest, at slow speed. We gave up our zigzagging plan and headed straight for Point Akroteri and, on reaching it, changed course to 340° and headed for the west tip of Aspronisi, the little island on the southwest. Reaching Aspronisi, we headed out to sea on course 225° toward the uninhabited island of Kristiana, 12 miles away, and proceeded until the water became 50 fathoms deep, about a mile offshore. Then we headed back to Akroteri. All this time, a paper recording of depth and subbottom detail was being made. The bottom here was not the flat muddy alluvial terrain on which the instrument had been used before but a very rugged sea floor covered with massive volcanic lava bombs, which had been ejected during the eruptions, and fragments of broken lava flows mixed with pumice. In places the bottom was flat and sandy, and here acoustic penetration was good and we could see beneath the bottom, where large objects appeared, some as big as a house, probably rocks similar to those on the surface. Later, in shallow water, we were able to take cores with a hand-driven coring tube, a device operated like a post-hole digger. Our findings showed that the bottom between boulders was a mixture of white ash and black lava sand. In some places there was mixed in a black organic constituent resembling peat. Here was a sure sign that once there had been land, now covered by the sea, which increased our hope of finding submerged ruins. We found later that the *Chain* had taken a core in the deepest part of the caldera, but the sandy consistency had permitted only a shallow, badly mixed sample to be drawn.

In the region between Akroteri and Aspronisi there appeared to be no ruins but, as I came to recognize in 1967, an experienced eye is needed to distinguish the natural rock from man-made structures, for the bottom is strewn with stones that could have been used for the building of walls or even remnants of walls themselves. We were on the rim of the caldera, on a part that had slumped relatively little, but still the sea was from 25 to 100 feet deep. Scuba divers were definitely needed to do anything further in this area.

At Point Akrotéri we anchored the caïque in 25 feet of water at the edge of the 200-foot cliff, beneath the lighthouse, and Loring, Davidson, Yorke, Lehman, and I dived to look over the bottom and collect geological samples. The boys, Robert Yorke and Dave Davidson, were like fish, completely at home in the water. Without fanfare, they repeated their 40-foot dives below the surface without scuba equipment. We took pumice and tuff in white, gray, red, and black from the bottom and shore, and sand from the bottom. I climbed onto the rocky shore in hopes of reaching the Minoan stratum, but it was high above me and would have to be approached by land, I realized. We examined an area 100 by 200 yards where the bottom was covered with pumice and lava boulders of all sizes up to 20 feet on a side—undoubtedly bombs thrown up in the eruption.

We could see the line separating the top 1500 B.C. ash layer from the Minoan land topography, and it was very irregular here, coming right down to the sea in places, which suggested to me that a bay had been located here in Minoan times. I was reminded of Fouqué's statement that clay had been found in this region. He surmised that there had been a pottery factory in the vicinity and perhaps a freshwater lake. Much of the pottery excavated at that time, 1867, was found to have the same chemical composition as the clay found near Akroteri. Our investigation of this area was prompted by our hope of finding evidence of a lake or marsh such as Plato had described in *Critias*.

While diving near the Akroteri cliffs, we were struck by the presence of small black sand patches between boulders, and the general scarcity of marine growth. Though they had lain there for 3,500 years, the smaller black rocks, 2 feet in diameter or less, were completely free of fouling, which is a boon to the underwater archaeologist. The origin of the black sand puzzled us for a time. Eventually we determined that it was merely an intermediate eruption layer, because the fine black material was seen all over the island in places where the ash had eroded away, on the limestone mountains and inside caves.

After weighing anchor, we streamed the pinger gear and traveled back to little Aspronisi, where we again anchored in about 25 feet of water just to windward of a monstrous, barely submerged rock, 25 feet high and 50 feet in diameter, on which the sea was breaking. We scouted the area over a 200-yard circle, looking for submerged houses reported by the fishermen. The bottom here we knew to be 75 feet beneath the Minoan stratum clearly visible on the cliff of Aspronisi. We were looking for any signs of pre-eruption dwellings or temples which would suit Plato's description. We were on what would correspond to the periphery of Plato's metropolis, an area he had described as heavily populated.

For knowledge of the underwater site we relied on the tales of the local fishermen. However, Greek fishermen have a way of often being right about such things; more than once, in the past, local tales led archaeologists to make important discoveries. There appeared to be no sign of regular structures but quite a lot of irregular and complex volcanic debris, including boulders and broken rocks. The first clue to ancient habitation is generally the presence of datable potsherds, but we were hardly in a position to find such evidence here without scuba gear, which we were proscribed from using. So our basic approach was limited to covering large areas and many sites superficially during this trip, with a view to selecting the more promising ones for a return visit.

In the evening of that first day of exploration, Loring displayed a treasure he had found, about which he had written me. It was a piece of lava formed, unmistakably, in the shape of a monkey's head, from the eastern beach of Thera at Kamari. Loring thought it was a fossilized skull, transformed during the eruption. If true, it would imply that monkeys lived on Thera during Minoan times. We know from frescoes in Crete that monkeys were kept by royalty as pets, so it follows that the monkey could have been brought from Crete by important persons during their visits to the metropolis of Atlantis. Loring made a gift of the head to Dr. Galanopoulos, who promised to have it examined by experts on his return to Athens. Sure enough, a leading Greek anthropologist, Professor Poulianos, arrived at the opinion that the fossil monkey head was indeed authentic, and could be further identified as *Cercophitecus callitrichus*, or West African green monkey, a type known to have been imported from Egypt to Crete for the amusement of royalty. An X-shaped skull fracture on top of the head indicated a violent death.

On August 29, a Monday, at 6:30 A.M., we left the harbor at Phira to examine reported underwater ruins on the north coast off Cape Riva. Again, the entire male contingent was aboard —Edgerton, Galanopoulos, Hoskins, Loring, Davidson, Yorke, Lehman, and I. The wind was from the northwest, 10 to 20 knots, and a sea was making up. We proceeded across the caldera to Therasia, the northwest island and home port of our caïque, the *Agias Trias,* or Holy Trinity. There were clouds in the sky, presaging the coming of fall and its rains, and 3-foot seas in the caldera made the going wet until we were under the lee of the shoal running due east from Cape Riva, or Cape St. Irene as it is sometimes called. From Saint Irene, who was martyred on Thera, comes the island's alternate name, Santorini. There are two locations here where underwater ruins have been reported: one on the Cape Riva shoal, and the other in deeper water, up to 200 feet, off the cliffs at the southern part of the deep cove between capes Riva and Tino. The shoal that runs about a half mile to the east from Cape Riva is very irregular, with the prevailing seas breaking on the north, and the southern edge dropping precipitously from a depth of only 25 feet down to 500 feet. We tried having a swimmer, Davidson and Yorke in turns, for it was a chilling process, towed alongside from a boom while the mud pinger was operating. The swimmer could see surface features of the bottom as they appeared on the acoustic record and the eerie drop into the bottomless abyss when towed over the precipice.

The captain of our boat knew his way well and guided us to a spot where, according to local tradition, underwater "windmills" had been seen. This was an intriguingly peculiar description for ruins, and indeed, from the surface, we could see circular stone structures, about 15 feet in diameter, which looked definitely unnatural. Our swimmers went down for a closer look, and found the rocks, again quite free of marine growth, to be irregular in shape and broken. The swimmers reported no signs of tool marks. Despite repeated dives, they were unable to investigate leisurely as they would have been able to do with scuba gear, and could come up with no potsherds or other relics. But then even if we had found any antiquities we would not have been permitted to touch them. The 1500 B.C. ash blanket meets the Minoan earth exactly at sea level here, so that the structures, if Minoan, would have slumped only 25 feet, a fact that makes the site very promising as one containing intact Minoan buildings.

Skirting the coast of the bay south of Riva and proceeding south, we passed a small settlement with a few fishing boats drawn up on the shore. An elderly man was walking alone along the beach carrying a basket full of grapes. From his wave we gathered that the grapes were intended for us. We could not land the caïque on the shore at this point, so Davidson swam in, presented the farmer with a pack of cigarettes, and returned with the grapes, green and sweet, from the nearby vineyards.

We continued to the south, about 100 yards off the beach, pinging in 100 to 150 feet of water, again towing Davidson and Yorke, but at the limit of visibility. Here it had been reported that red lava-stone window frames from ancient buildings had been retrieved by fishermen. No one knew where these recovered antiquities could be seen, but the story persisted. Our survey covered two tracks, parallel to the shore over the typically rough bottom, but our brief search was hampered by a lack of specific information.

We anchored the boat off the beach and swam ashore for a look at the Minoan stratum in the cliffs. At the north of Therasia the bottom of the great ash layer comes right down to the water's edge and gradually slopes up to a height of several

hundred feet on the cliff at the south end of the cove by Cape
Tino. Upon reaching the beach, we were struck by the great
number of potsherds at the water's edge. They were of red clay,
and some showed raised designs. They were beach-worn and
their condition precluded dating, but we did see one ceramic
lamp that appeared to be of Roman origin.

Loring and I climbed the cliff to examine the Minoan layer.
We found it to be well defined, a layer of brown earth 3 feet
thick, at one location about 100 feet above sea level. Therasian
earth, Fouqué had called it. It contained outcropping shards of
clearly pre-eruption antiquity and was a good site for excavation, for the cliff had been cut back by ancient quarrying. In
the same vicinity, we found six ruined buildings lined up
parallel to one another at the cliff edge. They were presumably
part of the quarry workings.

Continuing our search for antiquities on northern Therasia,
we went to the ancient and lonely chapel of Saint Irene, described in the journal of Lieutenant Leychester of the Royal
Navy, who toured the island in 1848 and wrote what is to this
day probably the best guide to Thera. The small chapel is built
with ancient marbles, the baptismal font an inverted Roman
altar carved with bulls and garlands. Leychester had remarked
with wonder on the number of churches he had counted on the
island—290. Religion is surely the major sustenance of the people
of this extraordinary place. I went behind the altar into a small
and dusty anteroom and saw, lying against the wall, a triangular
limestone anchor pierced with a single hole for the line. This
accidental find was most fortunate, because the anchor was unmistakably Minoan. Someone in years past had found this, perhaps on the beach, and brought it to the chapel for safekeeping
or, as was common in antiquity, made a votive offering of it.

I had hoped that we might see some evidence of an ancient
Egyptian sarcophagus of marble which had been reported by
l'Abbé Pègues. It had been found in 1836 by laborers in a field,
had on it non-Greek writing, and was decorated with figures of
birds and deer. But the farmers had broken up the sarcophagus

and buried the fragments; like so many other Theran antiquities, it was probably lost forever.

On my return to the beach for the swim out to the caïque, I met my first Greek farm dog, a breed known for their ferocity toward strangers. Though armed with a large knife, I was dressed only in sandals and bathing trunks and was rather vulnerable. Fortunately, the dog kept his distance and I reached the beach without incident.

That evening, in the comfort of Loring's home, we had our first opportunity to compare notes on our background studies of the Atlantis story. Loring, like Galanopoulos, saw it as central to a family of myths and related legends in various cultures. He found support for this concept in the origins of the Minoan or Atlantean people. Many historians agree that they came through Anatolia, where peoples of several languages, customs, and other ways of life lived, including the Hittites.

Within this century, Hugo Winckler excavated Bogazköy, the site of Hattushash, the ancient capital of the Hittite empire, and gave us our principal archaeological evidence of these curious people. Translation of the Hittite cuneiform script has shown that they were non-Semitic settlers who, in Asia Minor before 1800 B.C., had built an empire that lasted until about 1200 B.C.

Familiar European folk stories have been traced back to the Hittite legends, and Hittite or Hattian deities form a striking parallel with the Greek theogony of the poet Hesiod. The traditional genealogy of the Greek gods and the victory of the Olympians over the Titans is described in the Hittite myths. This prehistoric connection between the Hittites and the Greeks made Loring wonder if there were not more myths crossing cultural lines and in particular relating to Atlantis.

In about 1600 B.C., the Hittites came into contact with a people to the south, the Hurrians, who occupied a vast area from the Tigris to the Mediterranean, south to Babylonia, and to northern Syria. Loring told us of the "Song of Ullikummi," which speaks of Hurrian deities and is thought to be a Hittite translation from Hurrian. It is preserved in a number of cuneiform tablet fragments datable to about 1300 B.C.

Anu, the sky god, had ousted his father, Alalu, from the throne and then, in turn, was pulled down by his son, Kumarbi, father of the gods. Teshub, the storm god and son of Kumarbi, had then displaced Kumarbi as king of the gods. And with this sequence of events established, paralleling the Greek Uranos-Cronos-Zeus combination, the narrative begins. Kumarbi is conspiring to defeat his son, Teshub, and destroy his son's city, Kummiya. While so conspiring, he fathers a son whom he names Ullikummi—destroyer of Kummiya.

Impaluri, Kumarbi's messenger, is then sent to the gods of the underworld to convey the orders of Kumarbi regarding Ullikummi. Subsequently, they take Ullikummi deep into the earth and place him on the right shoulder of Upelluri, a figure camparable to Atlas, who holds up the world on his shoulders. Ullikummi then grows into a gigantic pillar of diorite stone. He rises from the sea like a tower until his height is 9,000 leagues and his girth 9,000 leagues. He reaches into heaven.

When he has grown so tall that the sea reaches to the middle of his body, the sun god sees him and is filled with anger. The sun god informs Teshub, the storm god, and Teshub with his sister, Ishtar, climb to the top of Mt. Hazzi, where they see the great Ullikummi rising out of the sea. Ishtar tries to charm the monster, presumably without success, for soon the storm god, Teshub, entreats, "Let them anoint the horns of Serisu the bull. . . . Let them summon the storm, the rain, and the winds. . . . Let them bring forth the flashing lightning from its sleeping chamber."

A battle then ensues between Teshub and his divine forces and Ullikummi. Teshub is defeated and goes to Ea, the wise goddess of the nether sea, for help. By this time, Ullikummi is not content with the defeat of Teshub but wishes to destroy all mankind.

Upelluri, in spite of all the activity, is unaware of the great pillar resting on his shoulder, and Ea turns him around so that he can see the diorite man standing there. Ea then asks the older gods to bring the ancient copper tool that had been used to divide heaven from earth and asks them to cut through the feet of Ullikummi, whom Kumarbi has made to oppose the storm god. This is done and Ea announces to the assemblage of gods that she has crippled Ullikummi and asks them to come forth to do battle with the giant monster. The storm god then reenters the battle and rides his chariot out to attack the wounded Ullikummi. The last part of the story has been lost, but we can be sure that the storm god wins the battle against the weakened monster and Kumarbi is defeated.

The possibility that Ullikummi was the personification of Thera in eruption excited me. Diorite is a dark intrusive volcanic rock chemically similar to the frothy andestic lava of which Thera is largely made. Here were described the phenomena we had come to know—the growth of a volcano from the sea, the stormy eruption and, finally, defeat and sinking into the sea, indeed the work of the gods. This could be another myth describing the end of Atlantis or perhaps the growth of one of the Atlantean volcanic cones previous to 1500 B.C. I was to learn later that during this same summer in excavations at Has-an-lin, in northwest Iran, a widely publicized gold cup was discovered which, Robert Dyson of the University of Pennsylvania thinks, is decorated with a relief of the legend of Ullikummi. The cup was dated eighth century B.C.

I recalled the writings of Cyrus Gordon, who believes strongly that the Greek gods are derived from those of the Hurrians. He believes that there was a Hurrian minority on Minoan Crete, that they introduced the myths of the Greek theogony to the Aegean, and that the cultures of Babylonia and the Nile Valley, as well as of several other Middle Eastern civilizations, were established on Greek soil and in the Aegean Islands well before the Greeks and Hebrews of the second millennium B.C. emerged as historic entities. From about 1800 to 1400 B.C. Greece was dominated by northwest Semites, writes Gordon.

So the Atlanteans, or Minoans, lived in a land with complex

cultural origins, their ties to Babylonia and the Nile going back perhaps for millennia. We could no longer think of the inhabitants of the islands of Atlantis as an isolated, primary culture, as some of the lore would have it.

Dr. Galanopoulos, who has lived all his life surrounded by the heritage of the Greek pantheon, felt that we need not go as far afield in mythology as the Hittites to find a battle between the gods that reminds us vividly of the Thera eruption. Hesiod, in about 800 B.C., wrote of a terrible war between Cronos and his brother Titans against Zeus with his five brothers and sisters. These deities parallel Kumarbi and Teshub, but the story is quite different.

This war, which almost wrecked the universe, as did the Thera cataclysm in the view of the ancient Greeks, was described as follows:

> A dreadful sound troubled the boundless sea.
> The whole earth uttered a great cry.
> Wide heaven, shaken, groaned.
> From its foundation far Olympus reeled
> Beneath the onrush of the deathless gods,
> And trembling seized upon black Tartarus.

Zeus defeated the Titans with the aid of hundred-handed monsters who used thunder, lightning, and earthquake and because one of the Titans, Prometheus, helped Zeus. Prometheus, who is credited with creating mankind and championing their cause thereafter, was always in trouble with his fellow gods and in their eyes surpassed all in cunning and fraud. Deucalion's flood was an affront to Prometheus because it was intended to destroy what he had created. As a result of the war, however, Prometheus' brother, Atlas, was condemned to bear the weight of the world and the vault of the sky on his back forever.

After the war, Galanopoulos continued, Earth gave birth to a frightful monster, a creature more terrible than any before, and his name was Typhon.

A flaming monster with a hundred heads
Who rose up against all the gods.
Death whistled from his fearful jaws,
His eyes flashed glaring fire.

Zeus fought the Typhon with his newly acquired weapons, thunder and lightning, and killed him. Apollodorus gave a description of the battle: "Zeus pelted Typhon at a distance with thunderbolts, and at close quarters struck him down with an adamantine sickle, and as he fled pursued him closely as far as Mt. Casius, which overhangs Syria. . . . So being pursued again the Typhon came to Thrace and in fighting at Mt. Haemus he heaved whole mountains . . . a stream of blood gushed out on the mountain, and they say that from that circumstance the mountain was called Haemus [bloody]. And when he started to flee through the Sicilian Sea, Zeus cast Mount Aetna upon him. That is a huge mountain, from which down to this day they say that blasts of fire issue from the thunderbolts that were thrown." Here Galanopoulos commented that there are two versions among the ancient authors of Typhon's fate. Some say that he lies beneath Mt. Etna and others that he lies beneath Lake Serbonis in Egypt.

Dr. Galanopoulos hastened to remind us of his theory that it was the entrance to this same Lake Serbonis that the Israelites crossed in safety during their exodus from Egypt as reported by the Old Testament. As the Egyptian soldiers, led by their pharaoh, tried to follow, a great tsunami from the Thera eruption, which previously had withdrawn the sea far out from the shallow shore, crashed in again, inundating the Egyptians.

The association of Typhon with volcanoes is clear, and the area bounded by the route of Zeus' chase of the Typhon interestingly enough has as its center Thera. Except for the active volcanoes of Italy, where eruptions have been minor compared with Thera, one must travel very far, indeed probably beyond the limits of the known ancient world, to find a volcano with even a suspicion of activity in the past few thousand years. The nearest reliably reported activity is found in Ethiopia and the southern tip of the Arabian peninsula. Thus the Thera catastrophe appears to be the only known event on which the well-known myth of Typhon could have reasonably been based.

As I studied the myths of great natural commotion, even those in which the meaning is obscure, the trail kept leading back to Thera, where we were gathered to search for archaeological answers to support the theories. A search for all the answers could take us to many lands over many years, but the basic question of what gave rise to these myths could be answered by evidence found on Thera.

CHAPTER 7

IN the early morning of August 30, Edgerton, Hoskins, Loring, and Lehman left Phira in the caïque to round the island, leaving the caldera by the southwest channel past Point Akroteri and turning to the southeast. They would put in at Kamari, after a journey of 22 miles following the striated cliffs to Cape Exomiti on the southeast and then north along the wide black beaches of the Perissa plain. The wind was from the north and the seas making up. The captain did not want to leave the security of the bay and was persuaded with difficulty to undertake the journey.

Meanwhile, Galanopoulos, Davidson, Yorke, and I drove in Loring's Volkswagen over winding and rocky roads worn into the pumice to the small village of Kamari. Kamari lies just north of Messa Vouno, the precipitous mountain atop which is perched the ruin known as Ancient Thera. We arrived at 8:30 A.M., planning to rendezvous with the caïque after negotiating with Manolis Kafouros the charter of a smaller boat, a varca. Manolis cheerfully announced that it was too rough to launch the boat that day. And with the north wind which sweeps this shore blowing at 20 knots and waves 5 to 6 feet high breaking on the beach, we were forced to agree with Manolis.

At about 10 A.M. the caïque appeared around the point of Messa Vouno, leaping from wave to wave. At one point she began to come right up out of the water, showing her red underparts, but she pounded on. Under these conditions, she dared not come closer to the shore than about a quarter mile.

Manolis tried several times to launch his 15-footer, but gave up, and the caïque turned around and left.

Since we had no way of knowing whether they would sail all the way back to the caldera interior or stop in the lee of Messa Vouno, a short distance to the south, Dr. Galanopoulos suggested that we visit Ancient Thera, the famous ruin on the mountaintop, 1,100 feet up, which had been excavated by Hiller von Gaertringen in 1900.

One of the most extensive island ruins in Greece, though not particularly well preserved, it dates back as far as 1100 B.C., or early Phoenician times. There is a legend that Europa, daughter of the king of Sidon, a Phoenician, was seduced by Zeus in the form of a bull. On the bull's back she went to Crete and there bore Minos, who later became king of Crete, and Radymanthes. Later, Cadmos, Europa's brother, was sent by his father, Agenor, to seek for his sister. Tradition has it that Cadmos, in his search, stopped at Thera and started the first settlement, presumably in the early post-collapse period. There he left the first knowledge of Phoenician writing in Greece, and from it evolved the earliest Greek writing. Afterward, it is said, Cadmos went on to found Greek Thebes. The Cadmos adventures are generally dated in the fifteenth or fourteenth century B.C., a bit early in the light of the geological situation at Thera.

We drove up the 45-degree slope on a zigzag road, about 4 yards wide with no guardrail, and finally had to walk the remaining few hundred vertical feet to the ruin of Ancient Thera.

It is a spectacular site, high atop Messa Vouno, and contains an agora, houses, cisterns, barracks and temple. Throughout the ages, the site has been important, strategically located as the island is—halfway between Greece and Turkey, with command of the trade routes from its height. The seven periods represented in this city, all built with the stones of the preceding cultures, are Phoenician, Archaic, Classical, Hellenistic, Ptolemaic, Roman, and Byzantine. Among the many stone inscriptions are some relating to the homosexual cult of Apollo, featuring phalluses and descriptions of buggery and fellatio. The script is thought to be the earliest Greek writing after the Minoan. This archaic script I found especially fascinating because I realized that it provided a striking piece of evidence to support the credibility of Plato's story of Atlantis as a historical document.

The Linear A and B scripts of Crete, Greece, and the Aegean Islands came into use during the second millennium B.C.; they disappeared from use after 1200 B.C. But no writing seems to have replaced them in Greece until about 850 B.C., when the archaic script which we saw before us appeared. The Greeks were apparently illiterate for 350 years. Whatever the reason for this cultural dark age, except for a single reference by Thucydides, the absence of writing was not noted until quite recently. However, in the story of Atlantis, told to Solon by the priests of Saïs and recorded for posterity in the writings of Plato, it is unmistakably clear that the Egyptians knew about the Greek literacy gap.

Plato has the priests say: "But in our temples we have preserved from earliest times a written record of any great or splendid achievement or notable event which has come to our ears whether it occurred in your part of the world or here or anywhere else; whereas with you and others, writing and the other necessities of civilization have only just been developed when the periodic scourge of the deluge descends, and spares none but the uncultured and unlettered, so that you have to begin again like children, in complete ignorance of what happened in our part of the world or in yours in early times. . . . You remember only one deluge though there have been many, and you do not know that the finest and best race of men that ever existed lived in your country; you and your fellow citizens are descended from the few survivors that remained, but you know nothing about it, because of the many intervening generations silent for lack of written speech."

The fact that Greek writing existed before the dark age was not discovered until the late nineteenth century, yet Plato tells us that the Egyptians knew about it and that it was a surprise to Solon to learn of it. Here, I feel, is another link in the chain of convincing evidence that Plato did not make up the story of Atlantis, but indeed received it through Solon and others from Egypt, as he reported and repeatedly maintained.

Dr. Galanopoulos drew our attention to the inscribed name *Eumelos,* which, he observed, was that of the brother of Atlas, king of Atlantis. Then he repeated a point he had made in our very first conversation. King Eumelos was given as his lot the island nearest the Pillars of Herakles, which would have been the Cycladic island of Mèlos, since, as Dr. Galanopoulos believes, the strait spoken of by the Egyptians was not Gibraltar but the westerly entrance to the Aegean.

From the top of Messa Vouno, 1,100 feet above the sea, we looked down on the great plain of Perissa, with its beach and town to the south. There we saw our caïque anchored jauntily just off the beach, almost directly below. We assumed that Doc Edgerton and the others would leave her there for the night, to be ready for an early attack on the eastern shore the next morning.

We saw not only the beaches but, through the clear green shallows, the sea bottom itself. The British Lieutenant Leychester, whose detailed account of "Santorin or Thera" accompanies the 1848 chart, had noted "submarine ruins" off Kamari to the north in water varying in depth from 30 to 90 feet. We could see dark patches scattered about the bottom in just this region, exactly as Leychester had said. Were they ruins of Atlantis? Of a later settlement? Or just natural rock? I knew that I would have to examine these "patches" close up.

Leychester wrote in his journal that in A.D. 1650, off the northeast coast of Thera, 3½ miles from Cape Kolumbo, a new volcanic cone had risen above the surface of the sea. This event was witnessed by the French Jesuit missionary Père Richard, whose observations were reported by Abbé Pègues. The growth of this volcano and its eruption caused disaster on Thera and the surrounding islands. On September 29, 1650, large-scale earthquakes shook the Aegean. Pègues provides one of the most vivid modern eyewitness records of how Thera looked and acted in process of a full-fledged, albeit still relatively diminutive, volcanic explosion.

On another occasion the sea is stated to have burst its bounds overflowing the neighboring lands and the houses upon them, also carrying away the cattle that were feeding there and swallowing them up forever. On this occasion 500 arpents [acres] of land upon the east coast were submerged. Quantities of fig and olive trees were torn up and five churches thrown down. Two ancient towns at Kamari and Perissa were disinterred at the same time which probably some previous earthquake had engulphed.

The road also which then existed around Cape Messa Vouno was sunk beneath the waters. At the island of Neo [now called Ios] 12 miles distant, the sea rose to a height of 60 feet destroying trees and shrubs and depositing vast heaps of pumice. At Zea [the present island of Tsia, or Kea, is 95 miles away], the sea rose equally high and was so agitated that a Turkish man-of-war broke from her anchor and was washed upon the shore.

The earthquakes which had been felt with such terrible violence produced the most disastrous effects. Père Richard says that Pliny truly remarks that there is no style of building so capable of offering resistance to earthquakes as those arched. All those on Thera are arched and built with a mortar of extraordinary tenacity. Those I have seen rock to and fro like ships in a gale and at times resume their perpendicular. More than 200 had their roofs split and each day one sees great rocks roll with impetuosity into the sea. On Monday, September 30, and on the three following days the inhabitants were seized with excruciating pain in their eyes. Few escaped this evil and most remained blind three days. Many sunk under the pain of this malady and others were suffocated by the pestilential vapors thrown out of the volcano. In the parts of the island nearest to it the number of persons killed amounted to 50 and of animals upwards of 1,000 of all kinds.

Leychester also observed that the island formed off Cape Kolumbo had disappeared leaving a 10-fathom bank (Fig. 9).

Of Perissa he wrote: "The quantity of ancient remains about Perissa would incline us to believe that it is the site of a city. It is close under Messa Vouno, around the foot of which before the eruption of 1650 there was a road. All the people young and old bear testimony to this."

The men on the caïque rejoined us at Loring's house, taxiing back from Perissa after their rather rough day. Harold Edgerton was having a bout with dysentery and was pretty shaky from five hours of bouncing about on the caïque. The sea had been calm enough until they rounded Cape Exomiti on the southeast, and it became very rough after rounding Messa Vouno, where they had hove into our view. Our main concern, the acoustic equipment, at least had survived. At Perissa, where they anchored offshore, the fishermen on the beach refused to send out a small boat to row them in. Our boat from Therasia, 7 miles across the bay, carried the stigma of foreigners. After half an hour of high-pitched argument, a man offered to go out for them for 50 drachmas. This was exorbitant according to Loring, 10 being a fair price. When no amount of talking would make the fishermen lower their price, Loring and Hoskins simply swam ashore and commandeered a varca. But an oar was broken in the process so they paid 50 drachmas after all to settle up.

Before landing, however, the group made two acoustic runs over the "ancient moles" of Cape Exomiti, which we later found to be made entirely of "natural concrete." This material, known geologically as beach rock, is formed here at the edge of a beach at sea level where fresh water has run over limestone beneath the ground and into the sea. The basic ingredients of cement—lime and silica—occur here together, the silica being the major ingredient of the lava and pumice. With the correct combination of these materials and low rainfall, the beach turns into a striated concrete. The material is common in the eastern Mediterranean, formed in different ways in different places. The deposits on Thera are particularly interesting because of their size and shape and their volcanic materials. At Exomiti

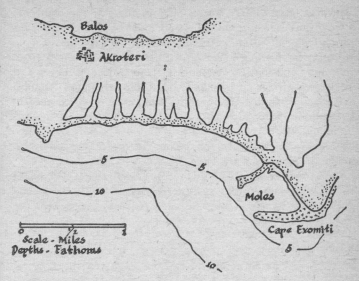

FIGURE 23. Southern Thera, Akroteri to Cape Exomiti, showing "ancient moles."

there were two giant submerged breakwaters or moles, formed of beach rock.

Leychester had reported that houses had been seen underwater in the shallows between the moles, their chimneys visible in calm weather. Galanopoulos was anxious to prove that the moles were only a product of nature because he felt that they were incorrectly oriented for any human purpose, since the opening faced the west, from which the prevailing wind blows. We came to the conclusion that the moles were definitely natural forms. Nevertheless, they could have had actual use in prehistoric times, especially since submerged ruins had reportedly been found between them. And the discovery of a large collapse caldera south of Akroteri showed that protective land may, after all, have shielded the moles from the westerly seas. The next day, the wind having slackened, we were able to use both our boats. There were clouds in the sky, the wind was west at only 10 knots, and our work site was off the east coast, in the lee of the island. Hoskins and Lehman took the caïque from Perissa, making long runs with the pinger off the beach 2 to 3 miles and south to Exomiti. Galanopoulos, Davidson, and Yorke were driven to Kamari to board the varca with Manolis. Loring and I joined the varca at Perissa, and we proceeded to the moles to meet the caïque. We had persuaded the indefatigable Edgerton to indulge himself in a day of rest and a dose of Entero-Vioforme, that marvelous astringent carried by so many Mediterranean travelers.

Our complex logistics this morning went smoothly, thanks to our radio communication—we had set up two walkie-talkie radios with hourly contact between parties. Range with the

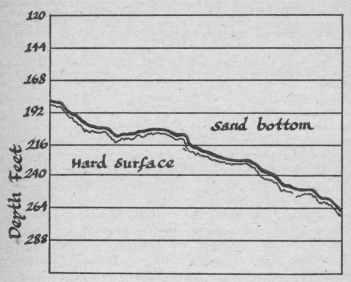

FIGURE 24. Edgerton mud pinger profile southwest of Cape Exomiti, showing irregular, sloping hard surface overlain by layer of fine black sand about five feet thick. (Linearized record after Edgerton 6 kc mud pinger, September 1, 1966, 1117–1137B. From H. Edgerton and H. Hoskins.)

little 100-milliwatt transceivers was remarkably good, 3 to 4 miles. In our attempt to detect any man-made objects that might lie buried in the bottom between the moles, we transferred the smaller recorder and the sound projector, better for resolving detail, from the caïque to the varca and used the larger recorder and longer-range projector on the caïque, which was operating in deeper water.

We now had two units going concurrently. The caïque continued offshore runs all day, returning to Perissa at 5 P.M. Hartley Hoskins reported that he had found a layer varying from 6 to 18 feet below the sandy bottom that became rough near the beach at Perissa. Whether this was the underwater buildings we were looking for, or just slumped and broken beach rock we could not be sure without excavation in this place, beleaguered by earthquake. But Leychester's journal spoke of a city exhumed here in 1650.

Those of us in the varca remained at the moles, where we swam over these massive slabs of concrete, cut off abruptly as if cast by some prehistoric giant. We took rock samples and underwater photographs and came to the conclusion that the moles were definitely beach rock of massive proportions, broken probably by wave action and by the undermining effect of the current running as much as one knot to the east. The two great moles were each a half mile in length and separated by a half mile, creating a large shallow harbor between. The bottom between the moles was a fine black and white sand, with sand waves covering all buildings. Here, too, excavation was required to determine whether Atlantean houses were buried here.

Loring and I swam ashore at Exomiti to explore the long beach rock slab running along the east beach for a mile and a half toward Perissa. Starting at sea level, it extends offshore about 100 yards, the water being but a few feet deep at that distance. It is one gigantic slab of concrete, presenting an aspect similar to a barrier coral reef. Loring showed me an exciting find here which he had made earlier, a mysterious ring of stones. The lava fragments were the size of fists and set in the beach rock two tiers high, forming a perfectly circular ring 3 feet in diameter. This formation was clearly man-made. Loring observed that the stones making up the circle were angular and not worn by the sea, as are those strewn loosely about the beach. We theorized that it could be part of an ancient structure that had been naturally concreted as the sea rose some 10 feet during the centuries since Minoan times.

More detailed examination could determine if the ancient circular structure was the base of an Atlantean watchtower. Perhaps the beach rock itself, in its Minoan form—for it has undoubtedly been built and rebuilt many times—was the Cyclopean wall that Plato said surrounded the metropolis of Atlantis. Identification of any structure or natural formation corresponding to that wall would "prove" the Atlantis-Thera relationship to anyone's satisfaction.

On Wednesday evening Dr. Galanopoulos had to leave for home. We were sorry to see him go, particularly before meeting the archaeologists who were due to arrive the following morning. We had at least verified, to some extent, his theory of the relation between the geometries of pre-eruption Thera and Plato's metropolis and examined the "ancient moles," which had particularly intrigued him. He told me that he did not see that land excavation could contribute much to verification of his Atlantis theory because the temples and palaces of Atlantis would have been on the central part of the island, which had collapsed thousands of feet into the abyss and were lost forever.

I did not share this opinion. To establish Thera as a great culture and population center might not require recovering antiquities from the parts of the island that had sunk into the sea. I hoped to find the outskirts, at least, of a large population center on the island itself.

On Thursday, Bill and Jane Biers of the American School of Classical Studies arrived on Thera with the paper from the Greek Archaeological Service permitting me to work on the island. I dutifully kept it on file but was never asked for it. The honeymooners had appeared at 6 A.M. and soon were hustled off

on the caïque with Hoskins and Lehman to observe the pinging process and see what archaeological interest it might have.
However it may have strained their good natures, they went
readily to work off the southeast coast while Loring, Edgerton,
and I took the varca to the moles for a second look. We planned
to rendezvous with the caïque at noon, when the Bierses would
transfer to the smaller craft to join us in diving to inspect the
bottom.

Before we left the beach at Perissa, a pleasant vacationing
Greek geologist named Vasos appeared. He had heard of our
exploration and joined us for the day. With the smaller recorder
mounted on the deck of the varca and Vasos looking on with a
critical eye, we made two passes at the moles and again saw a
rough stratum 8 to 10 feet beneath the sand which suggested the
underwater houses. This time, we swam over the area more
extensively than on the previous day, particularly over the
larger eastern mole, and the Bierses added their professional
eyes to the intensive search for exposed antiquities.

After this marine excursion, I explored the plain of Perissa,
where Père Richard had seen previously buried ruins exhumed
by the A.D. 1650 seismic wave. This large low flat plain lying
but 5 to 30 feet above sea level seemed strange to me, since here
there was no great thickness of ash which elsewhere blankets
the island. Perhaps before 1500 B.C. there had been a bay where
the plain now appears. I decided to make a seismic sounding of
this plain on my next trip.

At the end of Thursday's explorations, I instructed both
boats to be at Phira on Friday for a 7 A.M. start in the caldera.
After parting with the boat crews, the Bierses, Loring, Edgerton,
Vasos, and I drove to Exomiti to look for Minoan antiquities,
which the Bierses told us had been found by Marinatos. We
climbed the west face of Mt. Platinamos, a hill of shattered
limestone 567 feet high and badly fractured by earthquake.
The lone sign of ancient ruins was one large stepped limestone
block of uncertain date built into a modern retaining wall.

On Friday, September 2, the Bierses, Loring, Anna Brychaeas, and I took the varca to the harbor of Balos, the port of Akroterí. We landed and climbed the 250-foot cliff to the village looking for the Fouqué ruins all the way, but found nothing. The site is very rugged and badly eroded, hiding the Minoan stratum, and Fouqué's directions are obscure. We decided that a more extensive survey was needed to find these ruins. Even after the omniscient Dr. Marinatos and his party spent six weeks in 1967 digging for them, they remained obdurately hidden.

In the afternoon, we took our varca up north to the harbor of Therasia, where we examined a Venetian quarry building at the water's edge, and cruised north around Akro Tina to the beach some of us had visited previously and landed. Largely for the benefit of the Bierses, we returned to sites the rest of us knew. On our return to the Chapel of Saint Irene, the Bierses noted evidences of a buried village, probably one mentioned by the historian Ptolemy. Many potsherds dated the site at least as ancient as the fifth century B.C., and erosion ravines revealed the remains of cemented stone cisterns and plumbing systems. We went back to the cliff-face Minoan stratum that Loring and I had examined. There we noticed something we had missed before. Projecting from the white ash directly above the brown-red earth was a wall of black uncut lava stones. And it was clearly Minoan. I found this discovery exciting on two counts. First of all, it could be part of an outlying building of the Atlantean metropolis. Secondly, it indicated that we probably did not need to follow the diggings of Fouqué, after all.

Saturday, September 3, we devoted to the land. Hoskins, Edgerton, and Lehman visited the pumice quarry south of Phira, while Loring, the Bierses and I went to Akroteri by car to search the erosion ravines for the Minoan buildings excavated by Fouqué and Zahn. Dave Davidson and Bob Yorke had left for England by now—with some interesting underwater exploring to round out their summer's experiences.

To prepare ourselves properly, first we all visited the Thera museum. The museum is new and well designed, but unfortunately has no curator, and the many fine antiquities preserved

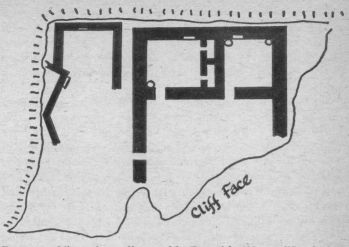

FIGURE 25. Minoan house discovered by Fouqué in 1867 on cliff at harbor of Balos near Akroteri. Building was sheared off by volcanic collapse in fifteenth century B.C. (After Fouqué, *Santorin et ses Éruptions,* Paris, 1879.)

there are either strewn about or stored in the basement; however, there are many fine examples of Minoan pottery on view of the type we could expect to find. We were surprised and pleased to meet Dr. Zaphiropoulos, distinguished "Ephor of the Cyclades," who happened to be on the island. It was curious that this influential Greek government archaeologist, who was in charge of all Cycladic archaeology and presumably must have endorsed our permission, had not made his presence known to us before. But he was a quiet, retiring man and did us the rare courtesy of permitting us to take photographs in the museum. After this brief meeting, he took no further interest in our work and disappeared. We were, I suppose, in his quiet opinion so many ανοητα ατομα (foolish persons).

On Thera most of the antiquities found during the excavations of Fouqué in 1867 and Zahn in 1900 were discovered near the village of Akroteri. Here the volcanic ash layer is notably thinner than elsewhere on the island, implying that the more violent eruptive centers were in the north and that the south was protected in some way. Deep ravines had been cut through the vineyards by winter rains and in the walls of these ravines, up to 75 feet deep, the layers of ash, pumice, and lapilli show clearly. Here and there, the Minoan layer of earth or flow lava can be seen.

For these reasons we drove to the village of Akroteri and from there walked over the fields and down into the ravines. Standing in the bottom of the most easterly ravine, 50 feet in depth, we could see, layer by layer, all the phases of the 1500 B.C. eruption. The top 35 feet was a stratum of very fine, almost powdery, uniform white volcanic ash. Within it were scattered layers, 1 or 2 yards thick, of small lava stones. At the bottom of the thick blanket of white ash lay a thin, 1- to 2-inch earthy-sandy weathered surface with no signs of civilization. This represented an interruption of volcanic activity that may have lasted for twenty to thirty years. Beneath that is a 10- to 15-foot-thick layer of pink angular pumice stones, 1 to 2 inches in size, the pink color deriving from flecks of iron oxide. At the bottom of the angular pumice lay the Minoan earth, a yard-thick layer of red, brown, or black soil, depending upon location, rich in decomposed vegetation. This layer lay on either broken slag lava or on smooth or ropy flows of reddish lava. In the pink pumice were supposed to be the buildings of Fouqué.

During our search of three ravines to the east of the modern village of Akroteri, each nearly one-half mile long, we saw potsherds of unmistakably Minoan date or earlier. Near the shore at the foot of two of the ravines, we found walls of uncut black lava stones projecting from the pumice cliff exactly at Minoan level, just like those we had discovered at the north end of Therasia, at the diametrically opposite end of the island group. These walls were undoubtedly part of a Minoan structure. They too could prove to be outlying buildings of Atlantis. We saw hollowed-out lava stones, used today as animal watering troughs, set near modern wells. I thought they might be Minoan mortars, a belief that was later given strong support. In 1967, while excavating in the same general area, artifacts identical to these were found that were positively identified as mortars from 1500 B.C.

Many retaining walls have been built and rebuilt in the ravines to hold the valuable, fertile surface layer of ashy soil in place for the scrubby vines, tomato plants, wheat, and barley that cover the fields. All loose stones find their way into the walls so that any exposed ruins do not remain standing for long. Changes in the landscape since the times of Fouqué and Zahn make the search difficult. For example, Robert Zahn, in 1900, published a photograph of the Minoan house he had excavated. Though we used this photo as a guide in our search for his house, we were unsuccessful in finding it. But a block of limestone built into a wall certainly means a building nearby, for the limestone is quarried only on Mt. Elias and Messa Vouno and is used only for buildings and the making of lime for cement. We saw some such stones in the Akroteri walls, probably clues to likely excavation sites.

We climbed down into the deep, narrow head of each ravine, where tall plants grow protected from the wind, keeping a careful eye out for the poisonous Egyptian asp, a small horned viper that is known to be found hereabouts, although Loring told us that they come out only at night.

Referring to Fouqué's notes while tramping the ravines, we rather expected to see walls jutting out from the pumice, as he had described and sketched; but a hundred years of weathering and farming had taken their toll.

Fouqué had seen very fertile humus giving support to rich vegetation, which we confirmed. He had also found vegetables in clay pots and olive-wood rafters in the houses in a remarkably good state of preservation. He concluded that the ash layer had been reasonably impervious to water filtration, a point that the islanders confirmed by building cisterns in it. Visions of a prehistoric Pompeii were forming in my mind. A city preserved under impervious ash would contain intact many important artifacts that had perished at other Minoan sites, and perhaps

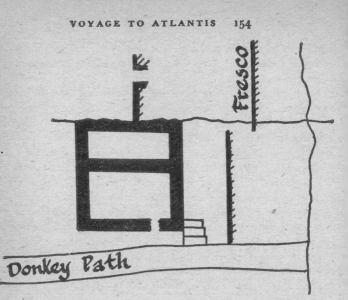

FIGURE 26. Minoan house of the flowered fresco discovered by Fouqué in 1867 in Akroteri ravine. After Fouqué, *Santorin et ses Eruptions*, Paris, 1879.)

even tablets inscribed in the Linear A script. On Crete, only those tablets that had been fired accidentally in a destructive holocaust had survived the ravages of time. Beneath the ash of Thera there should be intact unfired tablets and perhaps a written story of the Atlanteans.

Today the volcanic ash covering Thera is considered fertile for an Aegean island, but it is by no means as productive as the Minoan lava earth must have been. Though the surface ash is rich in plant nutrients, it is loosely compacted and will hold only stunted growth. The well-known Aegean winds, stronger on Thera than anywhere else, sweep the island the year round, blowing the loose ash about and tearing away the more adventurous grapevines. Even so, the land is now covered with vines, and the island's major industry is wine production.

The realization that it would clearly take more time and test excavations to make further discoveries at Akroteri fired me with the determination to find a way to start a full-scale excavation at Akroteri, so long neglected by archaeologists. The accidental finds of Fouqué showed me that there were bound to be many such buildings, and the antiquities he had found were certainly too elegant for simple farm dwellings. Behind these logical archaeological deductions was my firm belief in the credibility of Plato's description of Atlantis. It pictured the metropolis of Atlantis as densely populated, in particular around the outside edge of the circular island. Akroteri was the place to dig to find these Atlantean habitations.

We returned to Loring's house at the end of the day to hear what Hoskins, Edgerton and Lehman had discovered in the pumice quarry. It seemed that everywhere they looked there were Minoan antiquities. At times blinded by the swirling, wind-blown ash, the group had descended the steep access road down to the working level, where the sharp line between the pink pumice and the red-brown Minoan earth is clearly exposed and accessible intermittently for a half mile. Along the cliff face the line separating the pumice from the earth dipped and undulated in sand waves of Minoan times. The earth here was particularly rich in organic remains of all sorts, including wood, and it was sandy. This must have been a lake or marsh in Minoan times, Edgerton and Hoskins concluded. Plato had written, "provision for animals of every kind, both for those which live in lakes and marshes. . . ." Among the Aegean Islands, lakes have been known only on Crete, and now here was evidence of one on Thera. Here was important substantiation of Plato. Clearly more moisture had been retained on the land in prehistoric times.

In one location, Doc Edgerton made an unexpected find not directly related to our search for Atlantis—a burnished brown potsherd lying about 2½ feet below the Minoan earth surface. It was datable to the early Bronze Age, about 2500 B.C. This was the first sure evidence, to our knowledge, of a pre-Minoan culture on the island. To be sure, some Cycladic idols of the same date have been vaguely attributed to Thera, and one would expect that a pre-Minoan culture did exist there. The people known as Minoans, of interest to me as Atlanteans, are thought to have settled in the Aegean from Asia Minor about 2000 B.C., displacing and mingling with the previous inhabitants of unknown origin.

In addition to geological samples, the group took samples of wood fragments, which had lain for 3,500 years under the 150-foot blanket of ash, for carbon 14 dating, an expensive process not yet performed on the samples.

That Saturday evening was, for me, one of evaluation. We had visited many places on land indicating clear evidence of the Minoans, but these all called for archaeological excavation; and the underwater sites we covered had only whetted our desire to scuba dive. I was convinced that the island possessed a greater population in antiquity than had been heretofore suspected; clearly both the land and underwater aspects of our survey had been worthwhile in producing guideposts for future investigation. Even to give meaning to the acoustic pinging there had to be underwater excavation or, at least, inspection by scuba divers. Hartley Hoskins felt dedicated to putting as many miles on our caïque as possible, since we had brought the equipment here at considerable expense to Harold Edgerton. I felt that more land survey with a view to future excavation was equally in order. Our time was running out. We all had commitments at home and had to depart on the coming Wednesday boat for Athens.

Mythology had been my inspiration from the start and throughout my long journey. Now, in a reflective mood, I turned to it again. Galanopoulos had pointed out right at the start that Atlantis was really one of a whole family of related myths. One of these, he suggested, was the legend of Phaëthon, son of Helios, the sun god.

Of all the myths of ancient Greece, that of Phaëthon has been considered one of the most unique and inexplicable. Helios offers to grant any boon that Phaëthon would ask of him.

Phaëthon then asks to take his father's place for one day. Unable to persuade his son to desist, Helios sees Phaëthon off on the chariot at dawn. The steeds dart forward and soon notice that the load is lighter than usual and the chariot is tossed wildly around. They rush headlong and leave the traveled road. For the first time, the great and little starry Bears are scorched by the heat. Phaëthon is borne like a vessel flying before a tempest. He sees the monstrous forms over the surface of heaven, the menacing scorpion reeking with poison. Phaëthon can hold the reins no longer, and horse and chariot dash off unrestrained into unknown regions of the sky, among the stars high up in heaven, then almost to earth. The air he breathes is like the air of a furnace; the smoke is of a pitchy darkness. The Libyan desert is dried up. The earth is broken open, and through the chinks light breaks into Tartarus. The sea shrinks up. Wherever there is water becomes a dry plain. The mountains that used to lie beneath the waves lift up their heads and become islands.

The moon sees her brother's chariot moving beneath her own. The clouds begin to smoke and the mountaintops take fire. The fields are parched with heat and the trees are withered. The harvest is ablaze. Great cities perish; walls and towers fall. Whole nations with their people are consumed to ashes. The forest-clad mountains burn: Athos and Taurus; Molus and Ite; Ida, once celebrated for fountains, but now dry; Mt. Helicon and Haemus; and Etna, with fires within and without. Finally Zeus, in order to stop the rampage, brandishes a lightning bolt and launches it against the charioteer, striking him from his seat. Phaëthon falls headlong into Eridanus, the great river.

The array of catastrophes covering the known ancient world, taken literally, is hardly believable, I thought. But if we consider that it could apply to the greatest natural catastrophe known to man, the Thera eruption, many of the descriptions seem quite reasonable interpretations, given the unbridled imagination of the ancient people. It was indeed an event that would have struck many as the end of the world. With the birth of the volcano of Surtsey, off Iceland, photographs of spectacular volcanic lightning displays have become available. Even during this relatively minor event, lightning flashes like the branches of a great tree covered the sky and persisted for minutes at a time.

I recalled that the myth of Phaëthon is told to Solon by the Egyptian priests in Plato's *Timaeus*. It is described as a Greek myth known in Egypt. Egypt, they said, did not suffer from the two great catastrophes of destruction by fire, as illustrated by the Phaëthon legend, or by water, as illustrated by the deluge of Deucalion, and that is why in Egypt there is an uninterrupted historical record of great antiquity. It is curious that these two great myths appear in the same context as that of Atlantis, and that the Thera cataclysm was a destruction of civilization by both fire and water. I thought it more than accidental that the Egyptian priests associated these three stories, and that now there was more reason to believe they all actually described the same event.

Doc Edgerton and Hartley Hoskins proposed that we spend the next day making a depth chart of the caldera and coastal waters, even if we could not see below the bottom in deep water. This excellent idea, which would provide an aid to future underwater investigations, struck me as quite feasible if we divided into two groups again.

This time Hoskins and I went to sea and the others visited the quarry, Edgerton for the second time. Hartley and I made a chart of the southern half of the caldera, a remarkably flat plain at 900 feet below sea level with a very sharp rise to the central new volcano and a more gradual rise to the older caldera cliffs, where debris from the collapse and erosion had since accumulated. On this rise there might yet be identifiable Minoan antiquities, I thought. We attempted to drop a coring tube to the bottom, but the 900-foot line that we had carefully put together was not quite long enough. The weighted and empty coring had to be hauled up 900 feet by hand.

We had come to Thera unprepared for accurate navigation,

because we did not expect to do any precise mapping. Our equipment was designed for searching out subbottom features, but we could use it to chart the surface of the bottom. The decision to chart the deep waters now made accuracy important, because underwater features had to be located precisely in terms of surface points of reference. We attempted to fix our position at sea using a compass on board the boat and landmarks on the shore, but the rolling caïque and the great distances involved made for definitely unsatisfactory conditions. Nevertheless, we learned details of the shape of the bottom that were not evident from the latest navigation charts. In fact, though Hoskins and I would have liked to also navigate from shore, we later learned that our findings were actually corroborated by the sophisticated instruments on the *Chain*.

Our U.S. Navy chart showed a large scarp in the bottom, offshore to the south, and we were curious about it. Could it be an exterior volcanic collapse caldera? We knew that the land had collapsed on the exterior or south coast at Akroteri, but did not know its extent. The *Chain*, on her circuit of the island, proved that indeed there was a great volcanic collapse centered about a monstrous vent offshore to the southeast, but we had not heard of the *Chain*'s track or results at this time.

On Monday Doc Edgerton took the caïque to the south by himself, and on Tuesday he was joined by Hoskins on a similar track in search of the fault. As they rounded Cape Akroteri, we lost radio contact from Phira and saw them heading for Crete. By the time they were 3 miles offshore, we wondered if they had decided to follow the route of the ancient Therans who abandoned their island as the volcanic convulsions and earthquakes began. I thought they might be trying to mend a broken-down engine—they were now under sail with the northerly wind—until the craft finally turned into the wind and started back under power. When they returned, they told us of the huge near-vertical submarine wall 700 feet in height they had found. This fault could hardly be anything but a volcanic collapse caldera, further evidence of the enormity of the Thera cataclysm, but the *Chain*'s magnetics were needed to clinch the argument. On a traverse north of Nea Kaimeni within the caldera, they also had found the two volcanic cones that first appeared on the *Chain* trace and a third just north of Nea Kaimeni.

Our first expedition to Thera had come to an end.

All told, I felt that during these two weeks we had gathered enough evidence, when taken with that of earlier observers, to show that Thera had been heavily populated in Minoan times. The evidence was in little but tantalizing bits, potsherds, wall remnants, the mysterious "windmills," and more, some of it on land, some of it underwater. To develop these clues into undeniable demonstrations of a heavily populated Minoan Thera would be the task of a second expedition. Our pinpointing of likely sites for excavation laid the groundwork for not only that expedition, but many more. Thera would no longer be neglected; we had brought it into the archaeological limelight.

On Wednesday, September 7, we departed for Athens in the midst of a summer rainstorm. Loring came with us and was indispensable in helping to get our quantities of equipment, in many small and large boxes, on board the inter-island ship. A hectic few hours passed before they were all stowed securely in the hold. Loring, fluent in Greek and melodramatic in manner, conveyed to the captain, as he had done to the island officials, a sense of the importance of our mission and the eminence of our group.

We arrived in Piraeus at 5 A.M. in a pouring rain. For no apparent reason, the ship had to be unloaded immediately, and we gathered our boxes, suitcases, bags, and ourselves into a soggy encampment on the pier. Edgerton calmly woke up a Greek shipowner who had promised to meet us with a truck, and eventually we arrived back in Athens and called Dr. Galanopoulos without delay.

He had astonishing word for us—he told us that we were news, and announced that the U.S. Embassy had arranged a press conference for the next day. On the front page of the

Plate 1. Aerial view of Thera. *Photo by H. Edgerton*

Plate 2. Dr Galanopoulos aboard caïque. Nea Kaimeni and Cape Skaros, north of Phira, in background.

Plate 3. The research vessel *Chain* of the Woods Hole Oceanographic Institution.

Plate 4. Caïque pinging over reported Minoan underwater ruin in 120 feet of water in bay just south of Cape Riva, Therasia.

Plate 5. Archaic Greek graffiti on ruin of Ancient Thera, c. 900–800 B.C. This script is the earliest known Greek writing after the linear script which was last used c. 1200 B.C.

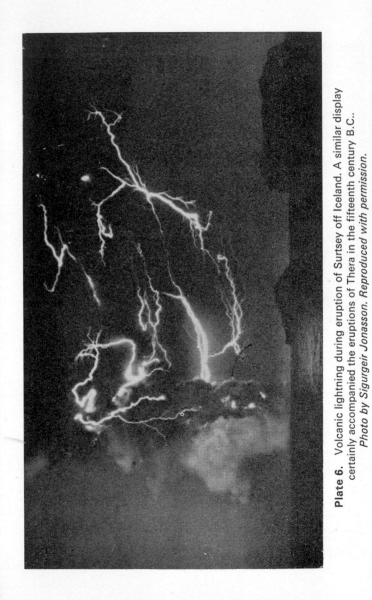

Plate 6. Volcanic lightning during eruption of Surtsey off Iceland. A similar display certainly accompanied the eruptions of Thera in the fifteenth century B.C.. *Photo by Sigurgeir Jonasson. Reproduced with permission.*

Plate 7. Excavation Bronos II soon after discovery of frescoes. Walls appeared within three feet of surface. Dr Marinatos on extreme left; Bronos III is starting in background.

Plate 8. Excavation Bronos II at advanced stage. Two- or three-story building of complex design, perhaps queen's chambers, is revealed. Mary Mavor, Dr Marinatos and Emily Vermeule examine well-preserved mud bricks of upper story.

Athens daily, *Ethnos*, was a photograph of the *Chain* with the headline that she had discovered Atlantis beneath the sea near Santorini! And in another newspaper, *Eleutheria*, appeared a large photo of Loring's monkey head beneath the headline: SANTORINI IS A PART OF LOST ATLANTIS, ESTABLISHED BY AMERICAN PROFESSORS MAVOR AND LORING. The press had reached Dr. Galanopoulos soon after his return and wrote enthusiastically of the results of our work, unbeknown to the rest of us.

The New York *Times*, on September 4, had written:

MOAT BELIEVED TO BE PART OF ATLANTIS IS FOUND IN AEGEAN SEA

Prof. Angelos Galanopoulos announced today the discovery of "most convincing proof" that the legendary city of Atlantis had been found in the Aegean Sea. The professor, who is a leading Greek seismologist, said that the outline of a wide moat had been detected 1,300 feet underwater in the submerged part of Thera island.

A Greek-American team of scientists led by Dr. James W. Mavor of the Woods Hole Oceanographic Institution in Massachusetts has been working for a week in Thera to explore the evidence of Professor Galanopoulos' theory that Atlantis should be identified with the Cretan empire that existed in the Aegean in 1500 B.C.

Prof. Galanopoulos said the moat was probably part of Atlantis' sacred island, the metropolis.

An announcement from the seismological laboratory of Athens University, which is headed by Professor Galanopoulos, said that the discovery had been made by the research vessel *Chain*, which belongs to the Woods Hole institution.

The *Chain* made a seismic profile of the Aegean island of Thera, two-thirds of which was sunk 1,300 feet below sea level by a volcanic eruption around 1500 B.C. Electronic devices aboard the research vessel traced the moat under a thick layer of volcanic ash.

These comments came as rather a surprise to us, for we truly had not thought our efforts were of world-shaking importance. The moat, in particular, was a source of confusion, which was not wholly surprising in view of the complexity of our operations. The use of the word "moat" was unfortunate—both as a concept derived from Plato's description of circular harbors and, in its more usual sense, as a man-made circular ditch that surrounds castles or fortresses. What we had found, of course, was a natural configuration in the caldera bottom, which could correspond to Plato's description of the Atlantis harbor. But my attempts at clarification fell on deaf ears.

Rudy Zarudzki and the *Chain's* scientific group, met at the dock in Rhodes by reporters, reacted coolly to the press reports. They did not feel that they had discovered a circular moat, since the *Chain* had not completely traversed the caldera. I don't know whether the use of the word "moat" originated with Galanopoulos; but if so, I suspect he was trying to emphasize the work of the *Chain*, without lauding his own efforts, and was generally misinterpreted by the press. That there was an internal harbor in Atlantean Thera he and I do happen to believe, but this belief is based on much more than the geophysical trace taken by the *Chain*.

On September 10, the New York *Times* reported my more detailed comments under the headline ATLANTIS EXPLORERS RETURN TO ATHENS. The story stated:

> Dr. James Mavor of the Woods Hole Oceanographic Institution in Massachusetts, who headed the team, said today: "There are shreds of evidence which, if put together, point toward a confirmation of the theory that the lost continent should be identified with the Minoan Empire, which ruled the Aegean archipelago and Crete about 1500 B.C."
>
> The team was working on a theory by leading Greek seismologist, Prof. Anghelos Galanopoulos, who believes Atlantis was a commonwealth of islands led by Crete that was destroyed by gigantic volcanic eruptions between 1520 and 1420 B.C.

We left Athens amid the furor of publicity, some of it regrettable but some quite welcome. I no longer felt alone in my enormous task of proving Galanopoulos' theory. The world press had become our ally. Once again the magic attraction of Atlantis was proving its spell.

Book III

CHAPTER 8

WE had come from far places to explore Thera together; now we were scattered and relied on the
mails to keep in touch. Doc Edgerton, in Boston,
and Rudy Zarudzki and I, in nearby Woods Hole, were the only
members of the expedition still physically near each other.
Hartley Hoskins had taken a position as professor of geology at
the University of Ghana, and had with him the acoustic records
taken by Edgerton's mud pinger, which he would analyze
through the winter. Hartley was bubbling over with technical
suggestions for improving our work. Loring remained in Greece.

Less than a month after my return home Loring announced
new discoveries that he had made after our departure. In the
quarry south of Phira he had discovered a Minoan riverbed
which he connected with the lake or marsh found by Edgerton.
Also, he had met two geologists, M. Norton and J. Green, who
were cruising the Mediterranean studying volcanoes, and the
three had traveled to the small uninhabited island of Kristiana,
where they had found a tomb or cistern containing some elegant
and well-preserved Early Bronze pots of c. 2500 B.C. Fragile and
beautifully shaped, they seemed to be ceramic copies of metal-
ware known from Asia Minor.

Loring wrote me that he had been in touch with Dr. Marinatos, back from Australia, who had invited Loring to assist him
in the field through the coming year. Marinatos planned in
November to search for the sunken classical city of Helice, in
the Gulf of Corinth, with the help of Doc Edgerton and his

underwater devices. After that, Marinatos would attend his excavations at Pylos, on the western Peloponnesus, and on his native Ionian island of Cephalonia.

In the meantime, I worked on a master plan, which I heroically called "Proposal for Certain Historical, Oceanographic and Archaeological Investigations of the Eastern Mediterranean Sea, Lands and People." This perhaps too ambitious document summarized the results of the 1966 Thera survey and described all the wonderful things that I visualized the future could hold, provided scientists and artists would cooperate.

I foresaw land excavations in the Akroteri ravines, for I was convinced that Fouqué had found a settlement elegant enough to correspond to Plato's Atlantis. I foresaw the digging of caverns deep into the pumice, supported by reinforced concrete arched ceilings. These horizontal caverns, I hoped, would reveal and preserve *in situ* Minoan buildings. I foresaw the use of a land magnetometer to detect buried walls, and a seismograph capable of measuring the thickness of the volcanic ash blanket which could also detect hidden walls and buildings. The deep submersible *Alvin*, capable of operating at a depth of 6,000 feet, the maximum known depth of the Aegean, could be used to search for Minoan shipwrecks, not one of which has ever been excavated. The proposal was published in November, 1966, with an attached budget of $320,000 for a two-year program, and was distributed to many people and organizations.

This was the starting point in my effort to raise expedition funds. In early November, John Lear, in the *Saturday Review*, published an article about Galanopoulos' Atlantis theory and my expedition of 1966, including a hint that money to support future work would be most welcome.

In October, Dr. Robinson of the American School of Classical Studies in Athens, whom I had queried about permission for excavating on Thera, wrote that his organization was unable to sponsor such a dig because of the limitation in the number of permits allowed the school. The Greek government places a quota on the number of excavations allowed foreigners, three per country, at any one time. He suggested that I approach the Archaeological Service of the Greek government or the Archaeological Society of Athens directly, or try to arouse the interest of Dr. Marinatos. These channels, if open, would lead to a Greek excavation under the direction of a Greek archaeologist, which could, however, be supported by American money. The excavation of the Minoan palace at Kato Zakros on Crete is so supported in part.

I was glad to have Robinson's blessing for what was already under way. I had suggested a dig on Thera in my letter to Marinatos the previous May as well as in my published proposal, and I hoped that Loring was also eliciting Marinatos' interest. But Dr. Marinatos was busy with Helice, a project that I thought exciting but beset by horrendous engineering problems. He had a long-standing interest in Thera, I knew, but to translate this into action might take some doing.

During the late fall of 1966, I tried various avenues of approach to the problem of starting an excavation in 1967. The University of Pennsylvania Museum is well known for its pioneering work in archaeological technology. I had sent them my proposal and was in touch with several of their staff, particularly the famous University of Pennsylvania underwater archaeologist George Bass, whose work I admire greatly. Dr. Froelich Rainey, director, and Dr. Elizabeth Ralph, associate director, who was eventually to go to Thera with our group, were most cordial and offered the sponsorship of the museum so that I could use the name in my attempts to raise funds.

Since my aims were, more and more, encompassing the techniques of archaeology, I decided that I must develop an association with a good archaeologist with a wide reputation who was also close at hand to my Woods Hole base and would be able to spend the 1967 summer season in Greece. I turned again to the Museum of Fine Arts, Boston, and to Mrs Emily Vermeule, wife of the man who had originally steered me to the right people for permission in 1966. It was not long before I realized that she was an ideal person for the project I had in mind.

Emily was fascinated by the prospect of excavating on Thera. A brilliant scholar, expert in the history and archaeology of the Aegean, she was intrigued by my broad proposal, which brought scientists of many disciplines together. And she is a delightful person. But perhaps most important of all, from the practical point of view, she had worked with Dr. Marinatos off and on for ten years and knew him well. As a classical scholar, Mrs. Vermeule was naturally skeptical about Atlantis, but I hoped that this would eventually change.

Doc Edgerton returned from Greece at the end of November and reported on the results of his sediment pinging at Helice, where he had been working with Dr. Marinatos. He reported that there were plans to start excavating the following June. Loring had been part of the work crew and Doc considered him most helpful; and apparently he had gotten on well with Dr. Marinatos. But Loring's Kristiana finds had developed complications. The story went something like this:

The fine Early Bronze Age pottery was discovered in a ravine and it seemed certain, in the opinion of Loring and the geologists with him, that if the cistern or tomb were not excavated immediately and the pots removed for preservation, they would be washed into the sea by the coming winter rains. Therefore Loring took some potsherds to Thera, reported the discovery to the chief of police, then took the shards to Athens, where he presented them to Dr. Zaphiropoulos of the Greek Archaeological Service. An expedition was immediately sent to Kristiana under K. Tsakos and a fine collection of well-preserved Early Bronze Age pots was removed to Athens and then to the museum at Thera, where I eventually saw them in 1967.

So far, all was well. It was not until February that I heard from Loring on the difficulties he had encountered. First, when he arrived in Athens with shards soon after the discovery, he was arrested and put in jail, apparently on orders from the Thera police. Dr. Zaphiropoulos came to Loring's assistance and had him released. Loring then was acclaimed in Athens for having salvaged the valuable pottery from the elements. During the next couple of months, a scandal in the Greek Archaeological Service erupted in the press. Some government employees had been caught smuggling antiquities out of Greece from the National Museum in Athens. Articles began appearing in the Athens newspapers criticizing the Archaeological Service for bad management and scandalous behavior. According to Loring, the handling of the Kristiana pot discovery was singled out for attack and both Loring and Zaphiropoulos were the subject of harsh criticism by Dr. Marinatos, who entered the scene as author of some of the articles. In effect, Loring had been made a scapegoat.

Soon Loring found himself mixed up in what was apparently a feud within the Greek archaeological hierarchy. He was charged, in keeping with the Aegean impulse to fabulate, with illegal removal of antiquities from Kristiana and apparently with being an accomplice in spiriting out of Greece some pottery that actually has been in the Brooklyn Museum for the past twenty years. No matter, Loring and Marinatos were completely at odds, and Loring decided to go to London to sit things out and study at the British Museum. I helped obtain permission for him to use the facilities, and he spent the winter studying Thera's history and, on his return in May, brought quantities of research material. In the meantime, his engagement to Anna Brychaeas collapsed, an idyll that did not make the epithalamial stanza.

Pieces of this complex story filtered through to me at the very time I was trying to establish some rapport with Dr. Marinatos by mail, with the aid of Emily Vermeule. The Loring fracas hardly helped, but I decided not to drop him from my plans for the summer of 1967. I would simply hope that things could be smoothed over come summer when Loring would be at his home on Thera and the problem would have to be faced. I had not met Dr. Marinatos at this point but I had heard from various sources that he could be a difficult person.

I rationalized by telling myself that personality conflicts are a part of any project that gets things done. Nevertheless, from what I knew of Loring and had heard of Marinatos, I could imagine a clash of natures, so I advised Loring to postpone his arrival on Thera if there was a chance of fireworks between Marinatos and himself.

More serious, I thought, was the possibility that Dr. Marinatos would not be able to secure permission to dig on Thera. His feud with the Archaeological Service seemed most untimely. Marinatos reportedly was far down on the totem pole during the liberal administration of George Papandreou. But with a change in government, his fortunes changed and he emerged on top. What I hardly realized at the time was that Loring had become an obsession with Marinatos, one that would, sadly, affect our every move the following summer.

But my summer plans were not entirely contingent upon a land excavation being set up. After all, it was sixty years since anyone had excavated prehistoric sites on Thera, and my chances as a foreigner of engineering such a project seemed slim, particularly with political and personality problems building.

I wanted Dr. Edgerton to return with his mud pinger, and hoped that our entire group of the previous year could return, this time with scuba diving permission. I wanted to take a land seismograph to determine the thickness of ash, mainly to find out how far we would have to dig to find ruins, and to survey Perissa and Kamari for underground remains. I hoped that an oceanographic ship could continue the work *Chain* had started, and that someday *Alvin* would go to the Aegean to study deep ocean currents. All these things I communicated to Dr. Galanopoulos, Dr. Marinatos, and Dr. Zaphiropoulos of the Archaeological Service. I was determined to remain completely neutral and above Greek politics.

Steady but slow progress was made on all fronts through the winter and early spring, during which time I was able to return to the study of history and the Atlantis legend, particularly Plato's description of the Atlantean and Athenian people, their identification with the Minoans and Mycenaeans, their customs and their great conflict. Professor Frost, in 1909, had noticed similarities between Minoans and what he presumptively and, in my view, prophetically called Atlanteans. The harbors, for example, with their shipping and merchants coming from all parts, the elaborate bathrooms, the stadium and the solemn sacrifice of a bull are all thoroughly, though not exclusively, Minoan. When we read in *Critias* how the bull is hunted, in the temple of Poseidon, without weapons but with staves and nooses, we have an unmistakable description of the bullring at Knossos, the very thing that struck foreigners most and gave rise to the legend of the Minotaur.

The description of Atlantis in *Critias* states, "There were bulls who had the range of the temple of Poseidon; and the ten kings, being left alone in the temple, after they had offered prayers to the god that they might capture the victim which was acceptable to him, hunted the bulls, without weapons, but with staves and nooses; and the bull which they caught they led up to the pillar (see Plate 23b) and cut its throat over the top of it so that the blood fell upon the sacred inscription. Now on the pillar, besides the laws, there was inscribed an oath invoking mighty curses on the disobedient." The similarities between this scene and those depicted in Minoan frescoes and on pottery are so great that one is inclined to forget that Plato was describing Atlantis and not Minoan custom, of which he knew nothing.

The period 1500 B.C., some 300 years before the Trojan War, is approximately the time when the Minoan culture of Crete and the Aegean Islands began to evidence strong Mycenaean, or mainland Greek, characteristics. Either as a result of conquest, cultural integration, or simply the cultural decay of an older civilization, the Minoans not only were losing their economic and political dominance of the Aegean, but were themselves gradually becoming Mycenaean in character. The Minoan culture was aesthetic in emphasis, devoted to art, craftsmanship, and the pleasures of life; the Mycenaeans appear to have been concerned more with the way society worked than the way it played. This change seemed unfortunate to me, since the Minoans had in many ways a better way of life, sprung from insular security, than the Mycenaeans who succeeded them on the islands.

Having evolved from the Neolithic during the third millennium B.C., Minoan civilization gradually developed into a peaceful, metal-using, mercantile society with a sensual love of pleasure and exquisite artistic skill, coupled with the affluence and leisure to indulge them. Controlling the seas, as they appear to have done, they had no need to fortify their palaces and towns, and probably preferred trade to war and piracy, though the difference may have been slight. Spared the time and expense most civilizations must pour into military preoccupation, the Minoans built a culture that is imaginatively echoed in Plato's description of the Atlanteans.

"For many generations," Plato has Critias tell us, "as long as the divine nature lasted in them, they were obedient to the laws, and well-affectioned to the god, whose seed they were; for they possessed true and in every way great spirits, uniting gentleness with wisdom. . . . They despised everything but virtue, . . . thinking lightly of the possession of gold and other property, which seemed only a burden to them; neither were they intoxicated by luxury. . . . But when the divine portion began to fade away, and became diluted too often and too much with the mortal admixture, and the human nature got the upper hand, they then, being unable to bear their fortune, behaved unseemly, and to him who had an eye to see, grew visibly debased, for they were losing the fairest of their precious gifts; but to those who had no eye to see the true happiness, they appeared glorious and blessed at the very time when they were full of avarice and unrighteous power."

The Atlanteans, we observe, were transformed from a wise and great people to a base and warlike one, just as the Minoans appear to have metamorphosed into Mycenaeans. At least this is how it appeared to the reporter who transmitted the story. We can imagine that, even as today, the real motives for a war, usually religious or economic, became clouded with emotion and fantasy.

Historically, a people living on a coast are vulnerable to attack from both land and sea. From the mountain hinterlands come marauding tribes seeking the fruits of agriculture and the sea that the coastal peoples have gathered. From the sea come colonists from insular powers. The Mycenaeans surely lived under these pressures and from them, in part, developed their warlike nature. The Minoans, their island empire spread wide over the Mediterranean, and perhaps beyond, must have indulged in military forays to secure and preserve their colonies. Most of these were, doubtless, minor affairs about which the population of the secure Cretan homeland knew or cared little.

But forays to preserve their colonies were probably not the basic ingredients of the conflict between the Atlanteans and ancient Athenians. I suggest that a much more profound force

FIGURE 27. Detail from the Silver Rhyton found in Shaft Grave IV at Mycenae. Probably a Minoan work, it shows an attack on a coastal Minoan town by mainland soldiers (in helmets). A similar scene was found recently at the Palace of Zakro on Crete. Note use of bows and arrows by Cretans.

was at work. The saying that East meets West in Greece was a truism in ancient times, as it is today. The Mycenaean Greeks were of European stock, aggressive individualists who had roamed at will through the thickly forested and more bountiful lands to the north. The Middle Eastern origins of the Minoans gave them a heritage of conformity and rigid discipline molded by their physical environment. A long history of civilization had produced great cities in the narrow river valleys and oases.

In the Aegean the two cultures met and fused in a spontaneous, colorful, yet controlled way of life that peaked in the height of the Minoan period in the fifteenth century B.C. Their religion combined the Earth Mother of the East with a male consort who eventually dominated in the time of King Minos, and who could well have been more Mycenaean than Minoan. Minoan art was a fusion of the individualism of the West with the techniques, materials, and religious ideas of the East.

The colonists who went west from Mesopotamia and Egypt migrated because of the demands for raw materials from the artisans of the cities and the attraction of rich mineral deposits. Thus rose the merchant princes of the Aegean. On the mainland, the Achaean city states evolved, helped by the Eastern influence. But these states, dominated by Europeans, were constantly at war with one another.

Finally, the aggressive, individualistic Achaeans of Greece came to permeate the Minoan culture, and Western ideas of religion and social structure dominated. The peaceful Earth Mother of the conformist Oriental culture was in time subdued. As Plato wrote, this society ". . . became diluted too often and with too much of the mortal admixture, and the human nature got the upper hand. . . ." Conflict between the islands and the mainland was the inevitable result.

The reality of Minoan Crete can be seen strikingly in the south of that island at the great palace of Phaistos, on the plain of Messara, with Mount Ida towering in the distant northwest. The palace was large, almost as large as Knossos on the north, in a more impressive setting, and elegantly constructed (see Plate 15a). It has yielded magnificent treasures, as has the nearby palace of Hagia Triada, which was built to replace it after the earthquakes of about 1500 B.C. From the palaces themselves and the graves have come beautifully wrought gold necklaces and pendants, seal stones, marvelous Cretan pottery, the famous steatite Chieftain's Cup, Harvester's Vase, and Sports Rhyton, or ritual drinking horn. Splendid frescoes were found —one from Egypt, by the way, showing two cats stalking a pheasant, and one with a marine design of fish and octopi.

All this is not quite as elegant as Plato's Atlantis, perhaps, but the two cultures are more alike than, say, the real nineteenth-century America and the one whose streets were paved with gold.

The Platonic accounts of the military might of Atlantis— the chariots, light and heavy infantry, slingers and sailors—all fit perfectly into our concept of the Aegean Bronze Age, particularly in its Mycenaean phase. It matters little whether this weaponry was typical of Crete or the mainland. It is characteristic of the armor and military skills known to have been practiced in the Aegean between 1500 and 1100 B.C. by two highly advanced cultures that were in conflict about the time that the island of Thera, strategically of the utmost importance to Crete, collapsed in a gigantic volcanic eruption and sank beneath the sea. It hardly strains good sense, I believe, to surmise that the Egyptian account of the Atlanteans and Athenians is actually a composite description of life at the palaces of Knossos, Phaistos, and mainland Mycenae. Probably included were folk memories of military adventures involving these peoples and recalling an earlier time when Minoan Crete, like Atlantis in its early days, had been a sensuous, prosperous, and peaceful place.

The Atlantis legend is not the only source of contact with the wondrous cities of the Greek Bronze Age. Homer described the country of the Phaeacians, a Crete-like island civilization which Thucydides identifies with Corfu, off the northwest coast of Greece. Whoever the Phaeacians were, they seem Minoan, Mycenaean, and Atlantean. "Our city is surrounded by high battlements," the lovely Nausicaä tells Odysseus. "It has an excellent harbor on each side and is approached by a narrow causeway, where the curved ships are drawn up to the road and each owner has his separate slip. Here is the people's meeting place, built on either side of the fine temple of Poseidon with blocks of quarried stone buried deeply in the ground...." Later she describes her people as having no use for the bow and quiver, but spending their energy on masts and oars and on the "graceful craft they love to sail across the foam-flecked seas." The Mycenaeans were famous bowmen, and the Minoans before them famous seamen.

As for the palace, Homer describes Odysseus as being awed as he crossed its bronze threshold. "For a kind of radiance, like that of the sun or moon, lit up the high-roofed halls of the great king. Walls of bronze topped with blue enamel tiles, ran round to left and right from the threshold to the back of the court. The interior of the well-built mansion was guarded by golden doors hung on posts of silver which sprang from the bronze threshold. The lintel they supported was of silver too, and the door handle of gold...." This description strikes us as realistic and is accepted as an historical account. Plato's account of the temples of Atlantis, while undoubtedly exaggerated, does not differ greatly from that of the palace of Phaeacia.

What were the origins of the Minoans and what does the archaeological evidence tell us of their widespread influence at the peak of their development in the fifteenth century B.C.? If these remarkable people were truly Plato's Atlanteans, strong ties with Egypt should have existed. Plato wrote, "Now, in this island of Atlantis there was a great and wonderful empire which had rule over the whole island and several others, and over parts of the continent, and, furthermore, the men of Atlantis had subjected the parts of Libya within the columns of Heracles as far as Egypt, and of Europe as far as Tyrrhenia."

Archaeology confirms what Plato said. The early Minoans

were Mediterranean in physical type, but culturally very mixed. Their pottery is similar to that of Asia Minor and in form similar to that of Mesopotamia. Egyptian inspiration is strong in the religious sphere, and there may have been an actual migration from the Nile. The origins of the written language, Linear A, are in doubt, but the idea may have come from Syria or Egypt. The famous double-ax cult of Crete comes from Syria and the Minoan seals from Iran.

Moreover, by means of trade and diffusion of religious ritual, in the second millennium B.C., the Cretan connection extended to northern and western Europe as well as to all the Mediterranean lands. And significantly, in all these places—Egypt, Italy, Spain, Sardinia—it ceased about 1500 B.C., just at the time of the Thera eruption.

The first millennium B.C. Phoenicians and the classical Greeks have been considered by many to be the earliest and greatest colonists of the Mediterranean. But the archaeological evidence now points toward a colonial empire 1,000 years earlier as great or even greater in extent than the Phoenician, and in many ways as culturally sophisticated, using bronze as the later people used iron for weaponry, tools, and money.

Trade in the rich silver and tin ores of Iberia, Tuscany, and Sardinia with the Aegean and the Levant flourished well before 2000 B.C. The eastern cult of the Mother Goddess was spread widely, and some believe that it was superstition and ritual that were traded abroad for gold, silver, and amber. The equipment, pottery, and physical type of the people who developed the farming communities of temperate Europe, including Brittany, Great Britain, and Switzerland, are related to the Mediterranean people as far away as the Nile Delta.

The famous megalithic structures of England, Scotland, Ireland, France, Spain, Sardinia, and Malta, the best known of which is Stonehenge, are evidence of funerary practice and a cult that probably was superimposed on a number of different cultures. This cult spread during the second millennium B.C. and again significantly died out in 1500 B.C., as we know from the associated artifacts, many of which, as well as designs on the megaliths themselves, are closely related to those of contemporary Minoan Crete. There appears to be no single megalithic culture, and many of the structures found all along the coasts could only have been inspired by sea voyagers, implying that the Minoans traveled by sea as far as Britain. The widespread influence of the Minoans throughout the ancient world could have been the historical basis for the extent of the Atlantean empire and the large size of its islands.

The well-known amber route from the Mediterranean, north through Rumania and Germany to the Baltic, was traveled in Minoan times. We know this from the finding of amber jewelry in tombs of Minoan Crete identical to that found along the route and as far northwest as England. Certainly, some part of the myth of Jason and the Argonauts is a memory of this trade.

Atlantis looms large in this picture of prehistory. If we assume that Plato's story was based on fact, archaeological finds of the period 2000–1400 B.C. should confirm the story and, conversely, the story, as well as many other contemporary legends, should point the way in the search for historical knowledge. Jason, Hercules, and Ulysses traveled in myth to far places which, the archaeological record has shown, their people did in fact visit and settle.

It is highly significant that in 1500 B.C. European cultures far from the Aegean lost contact with the Minoans and their civilizations experienced a discontinuity in the midst of rapid progress. That the eruption of Thera and the demise of the Minoans were in some way responsible seems to me an inescapable conclusion. In what way remains a mystery. Surely the megalith builders of England did not lose their skill and local sociological factors remained constant.

Perhaps this is how it happened. The bountiful northern European environment, abounding in space and rich resources, did not foster the building of cities until much later than the confined and traditional Mediterranean communities. Groups of people from these southern cities, all having urban-oriented ideas and missions, traveled to the north and west spreading their influence through the scattered populations of rural communities. Then, in the fifteenth century B.C., this united front, which had been pushed along by eastern Mediterranean economic pressures, ceased abruptly. The northerners, living in a culture where collective enterprise was not yet a natural part, reverted to their older ways.

In the spring of 1967 I was introduced to a remarkable book by Rhys Carpenter, *Discontinuity in Greek Civilization.* The book is concerned with the effect of climatic change on the movements of ancient peoples. Knowing about the Thera eruption, Carpenter was gripped by the theory that the kingdoms of Atlantis and the Minoans were one and the same. He wrote, to my great satisfaction, "I am accordingly prepared to maintain that in Solon's day there was preserved in Egyptian temple chronicles the mention of an island that had sunk beneath the sea during a tremendous natural upheaval, and that this island, for which Plato invented the name Atlantis, was none other than Thera."

Having positively committed himself, Carpenter went on to consider three events described in Plato's *Timaeus:* the submergence of the Atlantean island, the defeat of the Atlantean armies by the bravery of the ancestral Athenians, and the destruction of the Athenian civilization by "the sun's departure from its normal course." Carpenter writes, "Since the first two of this triad seem to have a firm basis in fact it is only reasonable to consider whether we may give credence to the third."

The demise of the Mycenaean culture took place rather suddenly about 1200 B.C., at least 200 years after the collapse of Thera destroyed the Minoans, or so goes the accepted Aegean chronology. Historians attribute the Mycenaean collapse to invasion by the Dorians, a mysterious people who came from the north.

Carpenter's evaluation of the evidence led him to the startling conclusion that there was no Dorian invasion at all. He points out that numerous migrations of people occurred all over the

Mediterranean at this time, which current opinion has attributed to military adventures of unknown motive. His examination of the circumstances of these events shows them, quite reasonably I believe, to be merely the abandoning of a homeland because of a natural catastrophe. This catastrophe, he believed, was a great drought.

To support his theory, Carpenter went on to explain the origins of Mediterranean weather. The hot and rainless Aegean summer is caused by the steady northerly trade wind, which blocks passage of the wet Atlantic Ocean storms into the region south of the Balkan mountain ranges. Dr. H. W. Willet of M.I.T. has noted climate fluctuations in historical times that caused shifts in the tracks of Atlantic storms and therefore in the position of the trade wind belt. From 1200 to 900 B.C. the Aegean was in a warm cycle, and it is quite likely that the trade wind belt moved north, making Greece that much drier and hotter than usual to destroy the agriculture which was, like any other, closely attuned to the natural environment.

Carpenter considered that the meteorological evidence and the archaeological evidence agree to support his theory of a Greek drought sufficient to cause the people to move east and west where better-watered land existed. His analysis, with which I agree, attributes great changes in the way of life of the people to the small but significant change in climate.

Is this climate change related to the Thera eruption? The story of Atlantis suggests that the drought can be equated to the statement about the sun deviating from its normal course. The archaeological evidence suggests at least the possibility of a tie between the great drought of 1200 and the eruption of 1500–1400 B.C.

I investigated quantities of published evidence establishing the date of the destruction of Minoan Crete, mostly in the form of Egyptian artifacts found on Crete and vice versa (see Appendix). While there are many artifacts the style and stratification of which allow us to be confident that the Thera collapse took place later than 1500 B.C., there are practically none from which we can confidently infer a date before which it occurred. This leaves open the exciting possibility that perhaps the Thera eruption and Cretan destruction both took place as much as 100 to 200 years later, tying in the great natural catastrophes of this era, the eruption and the drought. As Carpenter had written, "Until the preclassical remains lying buried beneath the thick mantle of ash on Thera have been adequately investigated, we shall have no certain guide to tell us the date of the disaster."

On the home front, the brand-new oceanographic research ship *Oceanographer*, owned by the U.S. government, was planning a round-the-world cruise to commence in the spring of 1967. Unexpectedly, I was asked by Dr. George Keller of ESSA, the Environmental Science Service Administration, which operates this largest of such vessels, to coordinate my Atlantis research with his general plan. He was interested in having the ship stop at Thera to continue the geophysical survey of the Atlantean harbors. Here was a godsend! Rudy Zarudzki and I prepared for another contour survey of the sea bottom, to get a better idea of what the area looked like before the 1500 B.C. collapse.

I continued to talk to scientists and U.S. Navy people about taking *Alvin* to the Mediterranean, though I knew this would require coordination with other projects to share the high cost of some $10,000 per day. Barring another lost H-bomb, the Mediterranean was out for this year. More and more of my time was spent in the tedious business of looking into prospective sources of money to finance the broad proposal. The horizons were expanding, but time was running short for 1967.

All through the winter and spring, Emily Vermeule and I corresponded with Dr. Marinatos. On February 27 I asked him to obtain permission to excavate, and on March 8 he wrote with encouraging news. He had presented my program to the Archaeological Society of Athens, an eminent group which sponsors all Greek digs, and received an enthusiastic response. "Unanimously they decided to help us in realizing your program," he wrote. He also informed me that Captain Jacques Cousteau wished to come to Thera in June and suggested that we start operations in late May. Marinatos was happy that his friend and colleague Emily Vermeule could come.

On April 12 I heard from Marinatos that he had his permission in hand, a paper from the Ministry of Education appointing him the director general for any excavation in Thera. He had indeed succeeded. In fact, the scope of his authority rather surprised me because I understood that Dr. Zaphiropoulos was in charge of Cycladic excavations and was himself working currently in a post-eruption site on Thera.

Dr. Marinatos announced that the Archaeological Society would put up $2,000 for the excavation and asked me to supply another $2,000 to cover 1967 expenses. I had not yet procured any hard cash, only the participation of several scientists who had their own sources of funding. In fact, my final request, of several, for modest foundation money had just been denied. I decided that, if necessary, I would put up the money myself.

The *Oceanographer* cruise looked encouraging until, suddenly, the route was changed and my hopes were shattered. She would not visit Thera because she had to make a diplomatic stop in Russia, at Odessa on the Black Sea. I did not accept this setback easily, and carried my appeal to Vice-President Humphrey, who had been put in charge of an oceanographic committee with a personal interest in the ship. But, as I might have expected, the appeal was in vain. Hopefully, there would be another opportunity, but I felt that they were missing a better one.

At this point, mid-April, in spite of discouragements, we did have a going concern, albeit small. Dr. Elizabeth Ralph of the University of Pennsylvania had agreed to come with her formidable cesium magnetometer which had detected walls, tombs and even large pots from 10 to 30 feet below the surface of the ground in Sicily. She was planning to magnetometer in Sicily all summer, so she could easily come to Athens, where she, Marinatos, and I agreed to meet on May 21. I would bring a land seismograph for search at our digging site of Akroteri and other probing on the island. My 1966 permission to do underwater work was still valid, and Doc Edgerton had agreed to appear in early June, depending upon Cousteau's schedule, to help with the Helice investigation and afterward come to Thera. Emily Vermeule would arrive about June 1, as would Robert Kane, a geologist and engineer whom I had invited. William Wetmore was also to come with me, as technical assistant and scribe, and my wife, Mary, would join us for three weeks after the excavation got going. Unfortunately, Hartley Hoskins' teaching schedule in Ghana kept him from joining us this year.

Dr. Galanopoulos, whom I had kept fully informed of developments and who was the central figure in all my work, was unable to come to Thera for the excavation. I would press him further when I arrived in Athens; for, if we did succeed in our groping validation, he ought surely to share in it. He gave me no reason for bowing out, but it is my guess that, in his wisdom, he suspected there would be personal and political difficulties. I also believe that this modest gentleman did not wish to experience more of the glare of publicity.

In addition, I worried about the possible effect of Greek politics. National elections, due in May, could change the whole picture. But as it turned out, there would be no elections. On April 21, 1967, reading the newspaper, I saw all my work and plans going up in smoke. The Greek government had suddenly been taken over by a triumvirate of military officers and thousands of people were imprisoned.

Where did my friends in Greece stand? For two weeks I heard nothing from Marinatos or Galanopoulos. I sent cables to Marinatos to find out if our plans were still active. Finally, on May 8, a letter from Marinatos stated: "The political situation here is excellent and in any case much more stable than before. I think sincerely that the conditions for work are much better and possibly they will be still better in the near future."

It was clear which side of the political fence he was on and that our permission was still valid. I was relieved on that score but apprehensive about visiting the country with violent revolution apparently about to break out at any minute. The Colonels, however, remained in firm control, and whatever armchair judgments I was tempted to make about Greek politics were sublimated by my desire to return to Atlantis.

CHAPTER 9

ON Monday, May 22, 1967, we confidently approached Athens on another leg of our search to confirm an Aegean Atlantis. But first we had to maneuver ourselves and our mysterious black boxes through customs. Bill Wetmore, our scribe, had met me in London for the flight to Athens; and what with the military coup, we were even less sure than usual what to expect. We had conflicting advice on whether to declare our instruments as professional equipment or not to declare them at all. We decided to say nothing. With us were the seismograph and a sensor for Beth Ralph's magnetometer, plus movie and still cameras and walkie-talkie radios.

We survived customs, but not without passing a large cage obviously designed for containment of malefactors. Athens was very different from what I had remembered on my two previous visits. There were too many soldiers, no tourists, and not nearly enough spontaneous noise and clatter. The military regime had cut the number of newspapers from twelve to three, causing a proportionate reduction in the number of newsboys hawking their wares. Then we found that not only the streets were quiet, but also the cafés, which I remembered as having been alive with continuous political discussion. Now, more than five persons were forbidden to gather publicly and no one dared discuss politics at all. Athens seemed a good place to get out of and we did, the day after our arrival.

Meanwhile we met with Beth Ralph, keeper of magnetometers, who had just arrived from Italy. By phone I talked with Dr. Marinatos for the first time. We also managed a meeting with Dr. Galanopoulos, who, sadly, for his own good reasons, would not be joining us on Thera. However, he had fitted some more pieces into the puzzle of a Minoan Atlantis, among them evidence that some of the destruction on Crete was not the result of inundation or other volcanic damage, but of earthquakes. Severe tremors may have struck Crete in advance of the Thera collapse, setting the stage for even more severe devastation. I made up my mind to look for evidence of this on Thera. He had also heard of pumice on the shores of Palestine at 15 feet above sea level, which could be traced to Thera. The physical evidence of the course of the tsunami was increasing.

There is no doubt that the waves hit the African coast. Two men from the Massachusetts Institute of Technology, Frank Press and David Harkrider, had recently come to the startling conclusion that sea waves created by the Krakatoa collapse were amplified by air blast waves which happened to be in synchronism with them. This means that sea waves are actually able to break on land, and then, propagated overland through the air, can be reestablished and again agitate the sea beyond. This phenomenon, to be sure, requires special but by no means improbable conditions, that is, an air blast of the same velocity as the sea waves. This resonance is a function of the ocean depth and the magnitude of the blast.

I applied their results to the Thera problem and found that Crete need not have been an obstacle to propagation of the waves that we know came from Thera. The waves, but not the water of course, could have literally jumped over Crete, transmitted by air vibrations which would then build up the sea on the other side. This being the case, Africa certainly would have been struck by substantial tsunamis, which indeed strengthens the case for the drowning of the Egyptian army from this cause.

Dr. Galanopoulos nodded and smiled at this commentary. He then reiterated his concern over the lack of enthusiasm archaeologists had shown for the Minoan Atlantis theory, but suggested that their interest might be warming up.

I brought up the heated differences that had arisen between Loring and Marinatos. What could we do to reconcile these two strong personalities?

"Everybody fights," said Dr. Galanopoulos and shrugged. "But I do hope that these differences do not disrupt your project."

Beth Ralph, Bill Wetmore, and I had dinner at the home of Dr. Marinatos. It was a smallish villa at the outskirts of Athens which, like Marinatos himself, was a little inaccessible at first. It took the cab driver an hour to find it and us a while longer before we managed to figure out the electric gate. Once inside, and having met his charming wife and daughter, Nani, the formality that seemed at first so impenetrable proved merely the cover under which was preserved a passion for good food and wine, charm and humor, and great knowledge. Under it was also preserved the cunning necessary for political survival in modern Greece.

The afternoon after our arrival in Greece, Dr. Marinatos, with the help of Jean Koutsogiannopoulos, whose name in English translation is "The Son of John Who Was Lame," had the five of us, plus Beth Ralph's overloaded Fiat, on board the motorship *Karaiskakis* of the Nomikos Lines, whose owner resides on Thera. I advised against taking the car because of the difficulty of landing it on the island, but Beth Ralph was more adventurous and preferred keeping the valuable, heavy and fragile instruments in her car to transferring them between rented vehicles and donkeys, as would turn out to be the case. I did not envy her the drive up that 1,000-foot, 45-degree cliff.

Jean Koutsogiannopoulos, a prominent Athenian lawyer who was born on Thera, was noted for promoting the well-being of the Cycladic islanders. A calm, understanding person with good humor and good sense, he had managed the Greek Red Cross. Almost as quickly as Marinatos' volatile nature could ruffle the waters, Koutsogiannopoulos smoothed them again. Unfortunately, he did not come with us to Thera this trip. He was to wait for the second foray.

The captain of the *Karaiskakis,* whose father managed the pumice quarry at Ia on the north coast of Thera, was excited by the project because he knew of some large Minoan storage jars that had been discovered in his father's mine.

At sea again, the forces of nature took over. The ship rolled and pitched as the *meltemi,* a northerly summer wind, drove spray aboard on the port side. The high black islands of the Cyclades loomed up ahead one after another and, as we passed Aegina, I recalled the story of Aeacus, king of the island, grandfather of Achilles and brother of the famed King Minos of Crete. He, too, lived at just about the right time to have witnessed the eruptions of Thera, a few generations before Theseus and before the Trojan War.

In the story, as told by Cephalus, the sky seemed to settle down upon the earth, and thick clouds shut in the heated air. For four months together a deadly south wind prevailed. The disorder affected the wells and springs; thousands of snakes crept over the land and shed their poison in the fountains. The force of the disease was first spent on the lower animals—dogs, cattle, sheep, and birds. The luckless plowman wondered to see oxen fall in the midst of their work and lie helpless in the unfinished furrow. The wool fell from the bleating sheep. The story goes on to describe the sufferings of a people overcome by plagues paralleling the Biblical plagues of Egypt in every detail. Volcanic vapors followed by pestilence and death are clearly the source of the myth.

We reached the Cycladic island of Melos around 7 P.M. but lost an hour while the captain engaged in some landing practice. A strong onshore wind made it difficult to approach the quay, built in ages past for much smaller vessels. Eventually, having dropped a bow anchor, the crew managed to get a line ashore and winch the stern in close enough to debark several garrulous passengers and unload cargo, all during a loud exchange of views between ship and shore regarding the captain's seamanship and the island's harbor facilities. This was more like the Greece that we remembered.

A large, peach-colored moon was rising. Brightly painted varcas gathered around us. Pale yellow lights illuminated the streets and white houses of the town. People milled and shouted and found each other and, though the crowd was small, there was more vitality here than I had seen in Athens. The ship cast off and faded into the dark, heading for Thera.

Melos, the other volcanic island of the Minoans, has no record of geological activity except for sulphurous fumaroles. In 1500 B.C. it must have looked much as it does today except that the land was more productive and there was a thriving settlement at Phylakopi, perhaps ruled, I could hope, by Plato's own King Eumelos, whose name we had seen inscribed on the rocks of Thera's Messa Vouno.

In the evening, Dr. Marinatos and I were the sole occupants of the ship's lounge. I was reading the report of Fouqué's excavations, for on the following day we would again search the ravines of Akroteri for those elusive buildings. Marinatos was also reading. He looked up and said, "Whenever I travel to Thera I read the *Timaeus* and *Critias* of Plato." He glanced at the worn volume in his hand. I, too, had an old copy in Greek which I treasured, dated 1829, left to me by my father. We began to talk of Atlantis and the Minoans. Marinatos soon changed the subject, but for that brief moment I felt we had achieved a sincere exchange of thoughts.

The next morning, when we arrived at Thera, the captain said conditions were too rough to land Beth Ralph's Fiat and, in any case, the lighter that was supposed to meet us for the transfer was nowhere to be found. Moreover, the cost of landing it, if it could be done, had increased severalfold. We would have to unload the little red rolling steamer trunk and leave the car on board to be returned to Piraeus.

The small boats that had come out to meet us and now hovered alongside were filling with people and baggage and rose and fell urgently with the swell, engines knocking loudly.

On the quay, donkey drivers waited to take us up to the town of Phira and to our hotel, named, impatiently, Atlantis. Loring had written me that he wished his home to be our headquarters this summer as it had before, but Loring was not yet on the island and I had refrained from broaching the touchy subject to Marinatos.

After checking in at the hotel, we left for Akroteri at 8:30, without changing out of our business suits into something more suitable for tramping the fields and ravines. I came to realize that Marinatos was accustomed to an atmosphere of pomp and formality, which doubtless helped him to command the respect of the local people. However, we were all eager to get to the site and immediately piled into our waiting Peugeot station wagon. It had no starter, so was always parked on a hill, a ritual easily followed on Thera.

At the village of Akroteri, we met certain elders who helped us in locating a suitable digging site. Our coming was anticipated, and the unobtrusive Mr. Koutsogiannopoulos the younger, nephew of the Athenian lawyer, acting as agent on the island to take care of business affairs for Marinatos, joined us. He had an auxiliary function, we were to discover, as Marinatos' chief spy and as confidant of the chief of police. Young Mr. K. did his work with a will and we soon learned never to start out anywhere without informing him or the chief of police if we wished to stay out of trouble.

As we left the hotel there occurred an incident that showed me another side of Marinatos. Mr. Giannacas, seventy-two years of age, had been custodian of the museum on Thera for thirty-five years. He was now retired and was government tourist adviser on the island, with a little office in town. He worshipped Dr. Marinatos and told him he would give up his tourism job in order to help. Marinatos agreed to this and offered him a job with the excavation. As we were about to drive off to Akroteri, Giannacas came running up with a large framed map of the island, a copy of an Admiralty chart, which he had gone to some trouble to obtain. Marinatos abruptly told him that we didn't need it, which was true enough, and curtly brushed Giannacas aside and drove off without him. Perhaps Marinatos had forgotten that he had engaged Giannacas.

The pumice was thinner at Akroteri than elsewhere on the island and deep erosion ravines had cut through to the Minoan level in places. Such geological conditions were bound to result in a higher incidence of surface finds than elsewhere and the Akroteri region was bound, sooner or later, to attract archaeological interest. As it happened, we were returning to Akroteri exactly 100 years after M. Fouqué's historic discoveries on Therasia and at Akroteri. Shortly after pumice mining operations were begun to provide cement for the construction of the Suez Canal, reports of prehistoric remains began turning up. Today, as then, in the Thera quarries walls, pottery, fresco remains, and other relics are being battered to pieces without protest, for cement from Thera is very economical. Removal of a small pot from the island without government permission can cause an international incident, and yet every year of the past century acres of antiquity-rich ash have been removed from Thera without a murmur of protest.

In 1870 there was enough evidence available to suggest a prehistoric civilization of high density and cultural accomplishment, plus the possibility that this may have been Plato's Atlantis, as Nicaise suggested in 1885. But the writings of Nicaise and Fouqué's monumental work fell into neglect. For the past 100 years, literally tons of antiquities have been shoveled into freighters while scholars smiled wryly when Thera was mentioned as a candidate for Atlantis.

But mining operations, besides destroying artifacts, led to Fouqué's discoveries. A geologist who had traveled to Thera to keep an eye on the volcano during an eruptive period begun in 1866, he became interested in ancient walls and pottery that had been found in the mines at Therasia. With the Minoan and Mycenaean civilizations yet to be discovered, it was difficult to date his finds; but they obviously predated the Greeks, and that in itself gave them importance. After excavating six rooms of what appeared to have been a large farmhouse and the remains of an old man who must have refused to heed the island's early warnings, Fouqué decided that the site, buried as it was under tons of ever-crumbling ash, was too dangerous and abandoned it for the less deeply shrouded site at Akroteri. There the ash was so eroded that Fouqué was able to spot walls projecting from the sides of the ravine as well as a number of pots, two gold rings, and copper and obsidian instruments, all pre-Greek.

Fouqué was denied a chance to excavate here by the peasant who owned the land, but at Fouqué's instigation two other Frenchmen, Gorceix and Mamet, were granted funds by the French and permission by the Greeks. They began excavating in the spring of 1870 and had immediate success. They found walls first, then a storage room filled with beautifully painted vases, many of which still contained carbonized food. Obsidian knives, scrapers, and saws were found, as were loom weights, mortars and pestles, kitchen utensils, murex seashells, and a number of bones of dogs, cats, horses, goats, and sheep. One shard with a painted linear script was found. Most significant of all from our point of view, concerned as we were with finding not just signs of human habitation but of wealth consistent with a major settlement, were the frescoes found just before they were forced to stop, once again because of possible collapse. Frescoes—large, lovely, intact on the walls, and of entirely aesthetic inspiration—certainly qualified as evidence of wealth and leisure, as did the elegantly turned and elaborately decorated pots found that same summer of 1870.

Gorceix and Mamet also found a second house at the same geological level, similarly filled with artifacts, and then a third near Balos, the port of Akroteri, on what is now the caldera side of the island. Here was found a pure copper saw, the only copper utensil found on Thera.

Fouqué certainly recognized that he had unearthed something far more significant than an isolated village, but he was not sure what. He noted that much of the pottery was similar to that found on Melos, Rhodes, and Cyprus. He also wrote of hearing on good authority that "there is in the Louvre an Egyptian painting depicting an Egyptian king receiving Greek envoys. The presents they bring [in the fresco] are similar in shape and decoration to the ones in Thera." This may have been the first modern reference to trade between the Minoans and Egyptians, a fact not acknowledged by historians until some years later.

In due course, it was confirmed that the linear script found at Akroteri was Minoan, that the architecture found there was Minoan, and that the pottery styles, fresco styles, sculptural styles, and living styles were also Minoan. The island of Melos had been occupied by the same people; in fact, there appeared to have been a great island empire in the Aegean during the second millennium which was destroyed when one of its member islands exploded in a terrible disaster. With so much new to consider, the possibility of a relationship between this island empire and Plato's Atlantis was still thought frivolous, even though it was apparently not considered frivolous to call a palace found at Knossos "the Cretan Labyringh of the Minotaur."

For many reasons, among them war, archaeological indifference, and lack of funding, Thera was virtually neglected for 100 years except for a brief dig in 1900 by Zahn. This neglect seems surprising in that Thera could prove to be another, much earlier Pompeii, a civilization packed in volcanic ash, preserved just as it had been when its people took flight. Intact, untouched by subsequent marauders, protected from wind, rain, and sun, it was, from the archaeologist's point of view, if not a Minoan's, the happiest of accidents. Excavation of such an ash-preserved site could add greatly to our knowledge of life in Minoan-Mycenaean times.

Today's village of Akroteri is one of the island's several hill-top towns, a monolith of neat white buildings wrapped around a hill, with churches and chapels everywhere, their blue domes nestled in among the houses. When a man as esteemed as Dr. Marinatos comes to town one either knows of it in advance or finds out very soon. A large gathering of Akroteriots materialized upon our arrival. This was important to us.

Research and theory may lead the archaeologist to a particular area, perhaps a particular square mile. Logic and common sense about terrain, exposure to the elements, protection against sea raiders, proximity to fertile and tillable land, may help narrow his search. But then what? Where in the square mile does one begin—by the fig tree, the donkey cave, near a ravine where the ash has been washed thin by erosion, or along that gentle lee slope? A farmer may have the answer, or at least part of it. He remembers when, following the spring rains, remains of large pots and storage jars were seen in a ravine south of his tomato field. And the fisherman remembers how, as a boy, his grandfather once took him to a field south of the village and showed him the site of the German excavation, where they had found an ancient house.

The first solid clue of this nature was given us by George Saliveros, an old man who remembered how the floor of a donkey cave had collapsed some years before, revealing what looked like a room beneath, and, nearby, a section of a field had sunk suddenly as though beneath the ash there were a cavity, another room perhaps.

The first job was to have a look at these and other such phenomena, so we set off along the sandy track that cut down through the fields. It was quite a procession. An old woman in a black dress rocked along with Dr. Marinatos, laughing, slapping her skirts, flashing two yellow teeth. The old men were pleased to demonstrate the uses of memory, and the young wanted work. The children ran ahead in fits of laughter, and retreated in sudden shyness. We foreigners, with our black boxes, were scattered through the long line, scuffing through the ash and stone, past cactus and nettle and scrub evergreen that lined the path.

There was haze and ash and a wind that erased our tracks an

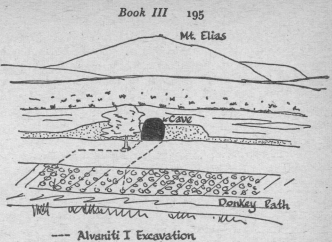

--- Alvaniti I Excavation
White Ash Stratum

FIGURE 28. View looking east from Akroteri ravine, showing cave and ash stratum shifted up by Minoan building beneath.

hour after we had passed. Here and there a peasant harvested his barley, gathering it roots and all from the loose volcanic soil, and everywhere were broken bits of pottery, the rubble of forty centuries or more.

Our procession stopped. Dr. Marinatos, who for all his sixty-seven years and considerable embonpoint is still as tough and quick as a bantam rooster, climbed on top of a 5-foot retaining wall and then descended easily, stalking the base.

"This peasant, he is a very intelligent man. He has observed that some of the stones in the wall are not natural."

"Yes," I replied. "They could be part of an ancient wall?"

"Very promising," Marinatos said cryptically.

"But I am afraid that with so many lava stones in the ash, the magnetometer will not record the walls," observed Beth Ralph. And, sure enough, it didn't, or not very well, a typical archaeological frustration.

A little farther on, by a solitary fig tree, was the cave in the ravine wall, partially filled in by wash and debris, but with a layer of ash and pumice over the entrance which suggested a building beneath. It was as though a large box had been buried in snow. The stratum of pumice suddenly rose a few feet, ran horizontally, then dropped down to its original level and continued on. The field above seemed a promising place to try out the magnetometer, so Beth Ralph, Bill Wetmore, and I got to work here while Marinatos moved on down the path, checking out other likely sites.

Fouqué had written of a ravine to the east of the village and 400 meters from the southern shore. Not very specific; but we tramped over the area. As in 1966, we found no trace of the previous excavations. They were completely obliterated by erosion and rebuilt retaining walls. The general region, however, was ideal for a Minoan settlement, comparable to the site of Gournia in eastern Crete, a wide sloping plain to the sea bounded on east and west by mountains. It was obvious to all that we should start digging near the bottom of the first ravine where the farmer had pointed out the cave and where tradition had it that pottery had been seen. The multitude of indications here in the field, as well as in the existing literature, pointed to this ravine or the next one excavated by Zahn. Either was promising. Fouqué's house containing the beautiful fresco was probably in the first or westerly ravine, we thought, and chose it for our exploratory excavations. In retrospect, I feel that we could have dug anywhere near the bottom of the ravines with success. Digging came so easily and antiquities appeared so rapidly that we could not record and preserve them adequately with our understaffed group and we had to stop to get our bearings.

I was anxious to use my seismograph, which both Beth Ralph and I felt would be more productive than the magnetometer, but Beth could stay only for a few days and Marinatos had fixed in his mind that the all-seeing magnetometer would find a palace. Even before leaving the United States, Beth and I had been apprehensive about the use of this instrument in this terrain of high natural magnetism, but it seemed worth a try and, perhaps more important from my point of view, the magnetometer held a fascination for Marinatos and probably helped to lure him to the site and keep him there.

It took three of us to magnetometer, so the seismograph would have to wait. We laid out grids the size of a tilled field and, marching back and forth between stakes flying red flags, took our magnetism readings, which later would produce a map of magnetic contours for the field and, we hoped, the locations of walls up to 20 feet beneath.

The magnetometer has the convenience of giving an instantaneous reading at each location so that if one takes many readings, one at each intersection of a grid, and writes them down in the proper location on a piece of paper, a map results. In one location, near Zahn's house, a promising magnetometer record did result, but time did not permit excavation in two widely separated areas, so Zahn was abandoned and there was no opportunity to vindicate the magnetometer. All day we paced in lanes 15 feet apart, through the vineyards and the tomato plants, the wheat fields and the barley, over walls and down gulleys, around somnolent peasants and snarling dogs.

On the way back to Phira by car after a day's magnetometering, Beth Ralph sought Dr. Marinatos' ear.

"We're in a very highly variable magnetic area, you know," she said, speaking with the too perfect diction we reserve for foreigners. "You can't pinpoint—*pinpoint*—the variants, because their force isn't enough to show."

Dr. Marinatos, looking out over the sea, nodded vaguely.

"As I was saying," insisted Beth above the rustle of the wind, "they don't *show*. But there is a chance—"

"Yes?" said Dr. Marinatos.

"A chance you might find some useful indications over the entrance to the cave."

"Ah hah!" said Dr. Marinatos deafly. "Excellent. Fine."

"How's that?" Beth inquired.

"Fine," said Dr. Marinatos, "wonderful to have a success already. Marvelous. It would be most interesting."

"What would be interesting?" said Beth.

"Having some indication," said Dr. Marinatos.

"I see," said Beth, her eyes rolling in her head.

That was the trouble. Too often we and Dr. Marinatos sailed on different tacks, not altogether divining what the other was driving at. It was basically, I think, a question of language. Marinatos spoke English well, but that was something of a snare and a delusion; for, in truth, a great deal of our mumblings and colloquialisms, meaningful though they might be for us, escaped him completely.

Our car horn put an exclamation point to the exchange. It yodeled delightfully, this time at a herd of goats, who were not impressed. A kind of hysteria was gathering about us, jammed in the little Peugeot, to which I was particularly sensitive, being 6 feet, 3 inches tall, feeling much too dirty, and with my knees up to my chin.

"And tomorrow if you can do your magnetometer work in the field across from the cave, it will be most interesting to see what is to be seen there," Marinatos suddenly resumed. Beth nodded helplessly. "I am most encouraged," Marinatos assured us, "by what the peasants account to us of finding antiquities all over. Not just here and there, but all over. I am most encouraged by these informations. It is very promising, I think. Oh yes, I am well satisfied."

Beth Ralph nodded and said she hoped the magnetometer would show something and let her doubts go at that for the time being. Later, as I feared, she was not very encouraging about the results, explaining to Marinatos that her earlier doubts had been borne out, that the area was so highly magnetic it was impossible to draw any conclusions.

Marinatos smiled, cocked his head, showed his palms, shrugged and folded his hands in his lap. He did not seem surprised, but it was not completely clear whether he had misunderstood or had simply expected as much.

I dozed fitfully. Travel fatigue had caught up with me at

last. Dreams of Loring arriving too soon were all that kept me from sounder sleep. Archaeology can be hell.

During dinner on May 24, Dr. Marinatos smilingly toasted the success of our dig, as the hotel proprietor arrived with a cablegram for me.

I opened and closed it and put it in my pocket, but not before I had a glimpse of the sender.

"Not bad news," Marinatos hoped.

"No, no," I assured him, "just a note from my wife. She is coming in a few weeks, you know."

"Ah, very good, and now I think if we are to begin early in the morning we would do well to have a good night's sleep."

We would if we could.

"When?" asked Bill as we were heading upstairs.

"Will phone from Athens Sunday," I whispered, "signed Loring." That meant that he could not arrive before Wednesday, a week away.

From my brief personal contact with Marinatos, I was now sure that he and Loring would not get along. I could see no recourse but to try to stall off a confrontation and prepare Marinatos for the shock. Loring fortunately had given me some time.

En route to Akroteri the next morning, we stopped to inspect

FIGURE 29. Archaic Greek tombstone with name Akryptos found at Megalokhorio, Thera. (30 inches high).

a large ancient stone reported to be in a wall in the village of Megalokhorio. It was a lava tombstone with a name on its face.

Dr. Marinatos circled it, moved in close, and kneeled, tracing the letters with his fingers.

"Akryptos," he said at last and we sighed. "It means 'the man who was not secret.' That may have been his battle name."

"Archaic characters," I commented hopefully.

Dr. Marinatos traced the letters again. "It is possibly late archaic," he decided, "around six hundred B.C. because the letters read from left to right." He turned as an old peasant came riding up on a donkey.

"The owner," Marinatos explained. "He says he found it ten years ago. I have made an appeal to his patriotism in the hope he will give to the museum this antiquity." He smiled. It was not a paltry gift, to say the least. It must have weighed over 300 pounds and was right in the middle of the man's wall. To dig it out without the rest of the stones toppling and to haul it by donkey cart some 10 miles to the museum was at least a day's work. On the other hand, these days, patriotism in Greece is a summons not lightly ignored.

Excavation was commenced on Thursday, May 25, at a site later designated Bronos I after the owner of the land. It was on the lowest terrace of the ravine (see Figure 35) and adjacent to a place that a farmer had pointed out to us. A second trench was started a couple of days later at the donkey cave, where my seismograph had indicated a rough stratum at about 15 feet under the surface. This later revealed our most spectacular finds.

Seismograph operation requires the instrument itself, including two geophones or electronic ears, one remote with a radio transmitter, a rock or steel plate, a sledgehammer, and two people. The refraction seismograph sends a sound wave into the earth which strikes a layer of bedrock, bends, and travels along the rock and finally returns to the surface some distance away, where it is picked up by a geophone and the sound travel time is measured. By moving the geophone away from the sledgehammer source along a line about 100 feet long, a number of travel times are recorded. From this information, the average depth of bedrock over the distance traversed can be calculated. Thus a great many seismo lines must be run back and forth and across to define local changes in substrata. Indeed, in unfamiliar terrain we found many lines must be run to establish consistency and confidence in the simplest results.

"Mr. Mavor, I observe the lighted numbers on your instrument. What do they tell you?" queried Dr. Marinatos. I answered that he had noticed the high-speed counter, which measures the time taken by the sound wave to travel from the sledgehammer to the geophone some distance away.

"And can you tell me how a computer works?" he continued. Pleased by his interest in technology, I told him that a digital computer is basically a group of very-fast-acting on-off electrical switches which can be wired to solve an arithmetical problem.

Dr. Marinatos meditated on this, then walked away.

Seismo runs made on the terrace in front of the cave at site Alvaniti I gave consistent readings of a substratum 12 to 15 feet down. Dr. Marinatos seemed impressed because it gave some hope that the ash thickness was not too great here.

Runs were made over the top of the cave as well, and the readings definitely showed the presence of the cave, as they did over another known cave. I concluded that in the future this ability would be valuable for locating in advance unfilled Minoan rooms. Elsewhere, we obtained consistent depth readings to the lava base in many locations, varying from 12 to 30 feet, which were confirmed in the places where trenches were dug.

Our use of the seismograph, while so promising, was limited, as it turned out, only because our archaeological success was so immediate and extensive. We soon fell to drawing plans of the architecture, photographing and recording the finds, and local geological survey. Having determined the local ash depth, further use of this instrument at the excavation site was put off.

"Still the best archaeological tool is the shovel," Dr. Marinatos advised. "It works well and does not speak."

After an exhausting session with the seismograph, swinging the 15-pound sledge, I returned to the first trench, where Marinatos stood looking intently into the 3-foot-deep hole.

"Hello," he said. "I do not need you anymore, not you or your friends."

I did not know how to interpret this remark.

"But do your tests anyway." He laughed, which I was pleased to see, and he waved his hand across the ditch. "Here we have found the walls of a house and here the burned brick of the upper stories."

It was seven minutes after three on Thursday, May 25, 1967. We had been on the island for thirty-three hours.

Optimistic as I was, I tended to be leery of such a great success so soon. I feared that it was a dream. Was it really a house? Was it a palace? Was it proof, along with Fouqué's and Zahn's houses, that a great prehistoric city lay beneath us? Could one even be sure at this stage that it was truly Minoan? If such a large settlement existed here, what wonders must have stood on the commanding highland site that once filled the great Thera caldera.

Potsherds were beginning to pile up around the hole. Dr. Marinatos reached down for some pieces that seemed thinner, more delicate, than the rest.

"Genuine Cretan pottery," he said, with a sagacity I was highly disinclined to dispute, "imported, not copied. This is to suggest that wealthy people were once living here." He smiled.

I watched the workmen. Some were using a hand tool like an adz except that the blade was spoon-shaped. It worked like an extension of the arm and hand, scraping, scooping, sifting, whisking the loose ash back to the shovelers behind. Though untrained in the arts of archaeological excavation, except for the foreman, Nicholas, they worked with surprising delicacy.

I wandered off, wishing to know what to make of the find. The stone and the bricks were there to see. So was the Cretan pottery, but could one really be sure it all signified a wealthy home? Merely finding evidence of pre-eruption habitation was not enough. I needed signs of wealth, of extensive and advanced habitation, further evidence that the Minoan civilization was even greater, even more like the Atlantean empire than had been imagined. I returned to the trench, Bronos I, again. Marinatos was ebullient with the imminent prospect of more exciting finds.

The Marinatos smile is not lavished but spent shrewdly and, when used, is as disarming and distracting as a magician's other hand. He is a short, stout man, but with gestures and stances that suggest slimness, agility, and grace. Before a smile he will often sit back, fold his hands carefully, and say, "Now, yes ... this is very amusing." Suddenly, as though to prove his point, *voilà*, the smile, from ear to ear, toothy, unflinching, frozen. "And now," he said, "let us get on with our labors."

At the site, Dr. Marinatos suggested that we seismograph the whole field in order to determine whether the Minoan layer was relatively level and therefore a logical town site.

"If it is so," he said, "we must consider expropriation of the entire field so we can be our own master and do as we please. Otherwise, pooh, it is impossible." I would have liked to seismograph the whole one-half square mile he envisioned, but we were able to do only a fraction. In addition, my auxiliary duties as photographer, draftsman, and recorder were becoming time-consuming and, indeed, more important.

Marinatos held up a stone object for my inspection.

"You know what it is," he stated rather than asked.

"No," I admitted cautiously.

"It is a lamp, of course. One may see, if one looks, that the signs of the fire are still visible. It is 1500 B.C. certainly. Probably they burned animal fat, for, except on Crete, the olive oil was too precious to burn. It was used solely for the purpose of anointing the body, as protection against the heat of the sun and for libation to the gods." He paused, then went on.

"Yes, it is as I expected, very likely a house. Perhaps not a very big one, but not humble either. Not a bit humble. We can say that for a certainty. The pottery, it is very well fired and well painted. No? It is also polychrome such as only the wealthy people would have in their homes. It is very promising.

"I am very pleased with your seismograph work," Dr. Marinatos confided. "It is extremely encouraging."

"Thank you," I said.

Lunch was under the fig tree at the mouth of the cave where we were planning to dig next. The tree, with its rich, thick feline smell, provided rare shade. The peasants were talking and laughing, fingers dipping into their lunch buckets, their wide, fat, flat, brown feet cocked and resting.

Marinatos explained to me what they were talking about. He paused, smiling, savoring what was to come. "You are of course aware that our language is much richer than yours. There are, as you say, many nuances." I took this as his little joke about an English lesson I had just conducted with a group of children who came to watch the dig.

"In Greek we have a saying," Dr. Marinatos continued. "To the rest of the Western world we say: 'You were swinging in the trees when already we were a civilization.' Very amusing, no? And now," he began, suddenly changing the subject, "I must have your expert advice. Suppose all is going well and we are at the point of excavating a great building or complex of buildings, there will be many problems."

I agreed, and suggested that, as I had written to him the previous winter, self-supporting caverns could be constructed where the ash is thick. This must be studied. And here in the ravines we would need bulldozers and conveyors to take the ash down to the sea.

"For us archaeologists it is to be ashamed to use bulldozers, but perhaps we can employ them to remove the surface until we reach the antiquity strata and then continue by hand. But the bulldozers are expensive, thirty-three dollars per day. It may be better to buy one and then at the end of the excavation we can sell it to get back more than half the money." He paused again to survey the site.

While I was sure Dr. Marinatos was visualizing the end product of the excavation of this vast site, I began to wonder if he really grasped how much was required to achieve it in terms of people, equipment, and money. But we were agreed on the objective and that was a good start.

Marinatos repeated to me that the government must buy the land before he could proceed much further. It seemed that we were digging now by *force majeure*. The peasants were pleased to have us here discovering antiquities in their fields, but the owner, who lived in Djibuti, Africa, did not know of our excavation. Marinatos said that in the event we had great success it would be important to purchase the land from the owner before he was aware of its value. And to make certain of our position we must arrange for government expropriation of the land, if necessary.

"Unfortunately," he said, "the high officials of a country are there not to solve difficulties, but to create them. I must go to Athens soon to arrange for expropriation. We will have work for several years. At least several."

"Perhaps even more," I said.

Beth Ralph would soon leave for Sicily. "Back in Italy," she explained, "they have planted melons and in a few weeks we won't be able to work in the fields."

"I am only sorry that you did not have better luck with the magnetometer," Marinatos said, and paused. "We have much help, we archaeologists, and from many sources. Did you know that in Crete the badger is for the archaeologist the best indication of a tomb? It is because he always burrows toward the soft areas that following him has led to finds of gold and other precious metals. Yes, the badger, we admire him very much."

"I shall remember that," I said.

I had hoped that the subject of Atlantis would arise and we could get into it in more depth than had been the case during our brief but pleasant chat on board ship. I finally asked Dr. Marinatos to give us his opinion of Atlantis.

"I have written regarding the legend of Atlantis," he said.

"It is quite simple. The Egyptians had intimate connections with the Cretans, but they were not, as the Cretans, seafaring people and had only a vague idea what happened outside Egypt. They considered themselves separate from the rest of humanity, referring to themselves not merely as men, but men of good origins, men born from lords. They knew there was an island in the middle of the great sea. They knew it was very prosperous, producing pottery and precious metals. Now suddenly they heard that an island had sunk beneath the sea. At the same time they lost contact with Crete for many years. Crete was of course still there, but the Egyptians, understandably, believed *it* was the island that had disappeared."

I was glad, to say the least, to hear Marinatos express the same views he had held when he wrote in 1950. While perhaps he did not accept all the details of Galanopoulos' theory, our goals in general seemed to be the same.

The car was late that day and, after trudging across the ash dunes, we had a long wait in the little square of Akroteri. The day's finds had been carried up by donkey and the peasants gathered around to finger the shards and listen to Marinatos' description of what had been done and how. They were pleased that we were finding antiquities near their town, and that they had a part in the excavations. The old woman with two eye-teeth brought us raki or tsipuro, a 40-proof sort of grappa, and Turkish coffee. The sun was behind the hill town now and there was a sudden chill.

We talked of other towns destroyed by nature, of Pompeii and Helice, which slid into the sea in 373 B.C. I told Marinatos about a Japanese village that slid down a mountain one night some years ago, but so gently that no one in the village realized it was happening. They simply awoke on a new site.

"Oh, fine," said Marinatos. "Tripping first class."

We were content. Our luck had been good so far and I looked forward eagerly to even greater successes. I enjoyed the company of Dr. Marinatos. I became less suspicious, as did he, or so it appeared, except that he did not sleep well.

CHAPTER 10

EDWARD LORING marched down the hall of the Hotel Atlantis, his heavy boots striking the tile with a doomful sound that reverberated through the building. His call, "Jim, Jim Mavor, rise and shine," at six o'clock on Sunday morning, May 28, was a shock, even though I was already awake.

What had happened? He was supposed to be in Athens, not Thera. With Dr. Marinatos scheduled to leave on Wednesday, I had hoped that they might miss each other, thereby providing two weeks of grace while Marinatos tinkered with the bureaucracy and tried to get the wheels of expropriation turning. That would be enough time to work something out; and, hopefully, after going through all the red tape, Marinatos would be eager to return, Loring or not. Now, in anger or spite, he might decide to drop the excavation just barely started, to return when the Americans were no longer around. But it couldn't be that bad. We were getting on well and, after all, my $2,000 for the excavation had not been spent and he could hardly back out of that.

"Edward," I cried, "how good to see you. But I didn't expect you so soon. How come?"

Loring seemed hardly the same person that he had been when we worked together in 1966. He was haggard, like a man who had been through an ordeal, as indeed he had, though I thought it was long past. More intense and loud-spoken than I remembered him, he came right to the point.

While I dressed, he embarked on a description of the importance of his Kristiana pottery finds and the difficulties they had caused him. They were indeed of fine fabric and design, dating from the Early Bronze Age, and indicated Anatolian ties. We had established this by correspondence. I had taken his report to an eminent archaeologist, who had been suitably impressed. Their importance was unquestioned. I did not see the relevance of harping on this just now. But his difficulties were real, and undoubtedly came about just because his finds were important. We were both aware that there is a long-standing attitude in Greek archaeological circles that frowns upon a foreigner making a discovery and receiving credit for it. Marinatos could be expected to uphold this tradition with singular enthusiasm.

Loring did not know that Marinatos was about to become director of antiquities, and therefore very powerful. I tried to convince him that to antagonize Marinatos at this time was folly. He halfway agreed and since there was so much to be accomplished, he proposed an immediate peace parley.

"Then," he said, great dark rings beneath his eyes, "we can archaeologize."

Loring insisted upon an immediate confrontation. He felt that he had been ill-used by Marinatos the previous fall and, after brooding on the matter all winter and spring, now was his chance to settle things.

I am sure that the incident would have been amusing to an outsider, but we all had too much at stake to be anything but apprehensive. As I told Loring later, I thought that both he and Marinatos were brilliant and dedicated but stood much too much on their mettle, too touchy altogether. I told him I did not advise the meeting he sought, that it would be better for him to remain in the background for a time. However, I could hardly expect him, or anyone else in his position, to stand by idly while the rest of us went ahead and developed an exciting excavation just barely started, one filled with significance and which he had an important part in bringing about through his work in 1966.

I agreed to mediate, and begged Loring to give me twenty

minutes with Marinatos at breakfast to ease the inevitable clash as best I could. For fifteen anxious minutes I briefed Marinatos on Loring's unexpected arrival. A stern silence gathered on his face, which became remarkably red as his Mediterranean temper grew. I knew he believed that the whole incident had been planned by Loring and me for his discomfiture. But Marinatos maintained a semblance of outward composure.

As it was, Loring arrived too soon.

"Ah, good morning," he said. "Welcome to my island."

I winced. Marinatos must have found it news that Thera was now under the sovereignty of Edward Loring of Chicago.

"So you are here," said Marinatos, his usually eloquent command of English momentarily deserting him.

Loring made it clear that he wanted peace, that he wished to work together for the benefit of archaeology with Dr. Marinatos, whom he admired and respected. He was very brisk and brusque and got on with it, in the American manner.

"We are going now," said Marinatos thinly. "Good-bye."

This day we had planned no excavation but a visit to Ia, the village so badly hit by the 1956 earthquake, and the site of reputed Minoan finds. Beth Ralph had left, four days of magnetometering being all she could spare. With Loring's status hovering in limbo, Bill Wetmore, Marinatos, and I formed an uneasy group.

That section of the village which the earthquake had destroyed was still a clutter of collapsed houses strewn down the mountainside, here and there one that had survived perched precariously atop the rubble.

"Look," Dr. Marinatos said, pointing to one of them. "What devil obliges them to inhabit that, right on the border of the abyss?"

It is a question that pertains to the whole island and it is never far out of focus. One wonders constantly what it does to those who live out their lives on the island. There is so much lava stone mixed with the ash, for example, that a man must always watch the ground when he walks, picking his way, his eyes always on the path. Then, too, a sense of isolation, of entrapment, is part of this island's soul.

Marinatos planned to drop by the museum that afternoon to cull, wash, and photograph our finds. Bill and I were to meet him there, but first it seemed a good idea to pay Loring a call. We still weren't sure how to read the auguries. Obviously Marinatos was not fond of his would-be student, but at this point he had yet to spell out the extent of his dislike for him. I had no idea how far either one was willing to be pushed.

In addition, while I did not intend to jeopardize the expedition, I was sympathetic to Loring's position. From what I knew of the row, Edward had had a pretty rough time. He had been very helpful to us the summer before and to Marinatos and Edgerton the following November. He seemed a decent fellow, if a bit melodramatic, and apparently he had landed in a pickle through good intentions. I wanted to do whatever I could to help set things right.

Loring was delighted to discover that we were en route to the museum. It was a wonderful opportunity to show Marinatos his Kristiana finds, which were locked in the basement, whether Marinatos wanted to see them or not. We descended to this basement where all the best things are kept, away from the prying eyes of the public, and located his controversial finds.

"Talk about being irresponsible," Loring muttered, plucking an alien shard from his boxful and throwing it away. "My God, it's awful." Then tenderly he lifted a round-ribbed trophy for our inspection. "You can see why I was excited," he breathed. "There aren't any pots like this in the world, not unless we can find some more here."

Marinatos was coming down the stairs with the museum guardian and Loring, maintaining his composure, kept talking while they came slowly our way. Loring addressed Marinatos in Greek, asking if he'd be good enough to look at his finds. Marinatos looked. He looked some more. He studied each piece, each pot, feeling them, turning them carefully, holding them close, then far, and at last he replaced them.

Silence.

Loring waited, his dark glasses cocked on his head.

After an exchange of conversation with the guardian, Dr. Marinatos moved on to other interests.

"What did he say?" I whispered. "To the guardian, I mean."

Loring's voice was flat with anger and disappointment. "He only asked how one of the pieces got there. He had the nerve to say he thought it was in Athens."

At dinner that evening Marinatos released his pent-up annoyance at last. "I must ask that Loring be persuaded to understand my position," he began. "I am very hopeful that the legal difficulties are cleared up and then, perhaps, he can work with us." He paused. I did not realize that the court case was still pending. I had optimistically hoped that during the six months since charges had been brought, and with a change of government, the matter might have been forgotten.

After the arrival of the usual fried fish, zucchini, and sliced tomatoes, Marinatos went on. "But, until then, no, it is quite impossible. What will people think to see that Loring accompanies us? They will think I am giving my support to a man charged with removing antiquities." He sighed heavily, broke a bit of bread, and washed it down with wine. "You Americans do not understand these things," he added. "In your country things are quite different. I have spent some time in Princeton and I know it is so."

Marinatos told me that he felt sure that Loring was innocent of the charges and would be acquitted, but this did not seem to affect his attitude. Apparently a charge was equivalent to conviction. In any case, I promised to have a talk with Loring after dinner.

"The whole village is talking," Marinatos continued. "Every year he comes with a different young girl. This the people do not understand. Not a bit."

We had heard that there was a girl named Adelphina with Loring, but she had been napping that afternoon so we had yet to meet her.

Edward and I entered into heated debate as soon as I arrived, which only ended with his marching off to the Hotel Atlantis and banging on Marinatos' bedroom door. Marinatos asked him to come back in the morning, and I watched him stalk off in silent frustration.

Dr. Marinatos was pale that next morning, spent with the rage that had robbed him of another night's sleep. He gave me a bitter look of reproach and commented that I had spent a long time at Loring's house the evening before. I thought to myself: How did you find that out? And why shouldn't I spend the evening with Loring? There is much to discuss. Even you can see that.

"Loring should go to Syros, where is the court," he said, "and ask that this matter be expedited. Can he not understand that I as a public official cannot work with him under these conditions? What is the matter with him?

"Perhaps you are not aware," Marinatos continued, "that this man, this Loring, came to my room in the middle of the night. I insisted that he must return in the morning, but now I do not wish to see him. Not at all." He paused to consider, shook his head and went on. "You Americans cannot, because you have complete freedom in your country, you cannot understand, cannot see the subtleties of public opinion. You must stop him from coming here this morning or I will say harsh things!"

"Please don't," I said, and all but wrung my hands.

I went to Loring and passed on what Marinatos had told me even though I hated the intermediary role. It was certainly no fun shuttling back and forth between two prima donnas. I urged him to go to Syros to find out what the charges were, and stand trial if need be. Marinatos had insisted that he would be acquitted, and I had the feeling that he was telling the truth. Loring agreed to go, in the expectation that upon his return he would be welcomed back. When I later relayed the news to Marinatos, he confessed that he had lost several days' sleep over this matter but now could regain peace of mind.

I began to see that, while I could accept Loring for what he

had to offer and overlook all complications, Dr. Marinatos
could not. He also could not or would not understand my con-
ciliatory attitude. He simply assumed that I was lying and that
Loring and I were in nefarious collusion. I was used to working
with all kinds of people and accepting them for what they
had to offer while getting the job done. Now I was rapidly de-
veloping into an ugly American. Meanwhile the precious hours
fled.

An archaeological undertaking usually requires many years
for excavation and preservation, but the first exploratory dig,
often the most crucial and most dramatic, is technically the
least complicated. It requires only the tools to dig, plus, of
course, the knowledge to use them skillfully and assess what is
found. From the column base, the brick, the stones, and the pottery found in trench Bronos I, we were satisfied that we had
found either a small palace or a villa. There was enough to
warrant a major excavation and we had not yet even dug down
to the ground floor of what was clearly at least a two-story
building.

Our second trench, Alvaniti I, begun at the cave mouth a
few days after the first, was not initially as generous of yield.
The stratification of ash and pumice was an infallible guide
to the depth required to dig. Above the Minoan earth level
lay 6 to 9 feet of coarse pumice stone. The top of this layer was
sharply defined and above it lay the fine white ash of the
long-ago eruption. A trench 30 feet long and nearly 10 feet
deep had yielded nothing, not even a shard, but we knew,
since we had passed the ash-pumice line, that walls should show
up soon. Indeed, the seismograph had predicted bottom at 15
feet.

Digging progressed rapidly through the loose and sterile ash.
Everyone had learned quickly to distinguish antiquities from
the natural terrain here. Our workmen toiled eagerly, talking,
observing. In the distance, a motorcycle was heard climbing a

steep winding road, and crows cried their gravelly cries. It was a saint's day and church bells rang.

There were always sightseers. The children and the old people whose memories served us so well browsed, also waiting for interesting disclosures. The old man who had called our attention to the cave watched and waited, fingering the stitches that held patches onto the patches of his trousers. Loring was not allowed to join us. He remained at home with Adelphina, awaiting the boat for Syros and his trial on charges he did not yet know.

The adz broke its rhythm and began to scratch and clatter. We leaned over to see what it was. A slab of limestone, cut by man, something at last. It was a tapered wall block typical of Cretan palaces, and near it the cylindrical stone base for a wooden column of the type famous in the reconstruction of the Palace of Minos at Knossos.

The following morning potsherds began appearing in abundance and walls materialized, finally revealing a large Minoan window frame, identical to those we were later to see at the Cretan palace of Mallia. It was hand-cut and grooved to accommodate vertical timbers and two swinging sashes as shown by the marks on the sill. By lunchtime our trench had revealed an upper-story room. Two exploratory trenches indicated a two-story building in each. We were elated.

We began to talk seriously of the requirements of a major excavation. Four-wheel trucks might be all right, the workmen believed, but a six-wheeler would be a lot more reliable in the loose ash. But roads would be a necessity in any case. They told us that, if great works lie beneath the ground, no one would

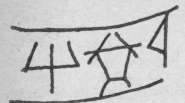

FIGURE 30. Minoan Linear A script on potsherd found by Fouqué on Thera in 1867. (Scale 3x.)

object to roads being made through his fields. We had to get a power shovel and perhaps a bulldozer, I told myself, and conveyors to take away the ash to the sea.

Marinatos scanned the site. "I see with the eyes of my soul a whole town here. I see a harbor one day with tourists approaching from the sea, perhaps a marina and landing made from the materials removed from the excavations."

In the afternoon, loom weights of clay 4 inches in diameter began to appear. Then we reached the doorsill, with scrape marks from the double swinging doors opening and closing still visible, and the impression where a large jar had once stood, packed in pumice. It had broken and collapsed, leaving a void in the ash. Intact and broken pottery was everywhere.

I still had the photograph of the site known as Zahn's house, and Bill and I tried to locate it by finding the place from which the photograph was taken. It showed the village of Akroteri in the background with certain hills and walls between, by which we could get our bearings, but even with that it proved difficult. It was strange to stand on a hill, looking at a photograph full of life, a scene much like our own with peasants and archaeologists and the scars of digging, a site that ought to have been there but was not. Only tomatoes, a whole field of them, met our gaze. One preferred to think we had made a mistake, that the real site was just over the next hill. But as we compared, it became obvious that we had found it. Akroteri was just where it ought to be and to the left was the same knoll, filled and graded now to make it arable, and on the right the hills and fields were all in proper perspective. We could even pick out an overgrown mound here and there where the previous excavators had dumped their ash. Only the people were gone.

At the same time, a peasant drew our attention to a tapered cylinder of red lava about 3 feet long and a foot in average diameter. It had been buried in his tomato field, he said, near Zahn's site. Marinatos joined us and examined the lava column.

"It is definitely prehistoric, possibly a lamp base."

With Atlantis more firmly fixed in my mind, I saw it not as

a lamp base, but as an Atlantean or Minoan sacred pillar. About 2200 B.C. on Minoan Crete, where mountain caves became places of worship, the stalagmites and stalactites may have been the forerunners of the sacred pillars found later in the Cretan palaces. The pillars of cut stone, usually incised with a double ax, are found intact in the palaces and represented on wall frescoes, pottery, and seals. Sometimes the pillars, as painted on the famous sarcophagus from Hagia Triada, look more like trees and may have been part of a tree cult. But, whether stone or tree cult, animals, including bulls, were sacrificed at the pillar and the blood poured at the foot of the pillar as an offering. This cult was associated with worship of the Mother Goddess on Crete and on the island of Malta as well.

Whether sanctity was inherent in the pillar is disputed by scholars, but, taking the Minoans of Crete and Thera and the Atlanteans as one and the same people, our scholarly question is answered by Plato. He tells us in *Critias* exactly how the pillar was used. "And the bull which they caught they led up to the pillar and cut its throat over the top of it so that the blood fell upon the sacred inscription . . . the rest of the victim they put in the fire, after having purified the column all around." Clearly the pillar was not inherently sacred, but required a blood sacrifice for sanctification. I did not doubt that our pillar of red lava corresponded to that of Atlantean legend and Minoan historical fact.

We pointed out our rediscovery of the site of Zahn's house to Marinatos.

"There is no doubt. It is Zahn's house," he said. I suggested that we should dig here and extend Zahn's excavation, but Dr. Marinatos preferred not to do this.

Dr. Marinatos would depart on the Wednesday boat, May 31, leaving Bill and me to fend for ourselves under the watchful eyes of the police chief and Mr. Koutsogiannopoulos the younger. Mr. Koutsogiannopoulos and the chief, we later learned, sent daily telephone reports of our activities to Marinatos in Athens at unimaginable expense. No matter, we would now have time to use the seismograph on the plain of Perissa, where I wanted to determine the ash thickness, which I believed to be small and the covering of Minoan buildings.

We touched on many topics at lunch on Tuesday, trying to overlook none of the things that could slow us up later on. In one week our dream of finding a major Minoan site on Thera had materialized, and with it my dream of proving the identification of Thera with Atlantis. Of course it would require years of effort by many people and large amounts of money to gather and assimilate all the evidence of our discoveries.

I reported to Marinatos that Loring was definitely leaving for Syros on the following Sunday.

"Yes, I think it is best,'" Marinatos said. "He may go alone but I would advise that he go with a solicitor without waiting to be summoned. But, in any case, to go is good because it is a gentleman's bearing. The judge always takes into consideration a man's bearing."

He advised us to visit the east and the north coasts of Thera while he was away. "It is terra incognita," he said. "As you have noticed, I have visited where the French and Germans visited because the pumice is thin, but I am exactly sure the same is true on the east and north."

"Perhaps near Kolumbo," I said, and he agreed. Kolumbo was a promontory on the northeast, offshore of which a new volcano had emerged in A.D. 1650. But, most important, Marinatos had given us permission to continue searching and to use the seismograph while he was away.

After bidding farewell to Marinatos, Bill and I arranged to visit the active volcano of Nea Kaimeni. We went down the mountain soon after lunch, for the brief varca ride across the caldera.

It looks like a huge coal pile, a spew of giant black chunks blown from the earth's interior, with here and there a steaming fumarole of pale green. Like an iceberg, most of the volcano is under the sea, and the part above is but a shapeless heap of cinders. The mass was formed at different times from different vents. But however it may appear, it is a single great cone and an angry one.

The two islands in the center of the caldera are called the Kaimeni, or Burned Ones. Palea (Ancient) Kaimeni was formed in 198 B.C. and, with five subsequent eruptions, has grown to an altitude of 300 feet. In 1573 the Mikra (Little) Kaimeni broke water more than a mile to the east and more than a thousand animals were killed, most of them by poisonous gases. Nea (New) Kaimeni, by far the larger and more ominous-looking of the two that can be seen today, and the one we explored, was formed between the old and the little volcanoes over a four-year period from 1707 to 1711. From 1866 to 1870 another series of eruptions, perhaps intended by the gods as inspirational music for Fouqué and his party, produced two new cones, which eventually grew and merged with Nea Kaimeni.

In 1925 a voluminous outpouring of lava almost completely filled the channel between the new and little Burned Ones, a job that was finally finished in 1928, when the two islands became one. Since that time, the volcano has been active on two occasions, in 1939 and in 1950, without a basic change in shape. But one need only glance at a chart of the Thera caldera to see that someday the new and the old will be one, and that a day will come when the caldera will be nearly filled again and Thera will be Calliste, the beautiful, as it was in Minoan times. When this has come to be, the complex pattern of inland waterways described by Plato will live again.

At the same time, we can imagine what must have happened in the gigantic volcanic chambers beneath the island to trigger the final collapse. Ash and lapilli periodically erupted from the magma chambers below, leaving less support for the island at the very moment that it was growing heavier and heavier from ash layered up to 500 feet deep near the center. One can easily visualize the island with its gas- or water-filled chambers below as the roof of a cave. Then came earthquakes which fractured the roof, and it fell thousands of feet to the bottom of the yawning abyss, shearing off the black cliffs seen today as the remnant of this event.

On Thursday, Bill, Loring, and I went to Exomiti with the seismograph. I felt, at this point, that it was rather silly of me to let Marinatos intimidate me to the point where I could not associate with Loring, especially as Loring knew the island so well and was so keen. I did, however, feel it best if we did not take Loring to the excavation at Akroteri. He would have seen nothing, in any case, because we had filled in the trenches before Marinatos' departure as a precaution against vandalism. To leave Achilles brooding in his tent until Agamemnon returned seemed hardly right to me.

At Cape Exomiti, at 200 feet inshore of the beach, a hard base was found a mere 6 feet beneath the ash. This was near extensive beach rock running offshore at sea level from the edge of the beach. The seismograph proved that the beach rock runs inshore under the ash, which has been eroding and encroaching seaward over the flat plain of Perissa. We looked again at Loring's ring of stones, nearly buried under the beach, which had extended 6 feet seaward since the previous year.

In Minoan times, much larger slabs of this natural concrete probably were to be found here and on the south shore, and perhaps were used by the people for some human purpose. The presence and location of underwater ruins off the south and east shores, in combination with what we know of vulcanology, point up my belief that the Minoan shoreline was seaward of the present one, a paradox explained by a land slump in the fifteenth century B.C. that moved the shore inland of the present beach. Now, the land is extending in places by ash erosion from the mountainsides, and in others it is being eaten away by wave action.

While exploring along the wave-cut cliffs west of Exomiti, Loring drew our attention to Hellenistic (300 B.C. to A.D. 100) shards exposed in the cliff face as much as 10 to 15 feet below the ash surface. This was the first time that we had seen this situation, which implied that a considerable thickness of the ash had eroded from the mountains above and washed down to the shore since 1500 B.C. This meant that the Minoan level, now some 30 feet below grade here, had been as little as 15 feet.

On Friday and Saturday, June 2 and 3, Bill and I explored with flawless decorum, or so we thought until dinner Saturday evening. We were about to dine at Café Loukas when we were informed that the chief of police wanted to see us immediately. On the way to the station we tried to fathom what appeared to be another contretemps, but in vain. Our sense of innocence was overwhelming.

We had visited the holy monastery on top of Mt. Elias, a sanctuary wrapped in howling winds from which we had actually seen the mountains of Crete, 60 miles away. And then we had visited the site known as Ancient Thera—the extensive ruin on the spur of Messa Vouno. We had done the mountain on foot this time, past marjoram, pepper, and a mountain spring, with its chapel and grotto shaded by an olive tree which grew straight down out of the roof. We went through ruined temples, streets, and houses, and down the mountain to the sea, where we found Manolis, the fisherman who had captained our varca in 1966. It was a warm reunion, accompanied by an invitation to lunch, music from a battery-operated phonograph, and dancing. Afterward, Manolis and several of his friends took us up the eastern shore in his varca to Monolithos.

We had underwater success this day at Kamari. Off the beach in 20 feet of water we discovered a tapered column of red lava exactly like the one we had seen in Zahn's ravine, the one which Marinatos had said was definitely prehistoric and which I thought could be a sacred pillar. This was a clue that the sunken city off Kamari might be truly Minoan, which would substantiate the extensiveness of the pre-eruption settlement.

And the next day we had taken another outing, this time to the beach at Perissa to seismograph the plain. Here we covered a large area and found the substratum at about 15 feet under the surface everywhere, even as much as 900 feet from shore, indicating another area for future excavation. We had a swim and lunch at a beachside café. There were English students camping, scented French ladies, and thunderous Germans. We were told that a group of tourists had, the day before, stolen eight icons from churches all over the island. Incredibly, one had been cut in half, the better to fit into a suitcase. On hearing this, I felt I could understand any harassment foreigners, including myself, might have to put up with. But not for long.

Theofanides Eleftenos, police chief at Thera, had black, close-cropped hair pressed flat and shiny. His aspect was early George Raft. He had a black moustache, black eyes, black tie, black trousers, and black shoes. But worst was his lack of expression. He was neither businesslike nor bullying, kind nor vicious, only watchful. A veritable basilisk.

He asked if we had been at Perissa, "using machine," as he put it. I said we had and asked what was wrong.

"Wrong," he shouted, raising his arm. "Wrong! To use machine in search of antiquities is wrong. Is very serious offense. Names please. Which of you is Mavor?"

"I am Mavor."

"Aha!"

"You see, before he left, Dr. Marinatos said it would be all right if we—"

"No, no, no, quiet please, quiet." We sat there awhile until he finished writing. "I have just talked to the esteemed Professor Marinatos here on the telephone to Athens and he has told me in no uncertain terms that you were not to do anything, anything at all, until his return to Thera."

Then, suddenly switching from menace to magnanimity, he said our association with "the esteemed professor" allowed us to be forgiven for our "serious" offense, and abruptly dismissed us. But we were effectively blocked from any further use on our own of the seismograph.

Association with Dr. Marinatos seemed double-edged at just that moment and I decided that, since we had planned a trip to Crete sometime during the expedition, better now than later. Dr. Platon's report of volcanic bombs at Zakros and hopes of finding ash or scoria from Thera, evidence of the eruption's widespread devastation, were our main objectives, but obviously not the only ones. Emily Vermeule and Robert Kane were due Sunday morning. There was a boat to Crete leaving Monday evening, and I booked passage for four.

Emily Vermeule and Bob Kane arrived at 6 A.M. on Sunday morning, June 4. Bill and I watched their ship come in. They were just what the doctor ordered, a bit of home to dispel the atmosphere of stealth and conspiracy that was growing on this island of mystery. Emily Vermeule, who speaks Greek fluently, brought a note from Marinatos giving us freedom of the island, or so we interpreted it. The sealed note, addressed to the chief of police, was duly presented to him, oozing charm this particular Sunday morning. We were assured that we could visit the Akroteri site and furthermore could use the seismograph in Emily's presence. Marinatos was susceptible to a woman's charm.

Shortly after being shown to her hotel room by the manager, Emily announced, to our horror, that he had tried to "hug and kiss her." I was quite taken aback. I had thought the unctuous, sixty-four-year-old quite harmless, to say the least, even taking his Mediterranean standards into account. Emily reported the incident to Mr. Koutsogiannopoulos the younger, who earnestly assured us it would not happen again. I had no idea that this minor incident would be blown up into a major preoccupation for us all during the remainder of our stay in Greece.

We left Phira as soon as possible to review the excavations at the ravines of Akroteri. We descended into one of the caves formed when the ash overburden had collapsed into the empty rooms of a Minoan house. The cave was even compartmented into small rooms as the house would have been, though nothing but ash was visible. Dutifully, all the shards and fresco pieces were taken to the museum for safekeeping.

Monday, we decided to take a boat to Therasia and, with the

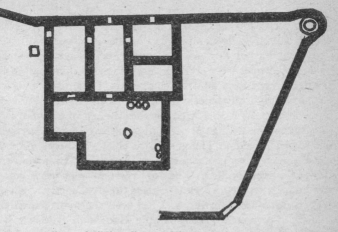

FIGURE 31. Minoan building discovered by Fouqué on Therasia in Suez Canal pumice quarry on cliff edge. (After Fouqué, *Santorin et ses Eruptions*, Paris, 1879.)

guidance of Mr. Giannacas, the retired museum caretaker, look for the Fouqué excavations on the south coast. Here, where a large house had been excavated on the edge of the cliff, and where the quarrying for the Suez Canal had taken place, Fouqué had made his first discovery. But before we could leave the hotel, we were all summoned to the police station and asked to bring our hotel bills. We did as we were bade.

The chief of police examined the bills with a great deal of snorting, head-wagging and other histrionics. He made a great deal of fuss about a three drachma overcharge on a lunch bill, a matter of ten cents, and about various ten drachma charges we could not explain. He began discussing these "crimes" with Emily in Greek. My Greek was not what I hoped it would be, and I had only a vague notion of their conversation. However, I gathered after a while that the subject had changed. The hotel manager's name came up ever more frequently. That much I could divine. The chief was laughing, shaking his head, then asking another question. Suddenly his face darkened, he pounded his desk, threw himself back into his chair, and went into paroxysms of outrage and disgust, probing for more information about Emily's encounter with the manager.

Alternately bullying and bellowing his outrage against the "*kakos anthropos*," the chief managed to extract enough, in his opinion, to write out a formal charge against the man. This was the last thing Emily had in mind, but the chief's outrage swept aside her demurs. I wondered whether we had unwittingly supplied the police with an opportunity to arrest the manager, who was not well-liked on Thera, or if the chief was merely promoting a stratagem to inconvenience us, engineered from above to prevent us from going to Therasia. We were released in about two hours, after we had acknowledged the chief's written charge to be substantially correct, and had seen the manager, in the custody of two burly officers, pass the window on his way to jail.

Therasia is seldom visited by strangers and the natives seldom travel, even the 7 miles across to Phira. Picturesque and primitive compared with the main island, its village also sits atop a cliff, reached by a steep donkey trail. On this island there are no roads and no transportation but the donkey. A 3-mile ride, sidesaddle on the traditional wooden frames that serve as saddles, over the fields and through rock-strewn gullies, took us to the quarries from which ash had been taken for the Suez Canal in the 1860's. We found abundant prehistoric shards, as usual, but no houses. There were places where shards were more dense than at others and we made note of these, piling up more sites for future excavation. According to Dr. Galanopoulos' projection, the canal from Plato's Altantean harbors to the outer wall ran through what was now the narrow strait separating Therasia from Thera. I was becoming satisfied that excavation almost anywhere would strike into the Minoan stratum and reveal buildings or, at least, signs of former life. It seemed best at this point, however, to concentrate on Akroteri, and I looked forward to establishing that site as truly an Atlantean palace.

Arriving back at the quay of Phira, we elected not to climb

the cliff again, but to wait there the two hours for the boat to Crete. Our luggage was to be brought down, anyway. The phone at the dockside café rang. The call was for Emily. The police chief demanded that she come up the 1,200-foot cliff immediately to his office. Emily was tired and anxious to leave for Crete. She suggested that he might come down to see us. The answering bellow shook the café. Emily and I meekly and silently started up the mountain.

The long, irritating climb was followed by another opera of outrage by the chief. The manager had mounted counter-accusations, and the chief decided that the two should confront each other. This embarrassing scene ended with Emily tearfully pleading with the chief to call Marinatos, which he did.

Marinatos seemed to have known about the incident. Emily objected to being inadvertently made the author of another's disaster. Marinatos insisted that the accused would not be treated harshly; but, from what I knew of Greek penology, this assurance did not impress me. During all this anguished exchange I sat by, unable to contribute because of my lack of familiarity with the language. We were released at last, uncertain of the outcome of the strange affair, and the manager was led back to his cell.

Down on the quay, we waited for the *Elli*, an ancient ship that stopped at Thera once a week to pick up a few passengers for Crete. A radio in the café was blaring, and we learned that war between Israel and the Arab countries had broken out at last. Russian warships were reported circling Crete. We wondered if the Cretan sea was the place to spend the night.

But, once on board, we forgot the war and the Thera police and our hotel manager, envisioning the Cretan palaces we were soon to see. At last I would be able to study firsthand the vestiges of Minoan civilization at its most magnificent—a civilization the memory of which, a thousand years after its destruction, Plato memorialized as Atlantis.

CHAPTER 11

NICHOLAS PLATON had recently found, at his excavation of the palace of Zakros in eastern Crete, some pieces of rock that he considered volcanic, and which Dr. Galanopoulos thought might be volcanic bombs from the eruption of Thera. For this to be so, the speed of ejection would have to have been more than twice that reported during the eruption of the Bezymyannaya volcano in Russia, the greatest on record. Dr. Alexiou, Ephor of Crete, was now the custodian of these treasures.

While we awaited an audience with this extremely inaccessible man at the Candia Museum in Iraklion, where the bombs were kept, we toured several Minoan palaces and villas. Though I was preoccupied with finding evidence of damage traceable to the Thera eruption, I clearly sensed the excellence of those ancients whose silent, sepulchral cities have yielded not only great treasure but an exquisite sense of life and an ability to enjoy it. In terms of spiritual, artistic, political, and social accomplishments these people were, if anything, more remarkable than Plato's Atlanteans.

Thanks to Emily Vermeule's vast knowledge and the dubious advantage of having arrived at 5:15 A.M., we were able to accomplish a great deal in the short time we alloted to "doing" Minoan Crete. But we found no signs of pumice, lapilli, or volcanic bombs at any of the excavations we examined. There is a powdered lime deposit on Crete which looks much like ash, but, simply by feeling and tasting the material, we discovered it to be of much softer consistency than the high-silica ash of Thera.

Nor did our inspection of the villa at Amisos help to reassure us in the matter of airborne pumice reaching Crete. This is the villa in which Marinatos reported finding sea-washed pumice back in 1939 and also indications that a wall had been pushed out by water force. Since the villa lies only 15 to 25 feet above sea level at a distance of 100 yards from the shore, it surely must have been inundated by the Thera disaster, and there were, indeed, two large wall blocks that had been tipped outward to the west by forces that could have been sea waves. Two large blocks were missing from the north wall parallel to the sea and I am inclined to agree that this was tsunami damage.

At Gournia lies a small Minoan palace surrounded by the best surviving example of a prehistoric Cretan town, having a location similar to that of Akroteri on Thera. It lies on a knoll overlooking the sea, 1,000 to 1,500 feet away, projecting from a sloping plain bounded on the east and west by mountains. I could imagine future excavations on Thera revealing better-preserved and more elegant structures in a comparable setting.

We were eager to see the Platon "bombs" but, after a brief excited look under Dr. Alexiou's guidance, we saw that they resembled nothing we had noticed on Thera. One showed metallic oxides in green and melted stone. The other was a white powdery material which looked like pumice but, unhappily, Bob Kane and I both felt that the first sample had been melted and fused together in an intense local fire. The second was lime, not a pumice deposit. Unless we were mistaken in our conclusions, the case for airborne bombs from Thera actually reaching Crete had yet to be proved. Pumice was another matter, for deep-sea cores all around Crete showed ash samples. Doubtless, almost all that had fallen on land had now washed into the sea. If we could find some inland basins or lake beds, they should still have Theran pumice.

The next day, we drove up into the mountains for a look at one of Dr. Marinatos' numerous restorations, the villa at Vathypetro. It is on the crown of a hill, in the lush hinterlands of Crete, where they grow choice raisin grapes. As we approached the villa, backed by a green wrinkled hide of mountains, I found myself staring at Bob Kane's outstretched palm. He was holding what appeared to be a volcanic bomb. But we were quickly put in our places by the guide, who told us that it was from a Minoan lime kiln that had been used to make whitewash.

Whenever possible, Dr. Marinatos prefers to leave the contents of his excavations *in situ,* an admirable policy that he intended to follow on Thera. Beautifully preserved vats and the press of a Minoan wine mill created a sense of presence, of intrusion on our part. So much so that I found myself trying to think up explanations should the owner suddenly turn up and wonder what we were doing in his winery.

After Vathypetro, we drove to Archanes for a look at the site, excavated by John Sakellarakis, of a palace believed to have been the summer residence of Minos himself. This is a recent excavation, uncomplicated by the hand of the restorer. It is small, less than an acre in extent so far, but the stonework is massive, comparable to the palaces of Knossos, Mallia, and Phaistos, and evidence of earthquake here was obvious. Huge building blocks had been knocked 8 or 10 feet out of position. Near Archanes, in 1964, was discovered the first unplundered royal tomb on Crete. Dating from the destruction period, about 1400 B.C., Mycenaean soldiers were represented but, in the main, the burial was tastefully Minoan. The presence of Mycenaean soldiers in this Minoan setting illustrated one of Plato's more allegorical statements about the Atlanteans. "When the divine portion began to fade away" in the Atlanteans, wrote Plato, they "grew visibly debased." This shift in character I had already seen as representing the historical shift in power from Minoans to Mycenaeans. Here was actual evidence of the Minoan-Atlantean change from peaceful to warlike nature.

Having never been to Crete, I had not had the opportunity to see and feel the beauty of Minoan art. I hoped to sense what these people were like, to test my feeling for them. Minoan architecture has a marvelous sense of proportion, managing to achieve a delicate balance of scale, texture, tone, and mood. The viewer is exhilarated rather than awed by the size of the palaces. They are large structures, but not overpoweringly monumental. The enormousness of the stone blocks is relieved by lightwells, pillars, terraces, interior courtyards, their drabness transformed by gay, brightly colored frescoes. Even the grim realities of a sarcophagus are balanced by other realities not so grim—gay designs of animals, birds, and fish, and frescoes depicting feast days, religious ceremonies, music, laughter, and life. This sense of balance, this effort to find some middle ground between what man is and what he would like to think he is, gives everything to do with their civilization, from the largest palace to the smallest seal stone, a natural, easy grace which seems intended not to impress, to exaggerate or overwhelm but simply and successfully to delight.

On our last day on Crete, Bob Kane, Emily, and I (Bill Wetmore having left for home) went to the tiny island of Dia, about 10 miles north of Iraklion. It is ideal as a location for a naval base, a shipyard, fishing settlements, and other maritime pursuits. There had never been, so far as Emily Vermeule or Dr. Alexiou knew, an archaeological survey or reports of any kind concerning antiquities on Dia, even though it is the isle where fair Ariadne was abandoned by Theseus, after she had aided his escape from the labyrinth. Dia lies on a straight line between the ancient Minoan port of Amnisos and Thera. Surely, if Thera was important, Dia must have been more than an occasional port of call. Jason is said to have stopped off there, where he was given a purple robe made for "Dionysus in sea-girt Dia." Dionysus is linked by many to the boy-god of the matriarchal religion of early Minoan Crete and the Cyclades.

In our brief wanderings around the harbor and up toward the promontory to the east, we discovered potsherds in such great numbers as Emily said she had never seen on any site in any period. We also found what is quite possibly a Cycladic or pre-Minoan town. Bob Kane was the first to see it, ruined walls of buildings laid out in streets. The island's rocky character and comparative absence of soil make it quite simple to excavate, though, for the same reason, it is not well preserved. After a brief underwater exploration, we found ancient moles or jetties, one of which contained parallel sections similar to the Minoan boat sheds found at nearby Amnisos. As a final crowning touch, Bob Kane found the timbers of one small boat sticking out from beneath one of the jetties.

That night we flew back to Athens, where we spent the next nine days, except for two delightful trips to archaeological sites in Attica and the Peloponnesus. One trip was in search of the ancient mines of Lavrion and Thorikos, where King Minos is said to have come ashore and conquered, probably in search of copper. The other trip, to the citadels of Mycenae and Tiryns, heightened my understanding of the "debasement" of the Atlanteans. These grim fortresses were quite different from the palaces of Minoan Crete. On both occasions, Emily Vermeule was our enthusiastic guide and provided a marvelous running commentary on historical background.

Marinatos' land acquisition proceedings for the Thera site we hoped to explore further were apparently bogged down. Legal notices had to be printed in the newspaper a certain number of times. In addition, Marinatos was busy trying to obtain the job of director of the Archaeological Service. In line with this campaign he gave a lecture on our finds to the prestigious Academy of Athens and published an article on our results in the Athens newspaper. But, though we begged him daily to return to Thera, he put us off with one excuse or another. Emily had to return home by the end of the month and, again, time was running out.

The closing of the Suez Canal during the Arab-Israeli war had prevented Cousteau's ship, *Calypso*, from reaching the Mediterranean, so his Thera plans were canceled. Doc Edgerton was also unable to come. He had hoped to work with Cousteau at Helice, as well as with us on Thera.

On June 13, Bob Kane returned to Thera alone. He had flown to Greece primarily to conduct a geological survey, but in the two weeks he had been with us he had been able to spend only two days on the island. Marinatos' return to Athens had not fitted in well with either Emily Vermeule's or Bob Kane's schedules. Thus we were pleased when Marinatos wrote to the police chief on Thera giving Bob permission to survey the island's geology, even though Marinatos would not be there.

Once on the island, Bob drew topographical maps of the Akroteri region, measuring distances by pacing and obtaining directions by hand compass. He laid out the ravines of Akroteri in much more detail than we had seen on any map heretofore. By walking along the south beach and studying the visible stratigraphy in the wave-washed cliffs, he was able to reconstruct the line cross section of the terrain in Minoan times, beneath the ash.

His finding, which was most significant, was that the Minoan settlement of Akroteri was built on the gently rolling floor of

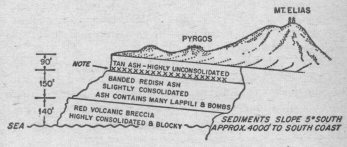

AKROTERI — VIEW DUE EAST FROM INSIDE EDGE OF CRATER
SHOWING SEDIMENTARY DEPOSITS OF ASH
& POSITION OF 1500 B.C. PUMICE LAYER

MT. ELIAS

PYRGOS

90'
NOTE — TAN ASH – HIGHLY UNCONSOLIDATED
XXXXXXXXXXXXXXXXXXXXXXXXXX

150'
BANDED REDISH ASH
SLIGHTLY CONSOLIDATED
ASH CONTAINS MANY LAPPILI & BOMBS

140'
RED VOLCANIC BRECCIA
HIGHLY CONSOLIDATED & BLOCKY

SEA

SEDIMENTS SLOPE 5° SOUTH
APPROX. 4000' TO SOUTH COAST

NOTE (XXX) = PUMICE LAYER 8 FEET DEEP – MADE OF ANGULAR PUMICE 1/8" TO
3" ACROSS – FINE DUST IS PRESENT AS IN OVERLYING LAYER
THE PUMICE LAYER DATES THE 1500± B.C. ERUPTION

FIGURE 32. Geological section of caldera cliff, Akroteri, surveyed by R. Kane. (After R. Kane.)

a shallow valley between the limestone Mt. Platinamos on the east and Mt. Styros, a mountain of andesite lava, on the west. In other words, it bore little relationship to the present-day ravine-cut slope. That meant that the Minoan landscape had provided a marvelous site for a palace.

The peaks of Mt. Platinamos and Mt. Styros project well above the ash blanket and are strangely free of the ash. Bob suggested a theory to explain this and the fact that there is so much less ash in the southern part of Thera than elsewhere. With northerly prevailing winds, one would certainly expect a violent ash eruption high into the sky to cover the southern as well as northern parts of the island. Bob was not satisfied with the argument that the southern mountains are so steep that all the ash has washed away.

He proposed that while much of the ash and pumice may have blown high in the air, at least some phases of the eruption produced ash that flowed over the surface of the ground like a very dense fog, finally settling in a thick blanket. This type of eruption has been observed with the Thera-type volcano and, indeed, would explain why an eruption in the northern part of the island could be kept from covering the south by the interposition of mountains, and why the valley of Akroteri is filled with ash but the adjacent mountains are free of the white blanket. In the cliffs on the south the intermittent phases of the great eruption were evident, layers of fine ash in gray, white and brown separated by concentrations of basaltic lava bombs and lapilli.

We were delighted to learn from Bob that the site we chose to excavate had been such an ideal location for a palace in Minoan times. We had started our excavations in the bottom of one of the ravines simply because the ash was thinner there. This did not mean, however, that there was a ravine there in Minoan times.

After completing his map and noting all the exposed volcanic products he could identify in the region, Bob took an adventurous swim along the south shore, all the way from Cape

Exomiti to Akroteri. Swimming a couple of hundred feet off-shore, but coming in to rest every now and then, he covered 4 miles of shoreline looking for evidence of underwater build-ings. Wave-washed and changeable, the beach was covered with black lava stones. It is likely that many of the underwater structures here have been broken up and covered by sand over the centuries. Nevertheless, the report of houses between the ancient moles of Exomiti sounded reliable. But Bob was not able to find anything here which he felt was a man-made building. As he approached the waters of Akroteri, however, off the ravine to the east of the one in which we had excavated, more rocks became exposed and the beach was less sandy.

About 200 feet off the shore, in 9 feet of water, he found what he sought, the wall of a house, made of cut stones placed one on top of another. At the bottom of this wall, among the smaller stones, were the telltale pieces of prehistoric pottery which identified the site as Minoan. The walls appeared to be extensions of those we had seen near the beach on June 4, long walls buried in the sand which appeared to run right out into the sea.

This was our first sure identification of underwater ruins seaward of our excavation site, where I thought the land had slumped either in the fifteenth century B.C. or in some later convulsion. The wall was in shallow water, and probably was a shore-front building in the days when the sea level was some 10 feet lower than it is today.

On June 14, Mary arrived in Athens, and shortly after-ward Marinatos gave us his promise that he would come to Thera on the following Tuesday. Preparatory to our re-turn trip to Thera, Emily and I had done what we could to insure a comparatively peaceful second stage to the expedi-tion, free if possible of the contretemps that had been such a nuisance on the first trip. We were disconcerted, however, to learn that we would be sailing to Thera on the *Pantelis*, whose captain was the brother of our unfortunate hotel man-

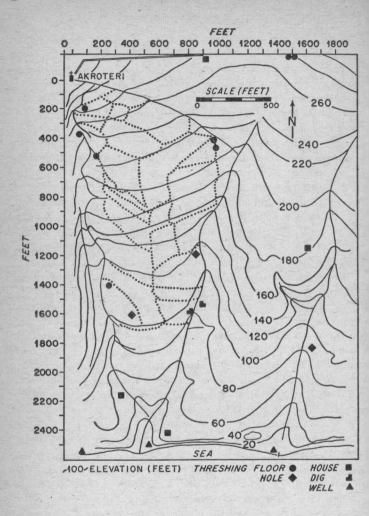

FIGURE 33. Plan view of excavation site, Akroteri. Surveyed 1967 by R. Kane. (After R. Kane.)

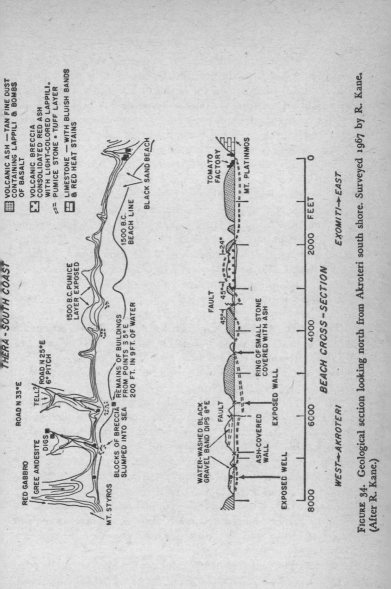

THERA - SOUTH COAST

VOLCANIC ASH — TAN FINE DUST CONTAINING LAPPILI & BOMBS OF BASALT

VOLCANIC BRECCIA CONSOLIDATED RED ASH WITH LIGHT-COLORED LAPPILI. PUMICE STONE = TUFF LAYER

LIMESTONE — WITH BLUISH BANDS & RED HEAT STAINS

ROAD N 33°E

RED GABBRO

GREE ANDESITE

DIGS

TELL?

ROAD N 25°E
6° PITCH

1500 B.C. PUMICE LAYER EXPOSED

MT. STYROS

BLOCKS OF BRECCIA SLUMPED INTO SEA

REMAINS OF BUILDINGS FROM POINTS S 5°E
200 FT. IN 9FT. OF WATER

1500 B.C. BEACH LINE

BLACK SAND BEACH

BEACH CROSS-SECTION

WATER-WASHED BLACK GRAVEL BAND DIPS 8°E

FAULT

ASH-COVERED WALL

EXPOSED WALL

EXPOSED WELL

FAULT

45°

45°

RING OF SMALL STONE COVERED WITH ASH

1-24°

TOMATO FACTORY

MT. PLATINMOS

WEST→AKROTERI

EXOMITI→EAST

8000   6000   4000   2000 FEET   0

FIGURE 34. Geological section looking north from Akroteri south shore. Surveyed 1967 by R. Kane. (After R. Kane.)

ager and whose first mate was the manager's son. We pictured ourselves tossed into the sea, an Aegean shiv in our kidneys. To top it all, what should we hear but that the manager himself would be boarding the boat at Syros, having been providentially released on bail. I visualized a sympathetic judge, one who felt that the victim of foreign intrigue should be allowed to orchestrate the family's revenge.

Fortunately, however, he did not come on board at all, and his family could not have treated us with greater courtesy while we were on their ship and their island. We arrived at the usual 6 A.M. landing time on Sunday morning, and, though the hotel was full, the family went out of their way to find us' accommodations for the next few days. When Marinatos arrived, we would be moving in with Mr. Koutsogiannopoulos.

We settled into rooms beneath the Café Loukas, practically next door to Loring, and planned a few days of scouting before Marinatos' arrival. Bob Kane would leave at 1 P.M. on the *Pantelis*, so Emily, Mary, and I were on our own.

The chief of police was fortunately in church when we settled in our rooms, so as quickly as we could we engaged Georgos Alvaniti, the faithful taxi driver of our previous session, and his Peugeot, and sped out of town, anywhere as long as it was far from Phira.

The three-day reprieve before Marinatos arrived was delightful. The chief of police ignored us, except for a leer as we unavoidably passed him on the street. Loring had gone to Syros for his trial. Mary, Emily, and I spent our time sightseeing, finding antiquities wherever we turned. Mary proved to have an unbelievably sharp eye for spotting prehistoric potsherds. It was at times like this that we regretted not being allowed to take even one small piece home with us. But we came to Greece to learn, to understand, not to take away from this wonderful land. To this day, we possess no Greek antiquities.

Monday and Tuesday, while waiting for Marinatos, we tried to spend our time productively. We chartered Manolis Kafouros' varca and visited a site off Cape Exomiti where a large collection of 3- to 10-foot rock slabs was to be seen on an otherwise sandy bottom in 60 feet of water. Looking through glass-bottom buckets, we could see them clearly, our sense of dimension aided by sponges attached to the rocks. They covered 3 or more acres and could have been beach rock broken into many small pieces. They were rather randomly placed as far as I could see, but Manolis saw order in them, and he had studied them longer than I had. He was convinced that they were underwater houses, a mile offshore. Further to the west off Akroteri, we followed the directions of Bob Kane's wall and, sure enough, prehistoric shards were to be found nearby.

On the east face of Mt. Platinamos is a relief rock sculpture of a serpent, 10 feet long. A local farmer called it an *exhydra,* a viper or adder, of ancient origin. Near it were cut rock tombs of the Hellenistic period, located only 3 to 6 feet above the ground. This was surprising, since these tombs are usually placed higher on a cliff, but could be explained by Loring's observation that ash erosion from the mountaintop tended to build up the depth of the ash surface over the plain at its foot through the years.

We met a farmer who asked us to look in his well, which he had dug the previous summer. It was a large cylindrical hole lined with stone, 8 feet in diameter, and he had dug 28 feet before he reached water. At the bottom of the well, he said, was a wall made with well-cut limestone blocks, fastened together with bronze dogs in Hellenistic style. The wall was similar to one on the hillside, which he pointed out. The wall was about 3 feet high and 18 inches in width, he said, and I could just make it out looking down into the well.

The elevation of the land at this point was 46 feet, so that the wall rested beneath ash on the limestone or lava base at 18 feet above sea level. We could not descend into the well and left frustrated by this enigma of a wall apparently Hellenistic in style but located where a Minoan wall should have been, under 28 feet of ash. The more I thought about it, the more certain I became that the wall had to be Minoan, bronze dogs and all.

We also traveled to Balos, the port of Akroteri, for my third try at Fouqué's elusive house. I had benefited by experience, and this time, with the keen eyes of Mary and Emily, we located the correct height on the cliff, a good start. With this established, we found prehistoric shards concentrated at one spot, one of the surest signs of habitation. But we could not dig without the presence of Marinatos, and thus could not verify our find.

Finally, however, he arrived, and with him came Mr. Koutsogiannopoulos, Mr. K.'s cook, and Herr and Frau Schloebke. Herr Schloebke is a retired architect who had volunteered to spend a summer with Marinatos as archaeological draftsman.

We all took up residence in Mr. K.'s elegant summer home. With a household staff of three to minister to our needs, we led a luxurious, formal, and somewhat strained existence. Dinner each evening, for which we all dressed—still a tradition in the more important German digs, I understand—was a formal affair with elegantly prepared food offered by our gracious host, but presided over by Marinatos. This was followed by after-dinner drinks on the veranda overlooking the main street of Phira and the caldera.

No sooner were we established amid this elegance and all seated in a circle on the veranda making polite conversation in English, French, German, and Greek as best we could—Mr. K. knew Greek and French, the Schloebkes only German—than a telegram arrived for me. It was from Loring, saying he was acquitted and that he was arriving the next morning.

Edward Loring did indeed arrive, in the midst of one of our formal dinners. Unexpected, unannounced, unkempt, but acquitted and therefore triumphant, he came for Dr. Marinatos' blessing.

"I have been acquitted," he announced excitedly.

Marinatos answered him coolly in Greek. "Congratulations."

Loring then announced that he had been waiting since 9 A.M. to see us; apparently he really had expected to be greeted with open arms by Marinatos. Mr. K. was a polite and reserved host, offering Loring a seat at the table, which he refused, but Marinatos was beginning to boil.

I hastily told Loring I would come down to his house after dinner and we could discuss the matter there. Loring clicked his heels, said quite needlessly, "I see I am not wanted here," and left.

After he had gone, Marinatos deplored Loring's grossly American manners. It was the first meeting with Edward for all except Marinatos and me, so his remarks fell into a rather incredulous silence. I announced to all that Mary and I would see Loring after dinner. Emily offered to come, too, but Marinatos would not permit her to go. "Absolutely not," he said, in a positive fury.

Mary and I later listened to Loring for over two hours. He was distraught, discouraged. He told us of the trial. There had been three judges. The young archaeologist Tsakos, from the antiquities service, had appeared and testified in favor of Loring. The Kristiana case was barely touched on, so Loring reported, but he was accused of stealing Cycladic vases now in the Brooklyn Museum. He was acquitted for lack of evidence and was to be kept under surveillance.

It was clear that Marinatos either forgot he had agreed to accept Loring after his acquittal, or had never intended to accept him in the first place. I advised Loring to leave the island for a while, since he was in a dangerous position if Marinatos became enraged again. We could do little to comfort Loring, who said that in the future he would devote himself to philosophy rather than archaeology. He had arrived this summer with quantities of research material on the Venetian period on Thera and we encouraged him to write a history. It was to everyone's best interest, I thought, to avoid meeting Loring again, and I did not see him after that evening.

CHAPTER 12

OUR next five days, charitably free of extraneous personal involvements, turned out to be most successful. They were also, in a manner of speaking, hauntingly successful. It was as though we had broken through the crust of time. Not just a Minoan palace and town, but the people themselves seemed to be materializing. Surrounded as we were by peasants, donkeys, primitive tools, Minoan walls, storage jars, and columns, it was not always clear which civilization was the living and which the dead.

The scene was our first excavation multiplied by ten. Some forty workmen had been provided by the owner of a pumice quarry, and these men plus our old Akroteri friends, at least those not committed to the tomato harvest, soon had the air filled with ash and the ground scarred with trenches.

We opened nine trenches in all, covering both sides of the ravine and strung out along a distance of 300 yards. Those on the west we called Bronos, and those on the east Alvaniti, and numbered them chronologically. After a trench began to reveal exciting walls and pottery on one side of the ravine, a companion dig was started on the opposite side, which invariably revealed a continuation of the settlement. Every one of the nine exploratory excavations paid off with rich finds, within a few hours of breaking ground.

The very first trench started, at site Bronos II, to the south of Bronos I, was begun with the expectation that we would have to dig down for yards before uncovering Minoan walls. But within 2 feet of the surface the picks hit limestone blocks. These tapered Minoan wall stones, typical of the Cretan palaces, were the same type as our first finds in trench Alvaniti I. The blocks were in disarray, having fallen out of place during an earthquake. Because the stones lay on top of ash, we concluded that the earthquake had occurred after some of the ash had fallen. We immediately enlarged the area of this excavation and began to dig down slowly and uniformly. Before another foot was cleared, the cry of "Wall plaster, frescoes" went up in several places at once. Frescoed walls jutted above the ash, in place, intact, preserved for 3,500 years. We had uncovered the first frescoes to be found on Thera since Mamet and Gorceix in 1870. Emily Vermeule immediately took motherly charge of this valuable site. Soon it was covered with little sticks identifying pieces of frescoes so that we would not accidentally damage them. She worked feverishly to uncover this two- or three-story complex of small rooms, passages and doorways, which contained many plastered walls still in place. We were surrounded by plaster, some of it in large panels, little having collapsed from the walls and ceilings.

Fouqué had reported a single painted fresco. While it was difficult for us to discern designed patterns, we obviously had uncovered more than one painting. The quantity of fresco, in fact, established this as a palatial building. Though richly decorated and appointed, the area seemed to be a place where food was prepared and eaten.

Mary set to washing potsherds and picking out the best painted ones. Intact pottery began appearing in quantity, and Emily and her three faithful precision workmen, who learned rapidly, gradually removed pumice. I took photographs and made drawings at each stage. A painted spherical water jug filled with pumice was found outside a doorway and was tenderly carried to our shelter, which had been constructed out of brush by the workmen. There it was carefully packed in a basket, with brush and grass for packing, loaded on donkeyback for transport up to the village, and put in our car, which would take it the 10 miles to the Phira museum over winding and bumpy roads.

A beautifully cut limestone doorsill in the upper story allowed us to enter a hall which was lined with three side passageways, each 2½ feet wide, with frescoes on both walls. We were mystified by this arrangement. Steps led down to a lower level, which we did not excavate. Our aim at this point was primarily to excavate around as many of the frescoes as we could, while clearing their surfaces of ash, looking for designs. This was done first with a shovel, next with our hands, then with a knife, and finally with a fine brush. In places where the edges of frescoed walls had broken off, we could see the pinks, greens and reds of several previous layers beneath, better preserved than the outer one. We wondered what paintings might be hidden by the outer layers, being able to see only black sponge prints on a buff background.

All of the kitchenware found in this site was of the very finest, painted in elegant Late Minoan design. Tapered cups and goblets, fine tripod braziers, animal bones, shells, and obsidian implements were found throughout the site. The end of the trench, at the edge of the donkey path down the center of the ravine, was cut away right down to the path. This area revealed much of the kitchenware. A large piece of stone, when turned over, proved to be a mixing bowl of very large size, cut from limestone.

As soon as the frescoes had appeared, a rush call went out to Athens, to the vast American excavation of the Athenian Agora, where Andreas Mavragiannis worked. He was known as an expert technician with experience in fresco preservation. In a few days he arrived and set to work helping Emily with the problem of what to do with the frescoes. At first it was thought that they could be removed to the museum. The edges were heavily coated with plaster of paris in preparation for this and to prevent crumbling during exposure. One fresco with a heavy backing of conglomerate, about 2 square feet in size, was removed and taken to the museum. But it was decided

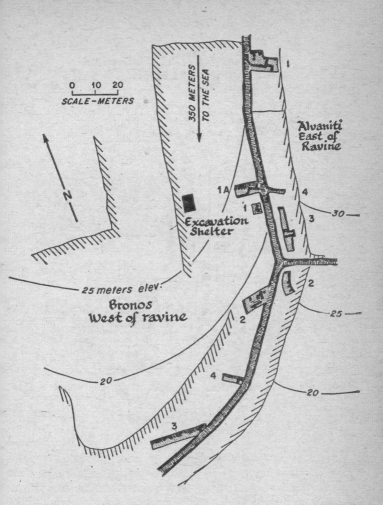

FIGURE 35. Plan view, excavation ravine, Akroterí, 1967. Numbered trenches radiate from donkey path which follows bottom of ravine.

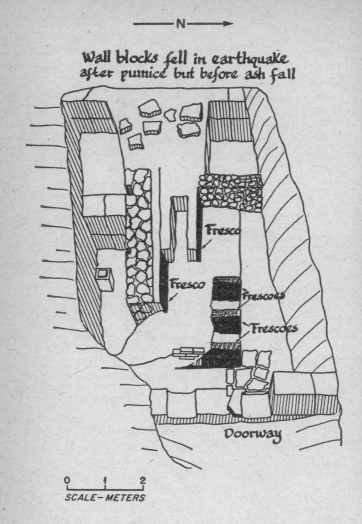

N→

Wall blocks fell in earthquake
after pumice but before ash fall

Fresco

Fresco

Frescoes

Frescoes

Doorway

```
0        1        2
SCALE—METERS
```

FIGURE 36. Excavation Bronos II, Akroteri, 1967.

that the other panels, most of them much larger, would be impossible to move without some better technique. Then too, there was a question of what would happen once the frescoes did reach the museum. Were they really better off there? It was decided that the best solution was to leave the frescoes in place for this season.

We dug down to the bottom floor in one place revealing a rectangular column, more elegant pottery, and well-cut walls. It looked as if some of the stones had fallen off walls before there was any eruption of ash. They lay on the basic weathered lava. Apparently there were two serious earthquakes which we could identify in the ruin. I should hardly call it a ruin, for even though it had been damaged by earthquake, preservation was still far better than in any previously discovered Minoan settlement. But, because this site was so near the surface, it had suffered the effects of weathering and erosion by water, and may even have been partially exposed at one time.

In the upper story of this building we found intact mud bricks, preserved through all the centuries under the ash, even though they were covered by only a few feet of ash when we discovered them. The finding of Minoan mud bricks is very rare because they deteriorate quickly in the presence of moisture. The prospect of finding many more in a fine state of preservation under the deeper ash is a virtual certainty. If

FIGURE 37. Tripod brazier found in excavation Bronos II, Akroteri, 1967.

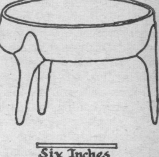

Six Inches

wood remains preserved to the extent that Fouqué leads us to believe, we will be able to know with certitude what the upper stories of Minoan buildings really looked like. On Crete, the palace of Knossos is reconstructed in large part on the basis of frescoes, pictures painted on pottery, and seal stones showing small details. None of the upper stories of the palace were actually left intact by the ravages of time.

Bronos II gradually revealed a picture, incomplete to be sure, of Minoan life on Thera. Perhaps this was the chamber of a queen or princess, domestic but elegant. We could see the inventiveness of the Minoans, their ability to imbue whatever they created with life, their love of bright colors. But we had barely scratched the surface. When we have excavated into the deep ash, where preservation should be the equal of that in the royal tombs of Egypt, we shall surely find the answers to the larger questions which Crete has not answered conclusively. Why did these people reach such a high point of civilization? Where did they come from and where did they go? Even Plato's story of Atlantis, which led us to Thera, doesn't tell us these things.

Bronos IA was started just to the north of Bronos I. Here, as in Bronos I, we ran into the top of a rubble wall only 3 feet below the surface. The line separating the fine ash from the coarse pumice stone told us that we would have to dig a good 15 feet down before we would come to the earth level. As we dug down at this site no pottery appeared, which struck us as unusual, but we did uncover walls that extended in several directions. Soon we came to realize that here we had come upon our first massive structure. When we reached the bottom, there was revealed a façade of great limestone blocks in ashlar masonry, perfectly fitted together, facing what was apparently a palace courtyard. In this wall a large wooden door had swung, and cuttings in the stones probably retained metalwork. Here again was the evidence of earthquake which I sought. There were cut limestone blocks that had fallen from the top of a wall and lay on the ground level covered by the angular

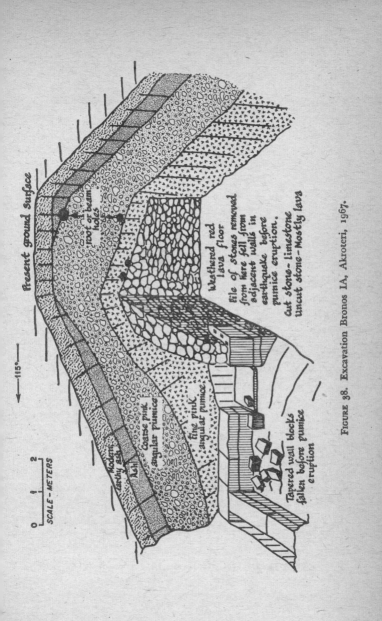

FIGURE 38. Excavation Bronos IA, Akroteri, 1967.

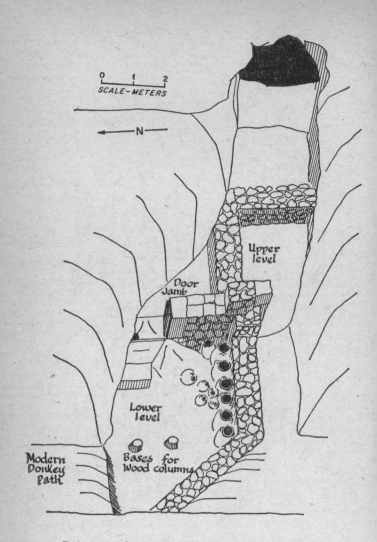

FIGURE 39. Excavation Alvaniti I, Akroteri, 1967.

pumice. This proved conclusively that there was a severe earthquake before any eruption. Nearby there were fallen wall stones lying on top of the angular pumice, showing, as we had seen in site Bronos II, that after the fall of some several feet of pumice, which partially buried the buildings, there had been another severe earthquake. Even some of the large and heavy stones at the bases of the walls showed some misalignment occurring before the eruption. Once the walls were buried in ash, however, they were preserved intact, even through earthquakes, and remained so for the 3,500 years since people lived and worked in these buildings.

Fouqué reported that the houses he had found were locked in the pumice and did not show earthquake damage. Since his statements seem based primarily on the house on Therasia, it is possible that the earthquakes were damaging at Akroteri, but not on Therasia, a not surprising situation in the light of more recent experience. If the epicenter were to the south, between Thera and Crete, this would add weight to Galanopoulos' theory that Cretan earthquakes before and after the collapse added to the cataclysm of volcanic ash and seismic sea waves.

With several trenches going at once, we were hard put to collect the shards, identify them as to location, and store them for washing and sorting. Mary did a great deal of this, shuttling from trench to trench. In the heat of early afternoon, she would sit in the shelter and the many dogs would gather. The Minoan door pivot from Bronos IA became a drinking trough for these friendly animals.

Trench Bronos III revealed something quite different from the others. Here was a wall buried in ash, but built on top of pumice. This was a bit of a shock, as we had not been aware that people had returned to rebuild the region after the ash started to fall. All we saw was this one piece of evidence, a small wall, possibly not part of a house. But it was clear; we could date it by the potsherds found with it. It had been built after some of the pumice had fallen, presumably during a lull in the activity of the volcano. We began to reconstruct a picture in which the early phases of the Thera activity featured severe earthquakes and even ash falls before the people were forced to flee their island permanently.

Of all the trenches opened during this busy week, the most spectacular discoveries were made in Alvaniti I, the trench by the cave and the fig tree. Here we dug down beneath the donkey path running along the bottom of the ravine to what seemed to be the earth level. At precisely the depth that the seismograph had indicated we should dig, we found a row of seven enormous storage jars, still standing and intact. Their colors were as bright as the day they had been painted, in red, black and brown. They even appeared to contain the remains of some vegetable matter. Nearby we found loom weights, 150 of them, and holes in the pumice where the wooden loom had stood. In the same room a hearth was uncovered surrounded by pots, stone lamps, palettes, and mortars.

I have described the findings in each of the major trenches, one after the other. Actually, all of us kept jumping back and forth among the nine trenches during this frantically busy week. In Bronos IV, we found pieces of a beautifully painted sarcophagus and, across the ravine in Alvaniti III, structures that were possibly tombs. With so little time and such incredible quantities of material to record and preserve, we were too busy to appreciate that we had actually found much more than we came prepared to find. I had hoped for a small palace at the most, with perhaps a few houses surrounding it, on the order of Vathypetro on Crete, but what we uncovered was far more impressive, far more extensive than that. Emily Vermeule was later to estimate the population of this town at 30,000 and Marinatos was to describe the find as "remnants of a grand city with immense palaces and streets and signs of old culture."

Such glorious discoveries have certain drawbacks. Mary and Frau Schloebke found themselves washing and sorting mountains of shards. Emily battled impossible odds in an attempt to get everything recorded before it was moved or covered up.

I made maps and fended off sightseers, who were beginning to arrive in waves. The chief of police and his wife paid us a visit. He wanted a ride in *Alvin,* and was improbably cheerful. The Schloebkes were busily drawing plans, each commenting on the other's conduct in Wagnerian tones. Dr. Marinatos roamed the sites, occasionally ordering everything stopped while the artifacts were cleaned and the excavations made attractive, at which point everyone had to climb out of the trenches. Then he would announce that it was time for photographs, and indulge his hobby. I preferred to take photos continuously, including people as well as pots.

Among our discoveries, not so dramatic but nevertheless significant, was the finding of some murex shells. The murex is a sea mussel that excretes a purple dye use by the Minoan nobility on Crete, and later by the Phoenicians. The dye had a special richness which made the purple robes of Minos and his noblemen famous all through the Aegean and beyond. It is worth noting that Plato's Atlantean kings, after hunting and sacrificing the bull, "all of them put on most beautiful azure robes, and, sitting on the ground, at night, over the embers of the sacrifices by which they had sworn, and extinguishing all the fire about the temple, they received and gave judgment."

This was the time of the cult of the Mother Goddess, in its latter phase when the king was beginning to become prominent. The Minoan family is thought to have been in the nature of a clan, rather than the limited group of today. Birth was a mystery and the sexual act was apparently indulged in for pure pleasure with no realization of its reproductive function. Thus so many mythological births have no father, and perhaps this is why Adam did not understand the origin of the strange creature produced by Eve. Here the queen was divine, attired in the well-known tight-waisted dress baring the breasts, as if to emphasize the role of motherhood. I looked for evidence of this cult among the antiquities that lay before us, but there was none. Signs of the Mother Goddess cult are plentiful on

Crete, and I felt sure that we would eventually find them on Thera.

We paced our excavating with a number of rest periods, during which Dr. Marinatos provided us with his views on some interesting points of history and mythology. He believes that two mythological references derive from the Thera eruption. First, the plagues of Egypt, in which case he concurs with Dr. Galanopoulos. Secondly, the Greek legend of Zeus and Hera. The two were married, but Zeus loved Alcmene, daughter of the king of Argos, who bore their son, Hercules. Zeus wanted to stay with Alcmene, so he had the night prolonged three days because he knew that only under the cover of darkness could he evade Hera. These three days of darkness, Marinatos feels, refer to Thera.

Marinatos believes that the Minoans came from Asia and that central Asia was the source of all civilization. He supports this by reference to the largely Mongoloid eastern Russian population, the isolated white Ainus of Japan, and the evidence of Mongol features throughout the world.

He also believes that before the Thera destruction occurred, the people moved to Crete, their parent land. When the Cretan destruction occurred later, he thinks that the Cretans mostly moved to Pylos on the western Peloponnesus. Since the Aegean shores probably saw great destruction, the Cretan people would be inclined to settle on the western mainland which had not been destroyed. This is confirmed by strong evidence of Minoan culture in post-eruption Pylos.

After the destruction on Crete was over, the Pylians may have returned, says Marinatos, contributing to the Mycenaean resettlement of Knossos. I was fascinated by his theories, and admired his willingness to enter controversial areas. The study of preliterate history is exciting but frustrating. It is open to, and filled with, so many theories, while offering such little ground on which to stand. Scholars in this field tend to shun mythology and mysticism in order to keep their art respectable. Because they were thus boxed in, the discovery of Atlantis passed them by and fell into the laps of physical scientists, secure in their solidly based professions and able to dabble free of professional inhibition in other fields.

As one of those thus freed, I took a stab at theorizing on the evolution of the Minoans in the Aegean, to further tie together these people and the Atlanteans of Plato. About 2000 B.C., the Minoan palaces of Crete first appeared, and what meager archaeological evidence there is tells us that the few hundred years before this were notably poor. It is as if the Cretan palaces flowered overnight. On the other hand, the Cycladic islands took a turn toward advanced civilization during just this same period and possibly were ahead of Crete, though again the archaeological evidence is meager.

If indeed, before 2000 B.C., the Cyclades, including Thera of course, were the center of this early culture, and Crete was an agricultural backwater, it would be consistent with the Atlantis theory in which Thera is presented as the religious center and cultural source. The Cyclades were particularly rich in graves and Mother Goddess figurines. Their art was individualistic, yet imbued with a peaceful and Oriental feeling. The Cyclades were also rich in resources, copper, tin, lead, silver, and obsidian, and the people were active in maritime commerce, later dominated by the princes of Crete.

A theory that fits the known facts as well as any, and Atlantis as well, goes as follows: During the third millennium B.C., people from the east and the south gradually settled the islands, probably seeking the natural resources. They brought their Eastern cult of the Mother Goddess and established Thera as rather special. They traveled west and perhaps did the same on Malta. As more people moved into the Aegean, Crete was settled and a peaceful mercantile culture grew and prospered and eventually built palaces. Crete became the population center but Thera remained a religious metropolis, just as Plato described, and all this was Atlantis. Confirmation of this theory will depend upon extensive excavation of the pre-Minoan level at Thera, and in the finding of religious objects, particularly some evidence of the Mother Goddess cult.

The last day of the excavation was given over to filling in, cleaning and tagging all the smaller finds and storing them in the museum. The Colonels of the now ruling junta in Athens had called Marinatos, so he was obliged to leave, bequeathing all this work to Emily, who presided, Andreas Mavragiannis, the frescoes expert, and Mary and me.

Evangelos Baikas of Akroteri had this comment on the excavations just concluded: "This summer, my family could not work in the fields because of the ghosts. In the mountain that came from the sea there are ghosts where now they make the excavations. I saw them. One morning when I went to collect the tomatoes and it was not yet sunrise, a big white light covered a great ghost covered with a shield. Then there were many, all in movement, yet they looked firm. They went toward the sea in the direction opposite from the sunrise to escape from the light which goes toward the west."

Ghosts are quite real on Thera, though you would not at first expect this to be the case in such an open, sunny environment. But there is unquestionably an atavistic feeling about this society, an unconscious awareness, in the manner formally described by Jung, of the very ancient past. I came to wonder if it was because of this collective susceptibility that visual hallucination was so commonplace. The Theran popular mind moves easily from fact to myth, from present to past. And indeed why not, considering the cataclysmic experiences which demonstrably occurred long ago and which the people see reminders of in the frequent vulcanism that has plagued the island through history? It must be that at least a fraction of these people are in fact descendants of the Minoans or, more precisely, Atlanteans. In consequence, it is not at all surprising that from time to time they should react collectively in a way that betrays their amazing antiquity, and by so doing provide all manner of fleeting intimations of the Atlantean reality of long ago. Now we had scientific evidence to confirm their insight.

Shortly after we left Greece, I later learned, Marinatos found time to return to Thera for ten more days of excavation. He spent this time expanding trenches Alvaniti I and II. In Alvaniti I, where the row of large and colorful pithoi had been found, he discovered stone column bases and a hearth with kitchen implements. A large, beautifully shaped tripod cooking pot, incised mortars and grinding stones appeared near the hearth. This room was identified as a storeroom and was roofed over to protect those finds not removed to the museum from the winter rains. An excavation was made back beneath the cave which revealed walls 6 feet below the floor of the storeroom. The situation was so precarious here, with more than 20 feet of loose ash towering overhead ready to collapse, that digging was stopped as soon as one wall was uncovered.

Pieces of wood from the Phira quarry were sent to the University of Pennsylvania, where Beth Ralph carbon dated them at 1750–1520 B.C.

The final excavation, an enlargement of Alvaniti II, began with the finding of masses of exquisite shards, more abundant than at any other location. The designs painted on them were more complex and interesting than any previously found. Goblets in this group were surely precious and reserved for royalty. Here, about 100 feet south of the storeroom in Alvaniti I, Marinatos discovered the most monumental structure of the season, a north-south wall, 50 feet long, made of careful ashlar masonry, as was the palace façade of Bronos IA. The preserved height of the wall was over 6 feet. It was built of large, extremely brittle stones having a reddish tinge, as if the limestone had been damaged in an intense fire. Most curious of all was the fact that, even though the wall was buried deep in ash, it lay on top of soft ash, showing that it was built after an eruption had blanketed Akroteri. To cast some further light on this strange situation, a hole 7 feet deep was dug beneath the wall. It revealed older large stone rubble walls built on the weathered lava Minoan surface.

Thus there is firm evidence of substantial rebuilding of the palace at Akroteri after an initial destruction by earthquake and a mild ash eruption that partially covered the ruined buildings. So people remained on or returned to Thera after the warning earthquakes and even after ash had begun to fall. What made these people stick to their island with such tenacity, even after the soil may have been untenable for agriculture? There must have been an extremely strong bond. Could it have been religious? That would fit in what Plato said of the metropolis of Atlantis.

In my view we had confirmed much of Galanopoulos' theory that Thera was the metropolis of Atlantis, a heavily populated cult center having wealth and culture the equal of Crete. It remained to excavate Thera further, which promised not only more evidence of its Atlantean identity but the answers to many unanswered questions about the preliterate world of the Mediterranean.

CHAPTER 13

ON Wednesday evening, June 28, we boarded the *Kanaris* for Athens. Before leaving Athens for home, Mary, Emily, and I attended a special dinner meeting of the Society for the Promotion of Cycladic Studies. This was a great honor and we were impressed. Dr. Marinatos lectured on the results of the excavations and accolades were given by a distinguished group of dignitaries including Hieronymus, the new Archbishop of Greece. We were flattered by their mention of the part we Americans had played in the excavation. Even Colonel George Papadopoulos was there, then "minister to the prime minister," later to become prime minister himself. Colonel P. was Marinatos' direct superior.

The future looked bright; we had found Atlantis, and I anticipated excavating it like Pompeii. In our final conversation with Dr. Marinatos, we talked of publicizing the fabulous results so as to raise funds. He said that he would write a report for the Athens newspapers and send us a copy, after which we could feel free to create our American publicity. Mrs. Marinatos and he presented each of the ladies with a box of candy.

On July 7, 1967, Dr. Marinatos sent me the clipping of his front-page announcement in *Eleftheros Kosmos* and a note as follows:

Now, I believe, you will be able to write anything you wish. Do send me a copy. Next week, I will be very busy, hélas, for

257

archaeology all over Greece. Very many greetings to Mrs. Mavor from me and my wife. Yours sincerely, SP. MARINATOS.

This, sadly, was my last communication with this mercurial Greek. We had in hand this and the written permission from the Archaeological Society of Athens to publish text, photographs, and movies. Feeling fully authorized, Emily Vermeule and I, on July 18, 1967, held a press conference at the Museum of Fine Arts in Boston, where we handed out brief statements, talked about the wonders revealed on Thera and answered questions. Fully aware that it was important to emphasize Marinatos and the Greek role, we did so at every opportunity. The press release we wrote was headed: "A Minoan Pompeii and the Lost Atlantis," and went on to say: "The discovery of a Minoan 'Pompeii' in the Aegean Sea is one of the most startling archaeological events of the generation. A complete prehistoric town by the sea has been found. . . . The joint excavations of the Archaeological Society of Athens and a group of scientists from several American Institutions, under the direction of Professor Spyridon Marinatos of the University of Athens, began. . . ." At the end were listed the key people and their institutions. There was no question that we had given top billing to Marinatos.

The American press naturally played us up, since we were Americans, as much as it did Marinatos. The story gained front-page headlines all over the world on July 19 and several days thereafter. *Newsweek* on July 31 featured a page of colored photos from the excavation and *Time* on July 28 gave full-page coverage to the story. Both magazines, incidentally, were reasonably accurate in reporting. But the Italian press mixed up Marinatos and Galanopoulos, and on the front page of a Greek newspaper, of all places, appeared a story without even a mention of Marinatos' name! The article that he had published on July 7 had not been picked up internationally, as had ours, because it did not mention the magic word "Atlantis." Or so I guessed.

Emily and I concluding correctly that Marinatos would be offended, immediately wrote to him explaining what had happened, apologizing profusely for the press, over which we had no control. I tried to make him understand the benefits of the tremendous publicity our project had received. I was whistling in the wind.

The roof fell in with a Minoan crash. I soon received a curt communication from the Archaeological Society of Athens in formal Greek, a masterpiece of asperity. The letter said:

> The Athens Archaeological Society finds itself in the regretful position to announce to you that according to the unanimous decision of its Council taken at its meeting, 7 August, it is discontinuing entirely its collaboration with you in its excavations at Thera.
>
> The Council of the society has decided that your goals are evidently different and not in the furtherance of true knowledge. We thank you warmly for the offer of 60,000 drachmas for the execution of the excavations at Thera, which you deposited in the treasury of the Archaeological Society. . . . Now, however, the gift is deemed unacceptable and its exact sum has been deposited in your name.

This message was followed by a document from the government archaeological service canceling my permission to do underwater research at Thera, obtained in 1966.

For some months after my official banishment from Thera Emily and I wrote letters to Marinatos. He answered none of mine. As a gesture of goodwill, we arranged to have him invited to the annual meeting of the Archaeological Institute of America. He declined to come, but sent a paper that Emily read to the prestigious assembly. Occasional press interviews became my principal source of information about his feelings.

The Athens press published a report attributed to Marinatos that was designed to correct "certain inaccuracies" that had appeared internationally. It pointed out that the excavations at Thera were conducted by the Archaeological Society of

Athens, under his leadership. And it disdained "any exaggerated attempts" to connect the excavations with tales about Atlantis.

However, in an interview published in an Italian magazine in September, 1967, he grudgingly took another position.

"Atlantis, Atlantis," he is reported as saying, "all want to know if this is Atlantis. I say only that these palaces could be also as important as Knossos in Crete. Atlantis. There are 2,300 years since Plato wrote. I used to think that Atlantis could be only a concept of Platonic perfection of the government of a state."

When pressed, he indicated a change of mind. He spoke of "the cyclopean walls, marvelously constructed," of frescoes, and of "a great cataclysm that buried a great city." The interviewer persisted, and there was this exchange between them:

"You are convinced that this is Atlantis?"

"I am convinced. . . ."

Eventually the New York *Times* reported, under a headline reading Non-Greeks Barred from Dig on Thera:

> Greek excavation of a prehistoric site on the Aegean island of Thera will be barred to all foreign archaeologists this year, Greece's Antiquities Department announced today.
>
> The ban was imposed because of an incident that occurred last summer, when an American scientific team was taking part in the digs. The team made public its results before the director of excavations, Prof. Spyridon Marinatos, had made his official communication to the Greek Archaeological Society. This is regarded here as a serious breach of archaeological ethics. . . .
>
> The American team, led by Dr. James W. Mavor of the WHOI was working to check a theory that Thera was part of Atlantis, the legendary continent. On returning to the United States, the team said that the discovery of a settlement had more or less confirmed the theory.
>
> Professor Marinatos, who is now Inspector General of Greek Antiquities, contests the American team's thesis.

Paradoxically I felt more of a kinship with Dr. Marinatos than with some of the other archaeologists I had met, for he did have a broader view than his colleagues of the needs of the Thera project, however difficult he found it to implement them. In spite of our differences, I hold great respect for this man's ability and historical insight.

Although I would not be returning to Thera, at least for a time, I hoped some foreign assistance would be accepted by Marinatos for coming excavations. I became convinced that much sophisticated technical support and coordinated effort in many branches of science will be needed to unravel the secrets locked in Thera, not only further evidences of Atlantis, but scientific data important to a reconstruction of the history of the entire Near East and, indeed, all Europe in the period 3000 to 1000 B.C.

I felt that the work at Thera had to be an integrated part of widespread archaeological, oceanographic, geological, and meteorological work, with communication between people in many countries in different fields. I hoped that government authorities might eventually see the Thera research in this light. Any piecemeal approach to this truly massive task would be a waste of time.

In the meantime there are other countries where the wide Atlantean sphere of influence might be explored. With Plato's story as a guide, there are trails to follow radiating in all directions from the Aegean. There are the ancient settlements of North Africa in Libya and Tunisia, the route of the megalith builders, Egypt, the Levantine countries, particularly the coastal Phoenician cities, Iraq, Iran, the Indus Valley, Afghanistan, and the lands surrounding the Black and Caspian seas. As we follow and relate the peoples of second-millennium Europe, Asia, and Africa, Plato's story of Atlantis becomes, conceivably, one of the most important historical documents of this period.

In 1965 I set out to find confirmation of Dr. Galanopoulos' theory of Atlantis. Since then, I have assembled many parts of this proof, some lying fallow in the literature, some from the thoughts of others, some from discoveries in the earth and under the sea. I have, in addition, extended the theory and shown some of the value of Atlantis as a historical document.

What has been contributed to our knowledge of Atlantis since that fateful day in 1965 when I met Dr. Galanopoulos?

First of all, there has been the gathering together of the geological and archaeological evidence that the eruption and collapse of Thera was truly an earthshaking event capable of destroying an Atlantis reduced to a manageable size from the exaggerated dimensions reported by Plato. Included in the material gathered were the results of the original research carried out during my expeditions of 1966 and 1967 to Thera, the underwater seismic profiles, geological surveys and archaeological discoveries on land and sea.

Having, then, a satisfactory explanation for this most crucial and unique facet of the Atlantis legend, I went on to seek confirmation of the remainder of the theory of Dr. Galanopoulos and, in the process, to extend it.

I have suggested that the Atlantis myth is the central one of a great body of related myth pertaining to the great Thera destruction, the Minoans and their sea empire, the Mycenaean Greeks and their conflicts with the Minoans, and the origins of the Aegean peoples. Also, I have proposed that the Atlantis story can lead us to an understanding of the migrations and other cultural dispersions of Near Eastern and European peoples as far from the Aegean, conceivably, as the British Isles.

In 1966 our expedition to Thera found that the island had been a complex of many volcanic cones before the great collapse and may have had internal waterways approximating those in Plato's description of the Atlantean metropolis. We showed also that there had been a great collapse to the south of Akroteri involving the entire south coast in a land slump. This would increase the size of the cataclysm beyond that estimated by Galanopoulos and also possibly provide a landing on the south for the Atlantean ships sheltered from the prevailing westerly winds.

Extensive habitation on Thera beyond what had ever been anticipated was proved in our 1966 land survey, as well as during the 1967 archaeological survey and excavation. Fertile soil, lush vegetation, lakes and marshes did exist on Thera in prehistory, as Plato said of Atlantis. The find of a fossil monkey head convinced me that royalty had at least visited the island.

In 1967 a Minoan palace and a large town were discovered buried in the ash blanket near Akroteri. This proved that royalty had lived on Thera and enjoyed wealth and a standard of living the equal of Minoan Crete. Why did they live on this small island? I concluded that they did so because Thera was a strategic center of maritime commerce and was probably a cult center, as Plato said of the metropolis of Atlantis. Thera, a pre-Minoan Cycladic center in the days when the Cyclades were culturally ahead of Crete, may have enjoyed a religious prominence, as the only active volcano in the Aegean, which persisted through Minoan times.

Having gathered the myths together, I then related them to each other and to the historical pattern derived from archaeological finds.

The relationship between the island-dwelling Minoans and the mainland Mycenaean Greeks was one of intermittent conflict, increasing as these Eastern and Western peoples intermingled and the islanders absorbed the European warlike habits of the Mycenaeans. The mainland was populated primarily by tribes from the north, whereas the Aegean islanders came from the east and south. This mixing, some say, created the highly individualistic Greek of classical times and today. As Plato said, the Atlanteans became base and warlike and made war on the ancient Athenians.

The Atlantean sphere of influence extended throughout the Mediterranean and north into the European continent, says Plato. So did the Minoans, say the archaeologists, even as far as Great Britain and Denmark. How the megalith builders transmitted their curious ritual we do not know, but it does seem to have originated in the Aegean with the Neolithic islanders about 3000 B.C. and to have persisted up to 1400 B.C. The Atlanteans, in their role as Minoans, could have influenced the spread of the megaliths.

The evolution of religious practices in the Aegean is known through artifacts, the worship of nature evolving to a mother goddess, a boy-god, the bull sacrifice and a divine queen with consort at the peak of the Minoan period. This is just the picture given by Plato's Atlantis. Some say that there is no surer way to trace the origins of an ancient people than through their religious beliefs and practices.

Plato's story of Atlantis, as recorded by Egyptian priests and brought to Greece by Solon, includes a geographical description of the islands and their people. It also describes the people of prehistoric Greece and the island empire, their political and social ways and their religious beliefs and practices. It tells of a conflict between the Atlanteans, who had changed from a virtuous and peaceloving people to base and warlike, and the mainland Greeks. After the Atlanteans are defeated in battle, their island sinks beneath the sea and the army of the Greeks is swallowed up by the land.

These are the essentials of Plato's story and I believe that our work on Thera has substantiated them as credible history. I am all the more convinced because, even as I write this in midsummer, 1968, word has just come to me from Greece that the throne room of the palace at Akroteri may have been found with its marble throne similar to that in the palace of Minos on Crete. If true, it is key proof of a flourishing pre-eruption Thera and identifies with the Platonic descriptions of Atlantis. The 1968 excavations by the Greek government have extended the trenches started the year before, and as we did then, have revealed more palace walls and more elegant pottery. A pharmacy was discovered with mortars, scales, weights, and pots with painted representations of the herb sage. Recent excavations at Zakros revealed similar finds. Plato said of Atlantis: "Also whatever fragrant things there are in the earth, whether roots or herbage, or woods, or distilling drops of flowers or fruits, grew and thrived in that land." In addition, our find in 1966 of a fossilized monkey skull was supported by the discovery of a painting of a blue monkey on a potsherd.

Unfortunately, the work is inadequately engineered, funded and staffed, and they have run into problems. The ash has caved in, preventing deeper and wider excavations. The winter rains have damaged last year's sites left unprotected. A few foreign observers were permitted in 1968. These included my friends Emily Vermeule and George Bass.

I am confident that in due course all manner of artifacts will be laboriously collected—religious statuary, inscriptions, frescoes of unparalleled beauty depicting Atlantean scenes, bits of pottery by the thousands—to provide the additive kind of proof peculiar to a subscience like archaeology. However, my excursions to Thera have convinced me that the Galanopoulos model of the origins of the Atlantean myth must of necessity anticipate actual physical findings, and that these, with the aid of shovel, earth-movers, mine railways and cars, cranes, conveyors and the like, will be brought forth and housed in museums.

The solution of the mystery of Atlantis should also, in my view, encourage the wider application of physical science to understanding these prehistoric memories, so as to re-create the topography, the weather, the climate, the ocean currents, the shorelines, the soil, the complete environmental situation out of which the myths sprang. This unquestionably can be done, in many cases, not only in the Aegean but throughout the world. Once this is done, the problem is at least oriented in space and time, with a clear set of coordinates established against which to test the conventional archaeological evidence. Such has been done with the myth of Atlantis.

MEGALITHIC TOMBS OF ANCIENT EUROPE

Appendices

APPENDIX A: Chronology of the Thera Eruption and Collapse and the Minoan Destruction

Introduction

The fifteenth century B.C. has been stated as the date of the Thera eruption and its effects. This is based primarily on stylistic and stratigraphical comparisons between artifacts found on Thera, on Crete, and in Egypt. But there remains the possibility, though a slim one, that the eruption and its effects occurred one or two centuries later, or that the volcanic cataclysms and earthquakes started before 1500 B.C. and continued into the fourteenth and thirteenth centuries B.C.

In any case, the most dependable calendar at the time of the Thera eruption existed in Egypt and our primary dating depends on how closely we can relate the eruption to this calendar.

Egyptian Chronology

Egyptian chronology represents our most accurate detailed statement of prehistoric chronology. It is better than carbon 14 dating. In fact the carbon 14 method was first verified using Egyptian chronology and is, in some areas, calibrated by it. Much archaeological spadework, study of hieroglyphs, and reference to astronomical observations have allowed us to construct a king list. The inscriptions give us the length of reign of most of the kings, and events were dated by the year of a given king's reign.

The best place from which to count backward from a well-established date to the Thera eruption is the Persian invasion of Egypt in 525 B.C. This is well documented in international records, and from it back to the beginning of the 18th Dynasty there is a quite complete record. Fortunately this is as far as we need go to date the Thera eruption and its effects.

Sirius, the Dog Star, which the Greeks called Sothis, came to be regarded by the Egyptians as related to the annual inundation of the Nile, and the annual rising of this star was called the opening of the year. We know that in Roman times a Sothic cycle, the coincidence of the rising of the Dog Star and the first day of the civil calendar, began in A.D. 139. We can calculate that the previous cycle started in 1322 B.C. and the cycle before that in 2782 B.C. Looking into contemporary records we find mention of the Dog Star on a date in the 12th Dynasty and again in the 18th Dynasty. Thus we have, at these two points, well-established dates. If we compare these astronomical dates wtih our dead-reckoning process, in which we count back by lengths of kings' reigns, we find that they agree.

Our date 1322, then, which is quite near that of the Thera eruption, gives us considerable confidence in the dates of any ties to the Egyptian dynasties in the form of artifacts found on Thera and Crete which can be established as of Egyptian origin or vice versa. This type of dating would be expected to be the most accurate and indeed it has been used as the basis for our best estimates of the date of the eruption.

Radiocarbon Dating

Most widely used and, to date, most successful of the modern scientific dating methods is the radiocarbon 14 process by which we measure the disintegration rate of radiocarbon in organic remains —a piece of wood, say. This rate when compared with that of the background inventory rate of radiocarbon 14 disintegration is a measure of the time since the organic material died.

Unfortunately, useful as this method has been, it has two drawbacks that render it inadequate for precision dating, which is required to date the sequence of and time intervals between phases of the Thera eruption. First, the probable error of the date given by the laboratory seldom falls below plus or minus 200 years for the period 3,500 years ago for a single sample. Second, the wood being tested may be from a tree that was felled and cut into beams hundreds of years before the antiquities were made with which the wooden beam was found.

The accuracy of radiocarbon 14 isotopic dating depends upon the accuracy of the counting of the particle emission rate of the sample relative to the background radiation. This is generally plus or minus 3 percent with a probability that the true value will lie within this range 68 percent of the time. It also depends upon the figure for the half-life of the radiocarbon 14 which is used.

Since the method was published in 1952, the best estimate of the half-life has been increased from 5,568 to 5,730 years. The accuracy also depends on variations in the radiocarbon 14 inventory on the earth's surface, which was originally assumed constant and has since been found, by tree ring studies, to vary from place to place and time to time. A current procedure for interpreting radiocarbon 14 dates in the absence of local specific information on the half-life and inventory is to add 3 percent to the value calculated in the laboratory and then to double the error calculated in the laboratory. In the case of a time about 1500 B.C., 3,500 years ago, the range of values within which the true value should lie about 75 percent of the time is about plus or minus 200 years for a single sample.

A way of improving the accuracy is to take more samples from the same circumstances, but this is expensive and removes only a part of the error. In other words, radiocarbon 14 dating is best suited to more general dating requirements and has, in some cases, resulted in a fairly extreme reassessment of the chronology of man. One of these bears heavily on Plato's Atlantis chronology. It is thanks to radiocarbon 14 that we now know that the last ice age ended closer to 10,000 years than 20,000 years ago, a fact that would have made things quite cold in the earth's present temperate zone and not at all conducive to the lush vegetation and luxurious climate that Plato describes: "Twice in the year they gathered the fruits of the earth." With radiocarbon 14 we can now be reasonably certain that the climate outside the Gates of Hercules 10,000 years ago was close to that of Iceland and would have required a way of life quite different from that of Plato's Atlanteans. For more precise dating needs, however, radiocarbon 14 is not so helpful.

Thermoluminescence Dating

Another laboratory method is thermoluminescence dating, which is used with potsherds and can determine the number of years from the time the pottery was actually fired to the present. Unfortunately, ceramic antiques were as fashionable in Minoan times as they are today. But some pottery, particularly kitchenware, was probably made by the people who used it. This method of dating, however, is less accurate than the radiocarbon 14 method, requires destruction of a potsherd, and cannot be applied to Greek pottery until there is a suitable laboratory in Greece.

Other Dating Methods

Historical and archaeological evidence provide most of the information used for establishing the chronologies of ancient times. Dating of artifacts by stratification and style remains our most precise and reliable dating method, though it is by nature relative and must be tied to an absolute reference established by history or radiocarbon 14 dating. On the whole, chronologies are established more by quantities of evidence than by quality.

The dates for the reigns of the Egyptian pharaohs have been established with some confidence, allowing us to date the artifacts found in their tombs. For example, comparing Minoan pottery found in the tomb of Senmut, contemporary with Queen Hatshepsut, who, we know with some accuracy, reigned 1504–1483 B.C., with similar pottery found elsewhere, we can reasonably assume that artifacts found with it date from the same period. After considerable evidence has been collected, a chronology emerges by which we may conclude that Minoan culture was in such and such a phase at such and such a time. Unfortunately, there exists considerable disagreement among archaeologists, historians, and philologists about the Aegean chronology from about 1500 to 1200 B.C. Perhaps one day it will be determined that Thera itself is responsible for this confusion, having so shaken the ancient world that many of the antiquities became interstratified.

But, whatever chonology is finally accepted, the fact of Thera's eruption and collapse cannot be denied nor its destructive power underestimated.

The detailed evidence of the dates of the Thera eruption and collapse is presented below in Tables I–VI. Dates are classified as follows:

AC   Absolute chronology
EARC   Established Aegean Relative Chronology
ERC   Egyptian Relative Chronology

Table VII summarizes the chronological picture.

TABLE I

Volcanic Destruction of Thera

The evidence of the date of the beginning of the volcanic destruction is given by six events.

1622–1422 B.C. (AC) From a tree found in the Phira quarry in 1956 by A. Galanopoulos, two RC 14 samples were dated by Lamont Geological Observatory. The first gave 3050 ± 150 before A.D. 1950. The material was then found to be contaminated by humic acid, which was removed from the second sample, giving a date of 3370 ± 100 before 1950. Applying a 3 percent correction and converting, the result was 1522 ± 100 B.C. with a probability of 68 percent.

1750–1520 B.C. RC 14 date from wood samples found in Phira quarry in 1967. Dating by E. Ralph, University of Pennsylvania.

1550–1475 B.C. (EARC) Thera excavations of 1867–1872 pottery was dated by Marinatos to last years of Late Minoan I period or 1500 B.C. (The LM I pottery style has been extended by some scholars as late as 1400 B.C. or the Cretan destruction date.)

1550–1475 B.C. (EARC) Thera excavations of 1967 revealed pottery of Middle Minoan and Late Minoan IA styles with a latest date of 1500 B.C.

1650–1500 B.C. (EARC) Inlaid sword contemporary with Mycenaean shaft graves attributed to Thera.

After 3000 B.C. (AC) Deep-sea cores radiocarbon-dated by ash and organic stratigraphy.

The dates above apply to the cessation of culture on the island, except for the last, which dates the great ash eruption. Probably, most of the inhabitants left after a large-scale earthquake. This was followed in a maximum of a few years by the first phase of the eruption, the fall of 3 to 5 meters of pink pumice stone.

A second earthquake then occurred and after that the large ash eruption in which up to 40 meters of ash was laid down on Thera and substantial amounts over other land areas of the eastern Mediterranean. The collapse of Thera, which followed the ash fall, was accompanied by great seismic sea waves (tsunamis), which were felt as far away as Egypt.

The date of the beginning of this period of volcanic and tectonic activity is most accurately given at present by the pottery style (1500 B.C.). The duration of the period is best given by the evidence of destruction on Crete, which occurs as tsunami destruction of coastal settlements and earthquake destruction of structures all over the eastern half of Crete. Agricultural destruction due to ash fall is indicated by ash in deep-sea cores and on Thera. However, there is no direct evidence from Crete as yet, though there is every expectation, in line with evidence offered by deep-sea cores, that such will be found.

Galanopoulos first provided the explanations for the time gap between the beginning of the Thera eruption and the Cretan destruction. He wrote that the eruption occurred in interrupted phases over a period of several decades with the *coup de grâce* coming at the end of the collapse and the tsunamis. His theory that earthquakes between Crete and Thera triggered the eruption were confirmed by my observations in 1967.

TABLE II

Dates of the Cretan Destruction

Let us examine the evidence of the date of the Cretan destruction. Here, dates are labeled A for more credible and B for less credible. A evidence directly relates Crete to the Egyptian chronology. B is evidence where a Mycenaean-Minoan link is required or it is necessary to assume that Egyptian tombs contained current pottery styles, considerations that make the evidence less credible.

After 1410 B.C. (ERC) (A) A seal of Queen Tye, wife of Amenhotep III (1410–1372 B.C.) is the latest datable object found on Crete stratified as predestruction. It was found in a chamber tomb with LM IB pottery at Hagia Triada, the palace in southern Crete. Hagia Triada was probably destroyed by earthquake before or after the Thera tsunamis. Thus this date represents the Hagia Triada destruction.

After 1410 B.C. (ERC) (B) An Amenhotep III inscribed plaque and a scarab inscribed to Queen Tye were found at Mycenae with Late Helladic III pottery. LH III pottery style covers the period 1400–1150 B.C. (EARC) and is considered contemporary with the post-destruction Knossian and other Cretan Minoan pottery. The dates 1400–1372 B.C., then, represent a time before or during the manufacture of LH III pottery. Assuming that the beginning of LH III and LM III pottery is contemporary, the destruction of Knossos and some other Cretan sites probably, but not necessarily, occurred after 1410 B.C.

Before 1358 B.C. (ERC) (A) Late Helladic III pottery was found at Tell el 'Amarna, an Egyptian settlement datable to 1375–1358 B.C., the period of the new palace of Akhenaton. The same type of LH III pottery was also found at Knossos immediately on top of debris from the great fire; therefore the Knossos destruction is datable before 1358 B.C.

After 1460 B.C. (ERC) (A) A Minoan alabaster vase whose inscription is inferred to mention Thutmose III in the period 1460–1450 B.C. was found at Katsaba, the harbor town of Knossos. The pottery style shows traces of LM IB, LM II, and LM IIIA, dating it just predestruction at Knossos. Thus, Knossos' destruction occurred after 1460 B.C.

After 1460 B.C. (ERC) (A) The tomb of Rekhmire, successor to User-Amon, grand vizier to Thutmose III, in Egypt, was closed about 1450 B.C. plus or minus 10 years in ERC. Keftiu representations therein were shown with LM IB vases, dating Cretan destruction after 1460 B.C.

After 1504 B.C. (ERC) (B) The tomb of Senmut in Egypt contains Keftiu representations with LM IA vases. Since Senmut was contemporary with Hatshepsut (1505–1483), Cretan destruction occurred after 1504 B.C.

After 1410 B.C. (ERC) (B) Faience vase inscribed to Amenhotep III (1410–1372) was found at Mycenae in a LH IIIA or IIIB pottery context. General Cretan destruction is therefore probably after 1410 B.C.

After 1450 B.C. (ERC) (B) The tomb of Menkhrperrasenb, son of Rekhmire, contains representations of Keftiu with well-advanced LM IB pottery. These date the destruction to after 1450 B.C.

After 1504 B.C. (ERC) (B) An alabaster vase of LM IB type was found at Sedment in Egypt in a Thutmose III context though not inscribed to him. This dates the destruction after 1504 B.C.

After 1504 B.C. (ERC) (B) A Hatshepsut scarab was found at Prosymna in Greece with LH I pottery. This would date the general destruction after 1504 B.C.

After 1450 B.C. (ERC) (B) A blue glass-paste ape was found at Mycenae bearing the cartouche of Amenhotep II (1450–1423) in an LH IIIA pottery context, or just before the Cretan general destruction. This dates the destruction, assuming the LH III-LM III link, to after 1450 B.C.

After 1504 B.C. (ERC) (B) Keftiu are represented in the Egyptian tomb of User-Amon with LM IA rhyta and cups. This places the destruction after 1504 B.C.

1511–1130 B.C. (AC) Destruction of the palace at Kato Zakro is dated by radiocarbon 14 to 1180 ± 120. If this is given a 3 percent addition and the error doubled, it becomes 1271 ± 240. Platon considers Zakro fell at the same time as other Cretan settlements and prefers the date 1450 B.C.

Archaeologists feel that the general destruction on Crete was complete in a relatively short time, a decade or two at the most. During this period the tsunamis and earthquakes occurred, but the effect of the ashfall remains uncertain. The ash was probably ejected during a number of eruptions over a period of decades, based on the analogy of Krakatoa, with one or more gigantic eruptions near the end of the period. The earlier phases, including the pumice fall, may not have disrupted Cretan life. Summarizing the destruction evidence:

1. Hagia Triada   after 1410 B.C. (A)
2. Knossos   " 1410 B.C. (C)
3. Knossos   *before 1358* B.C. (A)

4.	Knossos	after	1460 B.C.	(A)
5.	Crete	"	1460 B.C.	(A)
6.	Crete	"	1504 B.C.	(B)
7.	Crete	"	1410 B.C.	(C)
8.	Crete	"	1450 B.C.	(B)
9.	Crete	"	1504 B.C.	(B)
10.	Crete	"	1504 B.C.	(B)
11.	Crete	"	1450 B.C.	(B)
12.	Crete	"	1504 B.C.	(B)
13.	Zakro		1511–1130 B.C.	(A)

A preponderance of evidence sufficient for acceptance dates the destruction after 1450 and probably near 1400 due to the absence of data indicating a later date. Only one item of evidence specifies a date later than which it could not have occurred, 1358 B.C. This still leaves open the possibility that the destruction could have been later. After examining some of the later chronology, the possibilities of a later date for the destruction will be explored, keeping in mind its effect on the established framework.

Other major items of chronological evidence which play a part in a reasonable historical reconstruction are listed below:

TABLE III

Egyptian-Minoan-Mycenaean Ties

1570–1349 B.C. (ERC) 18th Dynasty scarab found at Koukounara with LH I-II pottery.

1301–1224 B.C. (ERC) Rameses II scarab found at Perati in a LH III B-C context includes the dates in the period of these pottery styles.

1550–1450 B.C. (ERC) Cups similar to those carried by Keftiu in Egyptian tomb representations found in LH I sites at Peristeria and Vapheio. This serves to date the LH I period.

1570–1545 B.C. (ERC) Minoan fresco themes first appear in Egypt during reign of Ahmose, first pharaoh of the 18th Dynasty.

Ties are established through artifacts found in the shaft graves, tholoi, and chamber tombs of Mycenae. The first circle of shaft graves,

A, found by Schliemann, contains 6 graves identified as I–VI. The other circle of graves, B, was discovered in 1951 and contains 14 graves. The dates of the two circles overlap and are given as 1650–1550 (EARC) with limited confidence. Vermeule reports beginning of shaft grave era MM III, with circle A terminating in 1504 (Hatshepsut) and circle B beginning about 1550.

1504–1480 B.C. (ERC) at Prosymna, a seal of Hatshepsut and infancy of Thutmose III was found.

1670–1570 B.C. (EARC) Disputed MM III shards were found in shaft graves IV and V at Mycenae.

Before 1670 B.C. (EARC) Shaft grave VI at Mycenae contains MH II pottery dating the graves at before 1670. B.C.

1530–1400 B.C. (EARC) Shaft grave I at Mycenae contains LH IB and LM II pottery dating this grave.

1450 B.C. (EARC) Earliest date of Knossos Linear B tablets, per Evans.

1200–1150 B.C. (EARC) Date of Linear B tablets found at Knossos, per L. S. Palmer. (Tablets probably were used earlier as well.)

1200 B.C. (EARC) Pylos Linear B tablets, per Blegen. On philological basis, Linear B tablets of Knossos and Pylos are contemporary, or Pylos' are earlier.

TABLE IV

Possible Historical Repercussions of Thera Eruption and Its Effects Which Can Be Dated Approximately or Better

1450 B.C. (ERC) A stela found by Riesner at Gebel Barkel in the Sudan, dated to 1457 or 1443 B.C., relates events of the first and eighth campaigns of Thutmose III. A description given may be an eyewitness account of a great eruption of Thera.

1406–1358 B.C. (ERC) Internationalism and monotheism in Egypt during reigns of Amenhotep III and Akhenaten.

1400–1300 B.C. (ERC) Habiru invasion of Egypt.

1450–1400 B.C. Plagues of Egypt probably occurred during reigns of Thutmose III, Amenhotep II and/or Thutmose IV.

1234–1222 B.C. Exodus of Israelites from Nile Delta if Merneptah was pharaoh (accepted by many but doubtful).

1314 B.C. Exodus of Israelites. Rabinnic date.

1440 B.C. Exodus of Israelites from Bible, Kings.

1572 B.C. Exodus of Israelites from Bible, Judges.

1451–1426 B.C. Exodus of Israelites if Amenhotep II was pharaoh.

1490 B.C. Destruction of Atlantis (Galanopoulos Theory).

1529–1382 B.C. Flood of Deucalion by Parian marble.

1450 B.C. (ERC) Thera tsunami may have coincided with death of Thutmose III.

TABLE V

Evidence of the Chronology of Other Events

1400–1300 B.C. Founding of the palace at Thebes and the Cadmian settlement on Thera. Traditional date (Parian marble) for the settlement of Thebes by the Phoenicians is 1519, but Herodotus implies a post-eruption landing and settlement on Thera by Cadmus with continuous habitation thereafter. Fourteenth century date for Thebes is based on artifacts.

1250 B.C. Destruction of Thebes given by Mylonas and consistent with mythology.

1234–1222 B.C. (ERC) Sea Peoples attack Egypt. Their identification is contested but they are generally thought to have come from Anatolia or as far south as Palestine.

1350–1275 B.C. In Syrian Alalakh, frescoes, lamps, and pottery imitating MM III-LM I designs.

1250 B.C. Nuzi pots like LM II palace style found at Alalakh in 1250 B.C. context. They were originally thought to be contemporary with Knossos originals but now are considered later copies.

1200 B.C. Alalakh destroyed by invasion of the Sea Peoples.

Soon after 1200 B.C. Founding of Posideium by Ampilochus reported by Herodotus. Posideium, considered port of Alalakh, Sabouni, and al Mina.

Tradition tells of many tribes and foreign rulers such as Cadmus the Phoenician, Kekrops at Athens, Danaos the Egyptian, Argos, and Aiolos in Thessaly before the flood. All these are traditionally ascribed to the sixteenth or fifteenth century. It is interesting that the highest period of the shaft graves at Mycenae was after 1500 B.C.

1450–1400 B.C. Destruction of Ugarit, possibly from the Thera tsunamis.

1200 B.C. Fall of Pylos.

1200 B.C. Beginning of the great Mediterranean drought, as suggested by Carpenter.

1200 B.C. The "Dorian Invasion," which may not have been an invasion at all, but the drought manifested in society. The "Dorians" are known only by their language, no pottery, no representations.

1580 B.C. Hyksos expelled from Egypt.

1184 B.C. Fall of Troy, Eratosthenes.

1260 B.C. Fall of Troy, Blegen.

1100 B.C. Fall of Mycenae, Mylonas.

1100–900 B.C. Dark ages in Greece.

The period 1400–1100 B.C., associated by most scholars with the LM III and LH III (Table VII) pottery styles, is controversial as to what occurred, and when and why it occurred, throughout the eastern Mediterranean area. It has been suggested that the period be shortened by 100 to 150 years, but the disruption which this would cause in established chronologies has discouraged serious analysis of its possibilities. This is a period of great international trade, yet in

Mycenaean Greece and Crete, art forms show stiffness of style, tradition, and less individuality than the pre-1400 Minoan. The styles are dull and do not change as rapidly as the Minoan. The assumption of a 300-year period of Mycenaean domination of Crete is in part responsible for the feeling of slowed change, and itself suggests that perhaps the period was in fact shorter.

L. R. Palmer, a philologist, has stirred controversy because he has questioned the accuracy of some of Evans' stratigraphic reports at Knossos. He believes that all the Linear B tablets that can be dated by stratification in a pottery context are of the end of the LM IIIB period (1200–1150 B.C.), and that they were baked in a destructive fire at that time. He accepts the great destruction of 1400 as well as the thesis that Linear B was in use on Crete as early as 1400 B.C. Only current tablets were preserved and only those baked in a destructive fire would survive more than a few decades. He agrees with C. W. Blegen that Knossos in the LM III period was a Mycenaean dynasty of importance and contemporary with Mycenae and Pylos, a widely accepted view. There was indeed a conflagration in the Knossos little palace datable to the end of LM IIIB or 1200 B.C.

There was much movement of peoples in the Near and Middle East from 1400 to 1100 B.C. This was probably the direct effect of economic and political factors, but over all hangs the pall of the known Thera catastrophe and Carpenter's theory of a great drought. Whether the two events were in any way related is unknown. Perhaps they were a part of a natural physical change having worldwide effects.

As for the possible compression of the period 1400–1100 B.C., the dating of the many events of 1200–1100 B.C. is much better established than the 1400 date of the Cretan destruction. However, the suggestion to compress remains speculative in the absence of a preponderance of convincing evidence.

TABLE VI

The Major Events from 1550–1100 B.C. Related to the Thera Eruption Are Reconstructed Below in a Tentative Chronology

1550–1500 B.C. A great earthquake shook Thera. On Crete this was perhaps felt as the division between the MM and LM periods which spurred development on Crete. The usually accepted date for this event is somewhat earlier, 1600–1550, however.

In *The Palace of Minos,* Evans stated that the shock, as in most Cretan earthquakes, came from the north as is shown by cracks in buildings which start at ground level on the north and travel diagonally south and upward. Hutchinson suggests that the epicenter was probably at or near Thera. The southern portion of Thera may have been evacuated or, at least, there was a large exodus of people after this quake. If this Thera quake and the MM-LM Cretan earthquake are the same, then Theran pottery would be classified MM rather than LM and show that Theran ware was at least as highly developed as the Cretan. Following the earthquake, the palace at Knossos was rebuilt. Platon calls this the start of the New Palace period and dates it at 1600 B.C. There followed a time of flourishing Minoan art and architecture, with mainland influence not being very prominent until LM II.

It is tempting to make the bold suggestion that many of the Therans (the island is now known to have been heavily populated) left Thera after the earthquake with their valuable belongings and moved south to Crete, to participate there in the rebuilding of the palaces and the resurgence of culture.

1525–1475 B.C. First phase of Thera eruption, during which 3 to 5 meters of pink-tinted angular pumice stone fell on much of the island.

1525–1475 B.C. Another earthquake occurred on Thera following a quiet period of a few decades during which most of the island was uninhabited.

1525–1440 B.C. The Thera volcanic vents erupted fine white ash and lapilli over a period of decades intermittently, but possibly over a very short period. At least one very violent phase occurred at the end of the period whose effects were widely felt.

1450–1390 B.C. Collapse of Thera followed immediately by gigantic tsunamis, possibly three or more in number. This probably was complete in hours, though a period of years is not excluded. Earthquake could have triggered the eruptions and/or the collapse, as Galanopoulos points out. Cretan palaces and towns were destroyed. The coastal settlements were probably destroyed by the seismic sea waves accompanying the collapse of Thera, as suggested by Marinatos in 1939. Earthquakes within a few years before or after this most likely destroyed the remaining settlements, notably Knossos, Phaistos, Hagia Triada, and Archanes.

1450–1400 B.C. Ugarit destruction probably caused by seismic sea waves.

1525–1440 B.C. Plagues of Egypt, most likely during the reign of Thutmose III and during the life of Moses.

1450–1400 B.C. Exodus of Israelites from Nile Delta, probably during reign of Thutmose III, Amenhotep II, or Thutmose IV.

1406–1358 B.C. Internationalism and monotheism in Egypt during reigns of Amenhotep III and Akhenaten, possibly related to Thera eruption.

1400–1300 B.C. Habiru invasion of Egypt, possibly related to Thera eruption.

1450–1350 B.C. Cretans find refuge in Levant, Pylos, Tyrrhenia, Africa.

1250–1100 B.C. Fall of Pylos, Mycenae, Troy, Thebes, Alalakh, etc.

1250–1150 B.C. Beginning of Mediterranean drought (Carpenter), and movement of people away from affected areas.

1275–1225 B.C. Sea People attack Egypt, probably during escape from drought.

TABLE VII

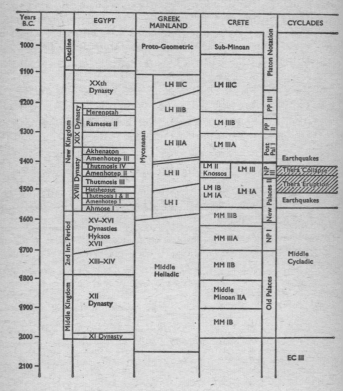

Years B.C.		EGYPT	GREEK MAINLAND	CRETE		CYCLADES
1000	Decline		Proto-Geometric	Sub-Minoan	Platon Notation	
1100						
1200	New Kingdom	XXth Dynasty	LH IIIC	LM IIIC	PP III	
			LH IIIB			
1300		XIX Dynasty — Merenptah / Rameses II		LM IIIB	PP II	
			LH IIIA	LM IIIA	Post Pal I	
1400		Akhenaton / Amenhotep III / Thutmosis IV		LM II Knossos / LM III	NP II	Earthquakes / Thera Collapse
	XVIII Dynasty	Amenhotep II / Thutmosis III	LH II			Thera Eruption
1500		Hatshepsut / Thutmosis I & II / Amenhotep I / Ahmose I	LH I	LM IB / LM IA / LM IA	New Palaces II	Earthquakes
1600	2nd Int. Period	XV–XVI Dynasties Hyksos XVII		MM IIIB	NP I	
1700		XIII–XIV	Middle Helladic	MM IIIA		Middle Cycladic
1800	Middle Kingdom	XII Dynasty		MM IIB	Old Palaces	
1900				Middle Minoan IIA		
2000		XI Dynasty		MM IB		
2100						EC III

Appendix B: Biblical References

The Exodus of the Israelites from Egypt

In Exodus 8:17 we read: "And it came to pass when the pharaoh had let the people go, that God led them not through the land of the Philistines although that was near, for God said, lest peradventure the people repent when they see war and they return to Egypt." Many scholars believe that the Philistines were people from

Crete represented in Egyptian inscriptions and paintings as ambassadors to the court of Egypt from the island of Crete or Caphtor, the people known as Keftiu. We can speculate that the Keftiu had left Crete because of the ash eruption and the deprivation of their land and settled in Egypt. Evidently, the Philistines or Cretans were considered enemies of the Israelites, who wished to avoid conflict with them during the Exodus.

After bypassing the Philistines, the Israelites camped before Pihahiroth, between Migdol and the sea over against Baalzephon. At this point the pharaoh pursued the Israelites with his army. He took 600 of his chosen chariots and all of the chariots of Egypt. Then occurred a strange event. Between the camp of the Egyptians and the camp of the Israelites there was a cloud and a darkness. It appeared this way to the Egyptians but to the Israelites it gave light by night. Presumably on the next day, and I quote from Exodus 14:21, "And Moses stretched out his hand over the sea; and the Lord caused the sea to go back by a strong east wind all that night and made the sea dry land, and the waters were divided."

Then in verses 22 through 30 we read:

[22] And the children of Israel went into the midst of the sea upon the dry ground; and the waters were a wall unto them on their right hand, and on their left.

[23] And the Egyptians pursued, and went in after them to the midst of the sea, even all Pharaoh's horses, his chariots and his horsemen.

[24] And it came to pass that in the morning watch the Lord looked into the host of the Egyptians through the pillar of fire and of the cloud, and troubled the host of the Egyptians.

[25] And took off their chariot wheels, that they drave them heavily; so that the Egyptians said, Let us flee from the face of Israel; for the Lord fighteth for them against the Egyptians.

[26] And the Lord said unto Moses, Stretch out thine hand over the sea, that the waters may come again upon the Egyptians, upon their chariots and upon their horsemen.

[27] And Moses stretched forth his hand over the sea, and the sea returned to his strength when the morning appeared; and the Egyptians fled against it, and the Lord overthrew the Egyptians in the midst of the sea.

[28] And the waters returned, and covered the chariots, and the horsemen, and all the host of Pharaoh that came into the sea after them; there remained not so much as one of them.

[29] But the children of Israel walked upon dry land in the midst of the sea, and the waters were a wall unto them on their right hand, and on their left.

[30] Thus the Lord saved Israel that day out of the hand of the Egyptians; and Israel saw the Egyptians dead upon the sea shore.

Biblical scholars have for many years supported the idea that the Israelites migrated through the Reed Sea or Yam Suf, not the Red Sea, as has often been thought. The Bible in fact says nothing about the Red Sea. It has been thought that *suf* means reed. If this is so, then the Yam Suf must have been a lake or lagoon, because it is well known that the reed does not grow in salt or brackish waters in the region of Suez. A script found at El Arish mentions that the reed sea was a lagoon between the cities of Romani and El Arish east of the Nile Delta. This lagoon extends parallel with the Mediterranean Sea (Fig. 40) and to the Kassion, today known as Kash Bouroun. In antiquity it was known as the Serbonis Sea. On today's maps, the lagoon is called the Sebcha el Bardawil. Herodotus, in his fascinating description of Egypt, says that the boundary of Egypt is at the Serbonis Sea, in which lived the giant Typhon, according to mythology. An account by Strabo states that the Serbonis Sea had a

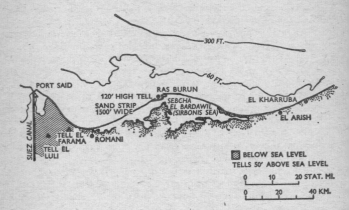

FIGURE 40. Sebcha el Bardawil. The Israelites are believed to have fled Egypt along the sand spit separating this lagoon from the Mediterranean Sea.

length of 200 stadia and a width of 50 stadia, that is 20 by 5 nautical miles, and was separated from the Mediterranean Sea by a narrow barrier. The lagoon was connected with the sea by a passage called Εχρηγμα or Echrima, and it was considered dangerous, in ancient times, to cross the lagoon or passage. Indeed, Diodoros of Sicily reported that many who were unfamiliar with the area disappeared, which indicates either an undertow or otherwise dangerous current or the presence of quicksand.

Galanopoulos, who researched the foregoing geography and accepts it, speculates that the Israelites in leaving Egypt passed along the narrow strip of land separating the Serbonis Sea from the Mediterranean and camped on the western shore of the passage to the sea. He suggests that one or more large tsunamis from the Thera collapse was capable of lowering or raising the sea level along the coasts of the eastern Mediterranean as far as Egypt. This could have occurred when the Israelites were camped on the Serbonis Sea. If the water was drawn out of the Serbonis Sea to the extent required to close the sea passage for a period of, say, thirty minutes to one hour this would have allowed some of the Israelites to cross, indeed perhaps all of them. Some Biblical scholars believe that the number of the Children of Israel was more likely 600, rather than 600,000, as reported in the Bible. They had probably been camped there for some years, so that the seismic waves from Thera need not have coincided in time with any particular travels of the Israelites other than the crossing of the water passage when the opportunity came.

Then, as the Israelites ran across the barrier with the wall of water on their right and left, the great flood wave arrived at their heels and drowned the pursuing Egyptian army. The Bible mentions that the chariot wheels stuck, implying soft ground or quicksand in the area. It is implied that Pharaoh died in this catastrophe. Certainly, if the pharaoh led his army and was killed in this venture, we have a means of dating the event, provided we can decide who the pharaoh was. Thutmose III, who died in 1447 B.C., is a possible candidate.

We must not ignore the statement in the Bible that a strong east wind blew the water out of the passage, but there seem to be reasons for not accepting this theory. It appears most unlikely that there would be such a lowering of the water level of the Serbonis Sea and nearby Mediterranean by a wind and that the waves would start or stop with the suddenness required to drown an army or inspire such a tradition. Also, strong easterly winds are uncommon in the eastern Mediterranean. It may have been thought by the writer of Exodus that, as the wind was divinely generated, it should come from the land of Canaan to the east, the homeland of the Israelite theology.

Vulcanism, Earthquakes, and Floods Described in the Bible

The references to volcanic eruptions, floods, and earthquakes in the Bible are remarkable for their great number and influence upon the people of the time and the chroniclers of history. They are all the more remarkable because earthquakes and volcanic eruptions are not common in the lands usually associated with the Bible— Canaan and Egypt. Thera is the most likely candidate for vulcanism, and the lands of Greece and Turkey for earthquakes. Extensive references that could well refer to Thera are to be found in the Old Testament books of Exodus, Amos, Jeremiah, Zephaniah, and Ezekiel. The Book of Revelation (the Apocalypse), according to tradition written by Saint John the Divine on the island of Patmos, 60 miles from Thera, is dominated by vulcanism. In short, there was in Biblical times an unmistakable tradition of writing in terms of volcanic reference.

It is interesting to note that there are several mentions of an active volcano in the Book of Exodus. Telling of the escape from Egypt, Exodus 13:21–22 states:

And the Lord went before them by day in a pillar of a cloud, to lead them the way; and by night in a pillar of fire to give them light; to go by day and night.
He took not away the pillar of fire by night, from before the people.

Later, in the third month, when the children of Israel were gone forth out of Egypt, according to Exodus 19:1, they came to the wilderness of Sinai and camped before the mount. On the mountain of Sinai, Moses received the Decalogue, the famous summary of moral fundamentals. From Exodus 19:18 we learn:

And mount Sinai was altogether on a smoke, because the Lord descended upon it in fire, and the smoke thereof ascended as the smoke of a furnace, and the whole mount quaked greatly.

Exodus 20:18–19 tells us:

> And all the people saw the thunderings, and the lightnings, and the noise of the trumpet, and the mountain smoking: and when the people saw it they removed and stood afar off.
>
> And they said unto Moses, Speak thou with us and we will hear: but let not God speak with us, lest we die.

And Exodus 20:20–21 relates:

> And Moses said unto the people, Fear not: for God is come to prove you, and that his fear may be before your faces, that ye sin not.
>
> And the people stood afar off, and Moses drew near unto the thick darkness where God was.

The spot where Moses proclaimed the law has been called Sinai and Horeb. Mt. Sinai is located by Biblical scholars either in a range in the south of the Sinai peninsula, between the Gulf of Suez and the Gulf of 'Aqaba, or at Elath, at the head of the Gulf of 'Aqaba, or at a third location north of 'Aqaba. In any case there is a tradition that God was manifested by an active volcano. We know of no volcanoes in the Biblical lands active in recent geological times. Thera in the Greek Islands, and the volcanoes of Italy are the nearest volcanoes active in historical times. Except for these, there is no active volcano within 2,000 miles of the Biblical lands, with one notable exception. Herodotus described an ancient trans-Sahara trade route south through central Libya to Lake Chad, in the present African nation of Chad. Some 800 miles south of the Libyan Gulf of Sirte lie the Tibesti Mountains and the lonely and impressive volcanic cone of Emi Koussi, rising from a desert at 2,000 feet above sea level to an elevation of 11,000 feet. According to Herodotus, the natives called this peak the "pillar of heaven," but the peak itself could never be seen. Whether this was due to cloud or eruptive gases is unknown. Herodotus gave it the name Atlas. The natives took their name from it, and thus were called Atlantes, from Atlas.

Just where did the volcanic tradition originate? Thera is a good possibility. The lone volcanic island on the trade route across the Aegean could well have been considered the home of the gods, and the tradition spread and magnified by travelers between the Greek islands and the Semitic lands.

Isolated references in the Old Testament appear to relate to the Thera eruption. There is no chronology associated with these other than the date of their writing, which gives us an indication of their antiquity.

In the Book of Amos, written in the eighth century B.C., we have:

[9:5] And the Lord God of hosts is he that toucheth the land, and it shall melt, and all that dwell therein shall mourn: and it shall rise up wholly like a flood; and shall be drowned, as by the flood of Egypt.

[9:7] Are ye not as children of the Ethiopians unto me, O children of Israel? saith the Lord. Have not I brought up Israel out of the land of Egypt? and the Philistines from Caphtor, and the Syrians from Kir?

This reference to the Philistines from Caphtor is a clue to the origin of the Philistines, who, this passage implies, came from Crete (Caphtor) to Egypt, very likely as refugees from destruction caused by the eruption of Thera. The Philistine migration is probably more complex than this, because their pottery seems developed from the post-destruction Cretan, which showed distinct mainland Greek or Mycenaean influence.

Amos was one of the later prophets. His prophecies were filled with such religious insight, political significance, and poetic expression as to raise his writings to a level different from that of earlier prophets, who were characterized more by ecstatic behavior, like that of the dervishes of Moslem lands or present-day revivalists. Amos lived about 785–745 B.C. and is known as the shepherd prophet of righteousness. Though Amos apparently is speaking of the destruction of Edom, these isolated references to flood and the travels of the Philistines from Caphtor represent the insertion of an older tradition. The Book of Amos is thought to include a number of parts hardly attributable to a humble shepherd.

Jeremiah wrote in the sixth century B.C. as follows:

[47:1] The word of the Lord that came to Jeremiah the prophet against the Philistines, before that Pharaoh smote Gaza.

[47:2] Thus saith the Lord; Behold, waters rise up out of the north, and shall be an overflowing flood, and shall overflow the land, and all that is therein; the city, and them that dwell therein: then the men shall cry, and all the inhabitants of the land shall howl.

[47:4] Because of the day that cometh to spoil all the Philistines, and to cut off from Tyrus and Zidon every helper that remaineth: for the Lord will spoil the Philistines, the remnant of the country of Caphtor.

[48:8] And the spoiler shall come upon every city, and no city shall escape: the valley also shall perish, and the plain shall be destroyed, as the Lord hath spoken.

[48:32] O vine of Sibmah, I will weep for thee with the weeping of Jazer: thy plants are gone over the sea, they reach even to the sea of Jazer: the spoiler is fallen upon thy summer fruits and upon thy vintage.

Jeremiah (c. 628–586 B.C.) was referred to by Jews of later generations as "the prophet." Chapters 47 and 48, in which we find such vivid descriptions of coastal destruction, are thought by scholars to have been the work of later poets. These are in the form of oracles against foreign nations. Again we have the Philistines mentioned as the remnant of the country of Caphtor, or the refugees from Crete, if we accept the identity of Caphtor with Crete or the Aegean Islands. The chapters quoted describe the destruction to be brought upon the Philistines. The destruction comes from the north and it involves all the cities of the Levantine coast, all the way south to Gaza. Sidon and Tyre, the great Phoenician centers, were destroyed. It is quite possible that these chapters refer to the seismic sea wave destruction from the collapse of Thera. The earliest dating of the Philistines is generally thought to be later than the fifteenth century B.C. but without convincing evidence.

Zephaniah was a contemporary of Jeremiah who appeared publicly about 626 B.C. His forebodings were gloomy, as were those of Jeremiah. It is thought that an invasion of Palestine by the Scythians was the source of much of the writings of both Zephaniah and Jeremiah. While there were many destructions in history, it is tempting to speculate that a bit of the tradition of the great Thera catastrophe found its way into the stories of Zephaniah.

Zephaniah, writing in the seventh century B.C., gives us the following:

[1:13] Therefore their goods shall become a booty and their houses a desolation: they shall also build houses, but not inhabit them; and they shall plant vineyards, but not drink the wine thereof.

[1:15] That day is a day of wrath, a day of trouble and distress, a day of wasteness and desolation, a day of darkness and gloominess, a day of clouds and darkness.

[1:17] And I will bring distress upon men, that they shall walk like blind men, because they have sinned against the Lord: and their blood shall be poured out as dust, and their flesh as the dung.

[2:4] For Gaza shall be forsaken, and Ashkelon a desolation: they shall drive out Ashdod at the noon day, and Ekron shall be rooted up.

[2:5] Woe unto the inhabitants of the sea coast, the nation of the Cherethites! the word of the Lord is against you; O Canaan, the land of the Philistines, I will even destroy thee, that there shall be no inhabitant.

Ezekiel 1:4 is intriguing in its implications.

And I looked, and, behold, a whirlwind came out of the north, a great cloud, and a fire infolding itself, and a brightness was about it, and out of the midst thereof as the colour of amber, out of the midst of the fire.

This has been considered to be an earry sighting of a luminous tornado. While there are obscure references to luminous phenomena in nighttime tornadoes in the scientific literature, the passage from Ezekiel sounds to me much more like a volcanic eruption or a subsidiary of one. Coming from the north it could have been Thera.

Appendix C: *Chain* Seismic Profile and Magnetometer Trace

Sound travels readily through the sea and is our most convenient probe for the study of the ocean depths. Underwater sound is created in the form of a pulse, a single wave or a few waves of sound or water pressure. We should not think of a pulse in terms of a musical tone, which is a continuous sound in which periodic repeated sound waves are created as the source vibrates. A better analogy is provided by simple carpentry. If a nail in contact with a board is struck on the head with a hammer, a sound or pressure pulse is created which, by traveling along the nail and back, drives the nail into the wood. The nail does not actually start moving into the wood until the pulse reaches the wood at the point of the nail, but then continues to move into the wood as long as the pulse is traveling back toward the head, causing the point to move forward by way of reaction. This reverberation continues for some time, driving the nail forward with diminishing result. Meanwhile the grip of the wood insures that the nail is held and does not withdraw as much as it penetrates. The nail is analogous to the sound source and the wood to the ocean.

For the purposes of the seismic profiler, a great deal of energy must enter the sea and travel great distances, and this is most effectively done by a series of pulses separated by a convenient time interval, say 10 seconds. On the *Chain,* pulses are created by the sparker having an electrical input equivalent to the energy released when an automobile strikes the ground after falling 30 feet off a cliff. The spark is made by immersing two very heavy wires in the sea, insulated except at the open ends, and passing an electric current between them. They are towed alongside the ship and, when fired, produce a gigantic spark and a loud explosive report.

The pulse rushes at one mile per second deep into the ocean. Some of the energy is reflected by the sea bottom and sent immediately back to the surface, and the time taken in this travel is our measure of the ocean depth. But most of the energy goes deep into the earth's crust as a fast-moving—faster than in water—pulse to be reflected back to the surface by discontinuities in the crustal rocks. Some 200 yards behind the ship, a sea microphone, or hydrophone, receives the returning sound pulses, which are then amplified and printed out on paper. The subbottom geological strata appear as dark lines along the length of the recording.

Also towed behind the *Chain* is the magnetometer, a small instrument which measures the strength of the earth's magnetic field by the behavior of very small particles, products of radioactivity. The location of a volcanic plug or vent can be pinpointed by the high magnetism of this type of geology.

The scientific results appear as strips of paper with time of day along the horizontal axis and depth below the ocean surface or magnetic intensity on the vertical axis. The *Chain* spent twenty-four hours at Thera, seven of which were spent within the caldera. After this, she circumnavigated the island clockwise.

A patient examination of the paper recordings helps us to un-

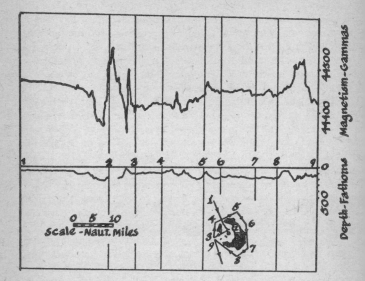

FIGURE. 41. Seismic profile and magnetic record during *Chain* track into Thera caldera and during circumnavigation of island. (After *Chain* cruise 61, August 27–28, 1966, Woods Hole Oceanographic Institution, E. F. K. Zarudzki. Reproduced with permission of U.S. Navy and E. F. K. Zarudzki.)

derstand that Thera was indeed a complex of many volcanic cones, with possible internal bays, which had collapsed into the sea. But these recordings, impressive as they are, tell only a part of the story and must be considered with the above-water geology and the archaeological evidence in a reconstruction of the history of Thera. The details are not difficult to understand, and we can see how they help Galanopoulos' identification of Thera with Atlantis.

The display, Figure 41, shows the magnetic field plotted above the depth soundings. The record starts before entering the caldera and continues until the circuit of the island has been completed and the ship has started on her way south toward Crete. Figure 42 shows an enlarged depth profile and the seismic subbottom profile for the portion of the track of Figure 41 from station one to sta-

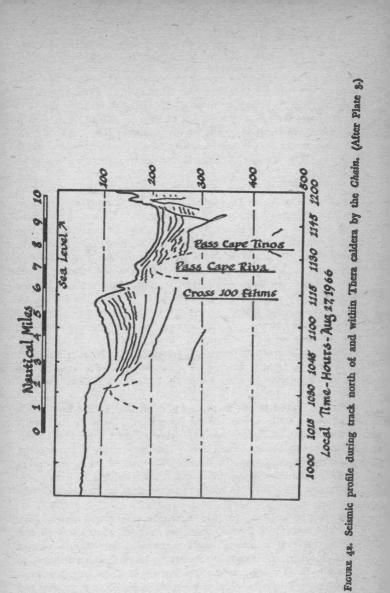

FIGURE 48. Seismic profile during track north of and within Thera caldera by the *Chain*. (After Plate 8.)

tion two, the radial track into the bay's center. The bottom, shown by the uppermost trace, and also in the chart, Plate 3, and the model, Plate 7, suddenly takes a dip from 60 fathoms down to 120 fathoms at 2 miles in the figure and then shoals to 80 fathoms at 5½ miles, before we enter the narrow northern passage. This probably represents a volcanic blowout, an explosive eruption, which blew to the north as well as vertically upward, though it could be a collapse.

The sea floor deepens as we enter the bay, passing two peaks on the ocean floor which are post-Minoan volcanic cones, as confirmed by corresponding blips on the magnetic record showing increased magnetism. Local complex bottom and subbottom surfaces here and farther on probably represent a collapsed portion of the island. For comparison, the photo in Plate 4b shows the stratification of the volcanic products as seen on the cliff faces of the interior of the caldera above sea level, a panorama running along the east interior from Ia to the principal town of Phira. Some of the lines which we see in the seismic record represent multiple transits of the sound pulses up and down and reflections from side surfaces and must be distinguished from real strata, but most of what we see is real.

The thickness of the pumice, representing the Minoan eruption, is difficult to identify because of variations in its thickness and its acoustic similarity to other materials. More data is clearly needed to be sure.

As we proceed to the south, the floor of the caldera flattens out at about 215 fathoms and 8 miles. Beneath it, a U-shaped line which is the bottom of a deep basin filled with volcanic debris of low magnetism, probably ash, is seen. This is a major volcanic vent, probably the largest one in the northern part of the island, which erupted quantities of ash in 1500 B.C. Afterward, a mountain collapsed into the great hole left by the voiding of the magma chamber below.

Measurements were stopped near the center and were unfortunately not resumed until seven hours later when the ship was leaving the caldera through the west channel, this shallow passage being barely deep enough for the magnetometer, which requires 60 feet of water. The track around the outside of Thera, which was followed after I left the ship, showed a rugged bottom profile and many peaks of the magnetic record. To the northeast, the ship went over the submerged cone of Kolumbo, which rose above the sea from the bottom in A.D. 1650 to subside shortly thereafter to 120 feet below the surface. We can see a great cone on the depth record, its vulcanism confirmed by the magnetometer, Figure 41. The next major feature appears on the south coast. There we find a large increase in the magnetic field in the vicinity of two curved cutouts in the coastline between stations 8 and 9, Figure 41. This increase, considered with the seismic record and the land topography above water, indicates a monstrous exterior collapse caldera, which was created at the same time as the interior disintegration, in the fifteenth century B.C. This knowledge suggests the possibility of a bay or harbor on the south facing Crete, the natural lee side of the island and berthing spot for the Minoan fleet. The topographic model shows this sunken volcano, collapsed into a great hole in the sea bottom, deeper than that within the island's central bay. The alignment of Kristiana, the great southwest vent, the central vents of Thera, Kolumbo to the northeast and Amorgopoulos farther to the northeast are evidence that Thera straddles a large linear fracture in the earth's crust running from southwest to northeast in the Aegean Sea.

In summation, the *Chain* profiles showed the presence of many volcanic cones including a major one in the northern part of the central bay and further evidence of a major fracture in the earth's crust. It is clear that the central portion of the former island collapsed into the sea. From this and other information, it can be inferred that the former outline included bays or estuaries which broke the roughly circular outline.

Additional data relative to the geophysics of Thera and its interpretation will be published by E. F. K. Zarudzki, Hartley Hoskins and J. Phillips in a forthcoming technical paper entitled "Geophysical Study of Santorini (Thera)." I quote from the abstract published in the American Geophysical Union Transactions, March 1967.

A suite of geophysical measurements within and around the Santorini volcanic caldera in the Aegean was obtained during the *Chain* cruise 61. The data consisted of precision echo soundings, continuous seismic profiles with 100,000 joule sparker, total magnetic field measurements and gravity observations. The magnetic data proved to be especially useful for elucidating sea floor morphology and the deep structure. A large positive anomaly of 1,000 gammas is associated with one of the central vents. Smaller magnetic anomalies indicate two external vents. One is the well known Kolumbos cinder cone northeast of the caldera; the other, a new discovery, is a submarine vent located to south-southwest and adjacent to the caldera. The latter has a positive magnetic anomaly of over 300 gammas. The magnetic, as well as seismic profiles, also reveal other volcanic plugs that did not penetrate the bottom, and several basalt sills and flows. The plutonic history of the island includes the development of a complex system of volcanic vents located within and outside the present caldera.

APPENDIX D: Use of the Refraction Seismograph on Thera, 1967

Description of Instrument (Seismiktron Model B)

The sound source for this instrument was a sledgehammer blow on the earth surface which generated a spherical wave passing into the ash. A 15-pound sledgehammer was used, striking on an anvil of lava stone, flat on top and imbedded in the pumice.

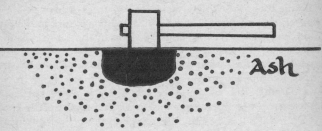

Two geophones, or sound pulse receivers, were used, one placed near the sledge and the other at a variable distance away. The near geophone signal, an electrical pulse, converted from sound by the geophone, was transmitted to the indicating unit by a wire and the signal from the far geophone by radio.

Procedure

The sledge blow initiated a pressure pulse which passed into the soil, where it propagated spherically. When it reached the nearer geophone the signal automatically started the time counter in the indicator. When the wave reached the far geophone, the counter was interrupted and a time reading appeared on the indicator in 1/1,000 second. By increasing the distance between geophones, a number of time-interval readings were taken which could be plotted on a graph of time versus distance between geophones. These were the basic data on which an interpretation of the subsurface materials was based.

The penetration capability of the unit at hand was reported to be 30 to 50 feet in compacted soil. It was anticipated that somewhat less could be achieved in the dry, loosely compacted ash and pumice stone of Thera because the sound waves tend to be reflected between the small pieces, causing reverberation and motion of these small pieces. This scatters and dissipates the energy in the pulse so that it cannot reach as far below the surface. I felt that test excavation along with the seismograph results would be necessary to establish confidence in the interpretation. This indeed turned out to be the case. Coupling between the anvil and the ash, or the ability for the sound to pass from one to the other without losing much of its energy in reverberation of the anvil and sledge, was poor. Another time, a more energetic source could be used, possibly a small explosive. Nevertheless, results on Thera were satisfactory in the thinner ash existing at Akroteri.

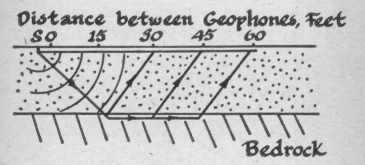

In the figure, the near geophone is at O and the sledge at S. The far geophone is located at varying distances 15 feet apart. The pulse travels into the earth radially, compressing the soil as it goes.

The near geophone at O receives the first signal, which triggers the counter. If the far geophone is at 15 feet, the counter stops as soon as the part of the pulse passing directly along the ash surface reaches it, traveling at speed V_1, the sound speed in the ash.

If the far geophone is located at 30 feet, again the near surface pulse stops the counter and we have a means of determining the speed of pulse travel in the loose ash. It is simply $V_1 = D/t$, where D is the distance between geophones and t is the time interval. At the same time, however, that the surface pulse is traveling horizontally, another part of the spherically radiating pulse penetrates deep into the ash and eventually reaches the bedrock beneath. There it is in part reflected back through the ash and in part refracted to travel horizontally through the rock.

The pulse that originally radiated downward from S now changes into two pulses, one traveling horizontally through the rock and the other radiating back to the surface. The velocity of the pulse in the rock is much higher than that in the ash so that, when the far geophone is at a certain distance from the near geophone, or greater, the pulse that has passed down to the bedrock, along it and back to the surface reaches the far geophone before the direct surface pulse. This causes the graph of time vs. distance to change slope and gives us a means of calculating depth to the bedrock, which we call H.

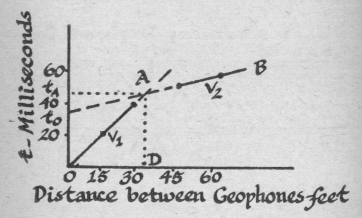

The distance, D, is called the cutoff point and represents the distance between geophones at which the pulse travel time by direct soil transmission and rock refraction are the same, t_A. The point, A, is found by continuing both straight lines until they intersect.

To calculate the depth of rock stratum, we must first find the pulse velocities. From O to D, transmission is direct through the ash and the ash sound velocity, $V_1 = D/t_A$. In the example shown, $V_1 = (35/45) \, (1,000) = 780$ feet per second. After the cutoff point, the pulse velocity is increased during part of the travel to V_2 so that the average velocity during the travel from the near geophone down through the ash to bedrock, along bedrock and back up through the ash is greater than V_1. The bedrock pulse velocity, $V_2 =$ slope of line $AB = D/(t_A - t_0)$. In the example shown, $V_2 = 35/(45 - 33) \, (1,000) = 2,900$ feet per second.

The refraction method allows us to measure the average value of depth, H, to bedrock over the distance traversed by the remote geophone and is given by:

$$H = D/2 \sqrt{(V_2 - V_1)/(V_2 + V_1)} = t_0/2 V_1 \, 1/\sqrt{1 - V_1^2/V_2^2}$$

where t_0 is the intercept on the time axis.

If the substratum is inclined, reversed lines must be run to determine the sense of this inclination. To reverse lines is good practice in any case.

Results

In three locations on Thera—Akroteri, Perissa, and Exomiti—the seismograph measured ash thickness in this manner. The final purpose of these measurements was hopefully to identify Minoan walls as well, but not enough data was accumulated, for lack of time, to permit this. In two places ceiling material over voids down in the ash had collapsed, revealing a surface cave-in, and good correlation between the seismograph record and the location of the void were made. This should permit future identification of voids representing rooms of Minoan structures.

A total of 32 seismograph lines were run. Analysis of a few samples is presented here.

2. Before the excavation at Alvaniti I, which later revealed a storage room with a row of large and beautiful pithoi on the lower of two floors at ground level 14 feet below grade, a seismograph run was made, No. 11, in which bedrock was located at 13.3 feet below grade.

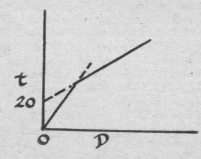

2. The Donkey Cave, which led to excavation Alvaniti I, was cut horizontally into the wall of a ravine. Above the cave was a vineyard. Two seismograph lines were run to determine if the cave could be detected. It was.

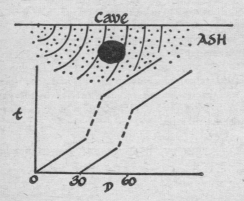

The two lines, started 30 feet apart, both indicated the cave at the correct location by a step in the time-distance plot. The sound pulse, passing horizontally through the ash, was slowed up in the region of the void.

3. At Cape Exomiti, bedrock was discovered but 6 feet beneath the surface 200 feet inland of the shore.

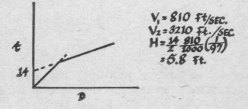

$V_1 = 810$ Ft/sec.
$V_2 = 3210$ Ft./sec.
$H = \frac{14}{2} \frac{810}{1000} \left(\frac{1}{97}\right)$
   $= 5.8$ Ft.

4. In a field north of the excavation Alvaniti I where a void was revealed beneath the ash by a surface cave-in, 12 seismograph lines were run. The typical displaced line over the cave confirmed that it could be identified. Bedrock was indicated from 9 to 15 feet beneath the field over an area of coverage of 75 feet by 150 feet. The region was not excavated.

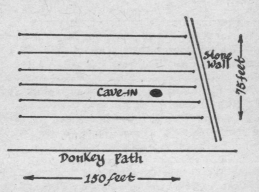

Selected Bibliography

Atlantis

Baikie, Rev. J., *The Sea Kings of Crete*. London, Black, 1910.

Bennett, J. G., "New Light on Plato's Atlantis and the Exodus." Autumn Lecture, Kingston-upon-Thames, Surrey, 1962, published, *Systematics* (1963).

Borchardt, P., *Platos Insel Atlantis*. Berlin, Petermanns Mitteilungen (1927).

Donnelly, I., *Atlantis, the Antediluvian World*. London, Sidgwick & Jackson, 1950.

Frost, K. T., "The Critias and Minoan Crete." *Journal of Hellenic Studies*, 33:189 (1939).

Galanopoulos, A. G., "Επι του μεγεθους και της γεωγραφικης θεσεος της Ατλαντιδος." Αθηναι, Πρακτικα της Ακαδημιας Αθηνον (Ετος, 1960), Τομος 35, Σελ. 401–418.

Heidel, W. A., "A Suggestion Concerning Plato's Atlantis." *Daedalus*, Vol. 68, Number 6 (May, 1933), pp. 189–228.

Marinatos, S., "Περι του "Περι τον θρυλον της Ατλαντιδος." Κρητικα Χρονικα, Ηρακλειον, Κρητης, Τευχος II (Μαϊος—Αυγουστος, 1950).

"A New View of the Atlantis Problem." *Geographical Journal*, Vol. LXX (July-December, 1927), p. 318.

Plato, *Kritias* and *Timaeus*, Jowett translation. New York, Tudor.

Ternier, Pierre, "Atlantis." *Annual Report of the Smithsonian Institution* (1915), pp. 219–234.

Von Humboldt, A., *Kosmos*, Vol. 2. Berlin, 1847.

Wetzel, W., "Vom gegenwärtigen Stand des Atlantis Problems." *Meyniana*, 17, Sete 111–115, Abb Taf Kiel (Okt., 1967).

History

Alsop, J., *From the Silent Earth*. London, Secker & Warburg, 1962.

Bacon, E., ed., *Vanished Civilizations*. London, Thames & Hudson, 1963.

Barnett, R. D., *Illustrations of Old Testament History*. London, British Museum, 1966.

Breasted, J. H., *Ancient Times*. Boston, Ginn, 1935.

Brugsch, H., *The Exodus and the Egyptian Monuments*. Leipzig, 1875.

Bunbury, E. H., *A History of Ancient Geography*. London, Constable, 1959.

Carpenter, R., *Beyond the Pillars of Heracles*. New York, Delacorte, 1966.

—— *Discontinuity in Greek Civilization*. Cambridge University, 1966.

Caskey, J. L., *Greece, Crete, and the Aegean Islands in the Early Bronze Age*. Cambridge University, 1964.

Childe, V. G., *Prehistoric Migrations in Europe*. London, Kegan Paul, 1951.

—— *The Dawn of European Civilization*. London, Routledge and Kegan Paul, 1957.

Clark, J. G. D., *Prehistoric Europe*. London, Methuen, 1952.

Daniel, G. E., *The Megalith Builders of Western Europe*. London, 1958.

Forsdyke, J., *Greece Before Homer*. London, Parrish, 1956.

Galanopoulos, A. G., "Die ägyptischen Plagen und der Auszug Israels aus geologischer Sicht." *Das Altertum*, 10 (1964).

—— "Die Deukalionische Flut aus Geologischer Sicht. *Das Altertum*, Band 9 (1963).

Gordon, Cyrus H., "The Phoenicians." *Orientalia* (April, 1968).

Helck, W., "Thutmosis III and Amenophis II." *Historische Inschriften* (1955).

Herodotus, *History*. London, Oxford Univ. Press, 1962.

Hood, S., *The Home of the Heroes*. New York, McGraw-Hill, 1967.

Lear, J., "The Volcano That Shaped the Western World." *Saturday Review* (November 5, 1966).

Mavor, J. W., Jr., "A Mighty Bronze Age Volcanic Explosion." *Oceanus*, Vol. XII, No. 3 (April, 1966).

Mavor, J. W., Jr., "Preliminary Proposal for Certain Historical, Oceanographic, and Archaeological Investigations of the Eastern Mediterranean Sea, Lands, and People." November, 1966, rev. 1967 (unpublished manuscript).

—— "Volcanoes and History." *Oceanus*, Vol. XIII, No. 1 (November, 1966).

McEvedy, C., *The Penguin Atlas of Ancient History*. London, Penguin, 1967.

Pausanias, *Description de la Grèce*. Paris, 1817.

Plutarch, *The Rise and Fall of Athens*. London, Penguin, 1960.

Mertz, B., *Temples, Tombs, and Hieroglyphs*. London, Gollancz, 1964.

Schleiden, M. J., *The Narrows of Suez*. Leipzig, 1858.

Schonfeld, D., *Die Halbinsel Sinai in ihrer Bedeutung für die Erdkunde und Geschichte*. Berlin, 1917.

Smith, W. S., *Ancient Egypt*. Boston, Museum of Fine Arts, 1960.

Strabon, *Geography*. Bibl. grèque de Didot.

Velikovsky, I., *Worlds in Collision*. London, Gollancz, 1950.

Vermeule, E., *Greece in the Bronze Age*. University of Chicago, 1964.

Woolley, Sir L., *A Forgotten Kingdom*. London, Penguin, 1953.

Oceanography, Geology, Seismology and Meteorology

Blacktin, S. C., *Dust*. London, 1934.

Eisma, D., "Beach Ridges near Selcuk, Turkey." *Tijdschrift van het Koninklijk Nederlandsch Aardrijkskundig Genootschad*, Deel LXXIX, No. 3 (1962).

Emery, K. O., and Y. K. Bentor, "The Continental Shelf of Israel." *Geological Survey Bulletin* 26, State of Israel (January, 1960).

Emery, K. O., and D. C. Cox, "Beachrock in the Hawaiian Islands." *Pacific Science* (October, 1956).

Emery, K. O., B. C. Heezen and T. D. Allan, "Bathymetry of the Eastern Mediterranean Sea." *Deep-Sea Research*, Vol. 13 (1966).

Emery, K. O., and D. Neev, "Mediterranean Beaches of Israel." *Sea Fisheries Research Station Bulletin* 28, State of Israel (January, 1960).

Galanopoulos, A. G., "On Mapping of Seismic Activity in Greece." *Annali di Geofisica*, Vol. XVI, No. 1 (1963).

—— "Tsunamis Observed on the Coasts of Greece from Antiquity to the Present Time." *Annali di Geofisica*, Vol. XIII, n. 3–4 (1960).

«ГЕОХИМИЯ ОСАДОЧНЫХ ПОРОД ИРУД ИЗДАТЕЛЬ-СТВО.» *НАУКА*. (1968), pp. 183–222.

Higgins, C. G., "Greece—A Sketch for Geologists." *Geotimes*, Vol. 10, No. 5 (December, 1965–January, 1966).

Hutchinson, G. E., "The Enchanted Voyage: A Study of the Effects of the Ocean on Some Aspects of Human Culture." *Journ. of Mar. Res.* (1955).

Loring, E., "A Fossilized Bronze Age Beach in the Aegean" (unpublished manuscript), 1966.

Mariolopoulos, E. G., "An Outline of the Climate of Greece." Athens, *Meteorological Institute of Athens*, 1961.

Mavor, J. W., Jr., "The Plain of Perissa" (unpublished manuscript), 1967.

Mellis, O., "Volcanic Ash-Horizons in Deep-Sea Sediments from the Eastern Mediterranean." *Deep-Sea Research*, Vol. 2 (1954).

Miller, A. R., "Physical Oceanography of the Mediterranean Sea: A Discourse." *Comité d'Océanographie Physique*, Vol. XVII, 3 (1963).

Miller, D., "The Alaska Earthquake of July 10, 1958: Giant Wave in Lituya Bay." *Bulletin of the Seismological Society of America*, 50, 265 (1960).

Neev, D., and K. O. Emery, "The Dead Sea." *Science Journal* (December, 1966).

Olausson, E., "Description of Sediment Cores from the Mediterranean and Red Sea." *Report of Swedish Deep Sea Expedition*, Vol. 8 (1960), pp. 286–391.

—— "Studies of Deep-Sea Cores." *Report of Swedish Deep Sea Expedition*, 1947–48, Vol. 8, 4 (1961), pp. 335–391.

Pfannensteil, M., "Reports of the Bathymetric Charts of the Eastern Mediterranean." *Bulletin de l'Institut Océanographique*, 1192, 18 (1960).

Powers, H. A., and R. E. Wilcox, "Volcanic Ash from Mount Mazama (Crater Lake) and from Glacier Peak." *Science* (June 12, 1964).

Shepard, F. P., *The Earth Beneath the Sea*. New York, *Atheneum*, 1963.

Sieberg, A., "Earthquake Research and Its Application to Technology, Mining and Geology." *Jena*, 60 (1933).

—————— "Investigations on the Earthquakes and Fragmented Bloc Layers in the Eastern Mediterranean." *Jena* (1932).

Sohlberg, R. G., and F. C. Allstrom, compilers, *"Chain* Cruise No. 61—North Atlantic, Mediterranean and Red Seas—Summary Cruise Report Prepared by Chief Scientists July 11 to December 17, 1966." *Report of Woods Hole Oceanographic Institution* (1967).

Zarudzki, E. F. K., H. Hoskins, and J. Phillips, "Geophysical Study of Santorini." (In preparation.)

Archaeology of Thera

Bratsiotis, P. J.,"Εισαγωγη εις την Παλαιαν Διάνηχην."Αθηναι, 50 (1937).

Fouqué, F., "Une Pompei Antéhistorique." *Rev. des Deux Mondes*, 39 (1869).

Hiller von Gaertringen, F., *"Thera."* Vol. III (1904).

Knidlberger, L., *Santorin, Insel zwischen Traum und Tag*. Schloendorn Verlags-G.m.b.H., 1965.

Lenormant, *Revue Archaeologique*, New Ser., Vol. XIV.

Mamet, *Die Insula Thera*. 1874.

Marinos, A., and N. Melidonis, "Περι του λοιοοντου θαλμεγεδος χυματος γατα την Προισοροχην εγρηξιυ της Σαντορινης." Ελληνιχη Τεωλογιγη Εταιρια 4 (1959–1961).

Perrot, G., and C. Chipiez, *Histoire de l'Art*, VI. Paris, 1894.

Renaudin, L., "Vases Préhelléniques de Thera." *Bull. Correspond. Hellénique* 46 (1922).

Stagirites, A., Ωγυγια η αρχαιολογια. Wien, 1818.

Archaeology and Philology (general)

Archaeological Institute of America, *Archaeological Discoveries in the Holy Land*. New York, Crowell, 1967.

Brice, W. C., *Inscriptions in the Minoan Linear Script A*. London, Oxford, 1961.

Ceram, C. W. (E. B. Garside, trans.), *Gods, Graves and Scholars*. London, Gollancz, 1952.

Chadwick, J., *The Decipherment of Linear B*. London, Cambridge Univ., 1958.

Diringer, D., *Writing*. London, Thames & Hudson, 1962.

Evans, Sir A. J., *The Palace of Minos*. London, Macmillan, 1921.

Gordon, C., *Ugarit and Minoan Crete*. New York, Norton, 1966.

Graham, J. W., *The Palaces of Crete*. London, Oxford Univ., 1962.

Hutchinson, R. W., *Prehistoric Crete*. London, Penguin, 1962.

Kenna, V. E. G., *Cretan Seals*. London, Oxford, 1960.

Loring, E., "A Protocycladic Community on Christiana Island" (unpublished manuscript), 1966.

Marinatos, S. "Amnisos, The Port of Minos." *Research & Progress*, 10 (1934), pp. 341–343.

—— *Crete and Mycenae*. London, Thames & Hudson, 1960.

—— "The Volcanic Destruction of Minoan Crete." *Antiquity* (1939).

Matz, F., *The Art of Crete and Early Greece*. London, Methuen, 1962.

Palmer, L. R., *Mycenaeans and Minoans*. London, Faber, 1962.

Palmer, L. R., and J. Boardman, *Date of the Knossos Tablets*. London, Oxford, 1963.

—— *On the Knossos Tablets*. London, Oxford, 1963.

Pendlebury, J. D. S., *The Archaeology of Crete*. London, Methuen, 1965.

Platon, N., *Crete*. London, Muller, 1966.

Vulcanology of Thera

Fouqué, F., *Archives des Missions*, 2d Ser., Vol. IV.

—— *Santorin et ses Eruptions*. Paris, Maison et Cie, 1879.

Galanopoulos, A. G., "Zur Bestimmung Des Alters Der Santorin-Kaldera." *Annales Géologiques des pays Helléniques*, 9 (1958).

Leychester, Lt., "Some Account of the Volcanic Group of Santorin or Thera." *Journal of Royal Geographic Society* (1848).

Ninkovitch, D., and B. Heezen, "Santorini Tephra." *Colston Papers* (1965).

Pègues, l'Abbé, *Histoire de Santorin ou Thera*. Paris, 1842.

Reck, H., *Santorin, der Werdegang eines Inselvulkans und sein Ausbruch*, Vol. I, II, III. Berlin, 1936.

Vulcanology (general)

Blanchard, D. C., *From Raindrops to Volcanoes*. New York, Doubleday, 1967.

Catalogue of the Active Volcanoes of the World—International Association of Volcanology, c/o Prof. Ing. F. Penta, Istituto di Geologia Applicata, Via Eudossiana 18, Roma.

Part I. *Indonesia* by M. N. Van Padang.

Part IV. *Africa and the Red Sea* by J. J. Richard and M. N. Van Padang.

Part XII. *Greece* by G. C. Georgalas.

Part XVI. *Arabia and the Indian Ocean* by M. N. Van Padang.

Part XVII. *Turkey* by M. M. Blumenthal and G. van der Kaaden.

Part XVIII. *Iran* by A. Gansser.

Furneaux, *Krakatoa*. London, Secker & Warburg.

Rigg, G. B., and H. R. Gould, "Age of Glacier Peak Eruption and Chronology of Post-Glacial Peat Deposits in Washington and Surrounding Areas." *American Journal of Science*, Vol. 255 (May, 1957).

Symons, G. J., "The Eruption of Krakatoa and Subsequent Phenomena." *Report of Royal Society* (1888).

Thorarinsson, S., *Surtsey*. London, Bailey Bros., 1966.

Verbeek, R. D. M., *Krakatoa*. 1886.

Archaeological Technology

Applied Science Center for Archaeology, University of Pa., *MASCA Newsletter*, Vol. 2, No. 1 (September, 1966).

Bass, G., *Archaeology Underwater*. London, Thames & Hudson, 1966.

Karius, R., et al., "Stereo-mapping of Underwater Terrain from a Submarine." *Science and Engineering* (June, 1965).

Lawrence, L. G., *Electronics in Oceanography*. Indianapolis, Sams, 1967.

Mavor, J. W., Jr., "Ten Months with Alvin." *Geo-Marine Technology*, Vol. 2, No. 2 (February, 1966).

——— et al., "Alvin, 6000-Foot Submergence Research Vehicle." SNAME transactions (1966).

Pollack, "Collection of Samples for RC 14 Dating and Interpretation of Results." *Australian Institute of Aboriginal Studies* (1966).

Rainey, F., and E. K. Ralph, "Archaeology and Its New Technology." *Science*, Vol. 153, No. 3743 (September 23, 1966).

Underwater Archaeology

Frost, H., *Under the Mediterranean*. London, George Routledge, 1963.

Throckmorton, P., "The Antykithera Ship." *Transactions American Philosophical Society*, Vol. 55, 3 (June, 1965).

——— "Wrecks at Methone." *Mariners Mirror*, Vol. 51, 1 (1965).

Ward-Perkins, J. B., and P. Throckmorton," The San Pietro Wreck." *Archaeology*, Vol. 18, 3 (1965).

Mythology and Ancient Writings

Barrett, ed., *Hippolytus of Euripides*. London, Oxford Univ. Press, 1964.

Bulfinch, T., *The Age of Fable*. Tilton, 1894.

Daniel, G. E., et al., *Myth or Legend*. New York, Capricorn, 1968.

Glueck, N. *Deities and Dolphins*. London, Cassell, 1965.

Grimal, P., editor, *Larousse World Mythology*. London, Paul Hamlyn, 1965.

Holy Bible.

Homer, *The Iliad*. London, Penguin, 1950.

Rieu, E. V., *Apollonius of Rhodes: The Voyage of Argo*. London, Penguin, 1959.

Sandars, N. K., *The Epic of Gilgamesh*. London, Penguin, 1960.

Index

Achaens of Greece, permeation of Minoan culture by, 174
Acoustic instruments, types of, 125
Aeacus, king of island of Aegina, 188
Aegean Sea: islands of volcanic origin, 26–27 (fig.), 59; scholars, on Atlantis location in, 51–55; oceanographic study of, by R. V. Chain, 102 (fig.), 103–17; thickness of earth's crust beneath, 110; island empire of, in second millennium B.C., 193
Africa, coast of: land and sea contours, 73 (fig.); from Tripoli to Cyrene, contour on land of possible flooding from Thera collapse, 74 (fig.); hit by tsunami from Thera eruption, 186
Akroteri, Thera: search of erosion ravines, 150, 151–54; excavations of Fouqué and Zahn, 150, 151, 192–93, 196, 197, 202; excavations of Gorceix and Mamet, 192; linking with Minoan culture, 193; today's village, 193; explorations on 1967 Thera expedition, 194–206, 213–16, 240–54; ravine looking east from, 195 (fig.); finding ruins of house in ravine, 202–4; review of excavations at ravines, 222; topographical maps and surveys by Kane, 231–35 (fig.); geological section of caldera, cliff at, 231 (fig.); underwater Minoan ruins, seaward of excavation site, 233; plan view of excavation site, 234 (fig.); geological section north from south shore, 235 (fig.); Bronos and Alvaniti trenches opened for excavations in ravines, 240; plan view, excavation ravine, 243 (fig.); excavation Bronos II, 244 (fig.); excavation Bronos IA, 247 (fig.); excavation Alvaniti I, 248 (fig.); collecting, identifying, storing of shards from ravine trenches, 249, 250; Marinatos' description of finds, 250; discoveries in trench Alvaniti I, 250;

making maps of ravine excavations, 251; taking photographs at excavations, 251; ghosts, and 1967 excavations, 254; Marinatos' excavations after 1967 expedition, 255–56; evidence of rebuilding of palace after earthquake, 255–56
Alaskan earthquake 1958 in Lituya Bay, seismic waves during, 67, 98
Alexious, Dr., 226, 227
Alvin: design and construction, 24, 25; investigation of caldera of Thera, 30, 41; search for Minoan shipwrecks, 166; study of deep ocean currents in Aegean, 170
Amber trade route, 178
American School of Classical Studies in Athens, 88, 101, 148, 166
Amnisos, Crete: excavations at, 62–63; inspection by 1967 Thera expedition, 227
Amorgos, sea waves created by earthquake on Aegean island of (1956), 67
Amos, Book of, and correlation of events of Exodus with eruption of Thera, 74–75, 288
Anastasiades, Michael, 23, 24
Ancient Thera ruin atop Messa Vouno, 139, 140, 220
Aneirousis, Euaggelos, 100–1, 121
Ansedonia, as location of Atlantis, Cattoi's theory of, 48
Archaeological Institute of America, 259
Archaeological permission from Greek authorities, and restrictions placed on 1966 Thera project, 88–89
Archaeological Society of Athens, 167, 181, 182; permission to publish text, photographs, movies of 1967 Thera expedition, 258; letter announcing discontinuance of collaboration with Mavor in Thera excavations, 259. See also Greek Archaeological Service

310